SIR LIONEL

SIR LIONEL

by
Fred Archer

Gift Publications
Costa Mesa, California 92626

Published by Gift Publications
Costa Mesa, California 92626

Library of Congress Catalog Card Number
80-67302
ISBN 0-86595-005-9

Printed in the United States of America

DEDICATION

From the New World he had discovered, Christopher Columbus wrote to Ferdinand and Isabella:

"I swear to your Majesties that there is not a better people in the world than these; more affectionate, affable, or mild. They love their neighbors as themselves and they always speak smilingly."

Columbus erred in thinking that he had found the real India. (The Indians of India came to the West Indies four centuries after Columbus.)

But, applied to the Luckhoo family today, the description cannot be bettered. To them this book is dedicated.

THE LUCKHOOS—
may their tribe increase.

CONTENTS

FOREWORD

Lionel Luckhoo is known to many as one of the most distinguished of a family of distinguished lawyers. His success in this field, particularly on the criminal side, is attributable not only to his deep knowledge of the law, but as well to an unusual understanding of human nature and an eternal conviction of the justice of his client's case which he had and has, and an inexplicable ability to communicate this conviction to judges and juries. This quality he has carried with him into other fields as a Trade Union leader, politician (he was Mayor of Georgetown on several occasions) and diplomat.

There have been many times and periods when we have been on opposite sides both professionally and politically, but never have I doubted his earnestness and commitment to the cause he has espoused.

As a diplomat, he was Guyana's first High Commissioner to Britain and the first Ambassador to be accredited to Paris, Bonn and the Hague, serving in the same capacities at the same time on behalf of a sister nation, Barbados. Again, in this field, his was an outstanding success.

He has been my political opponent as well as my political colleague; he has been my personal counsel; but to me the deepest relationship I have enjoyed with him has been, and is, that of friend. A man of character, integrity and a rapier-like wit, endowed with an infectious sense of humor combined with a physical and intellectual energy that outmatches that of his most junior juniors, he is undoubtedly one of Guyana's most outstanding sons.

May, 1980

(L.F.S. Burnham)
Prime Minister of Guyana

Characters and events in this book are real. In a few instances, names have been changed or omitted to protect the innocent, or the guilty, as the case may be.

Chapter 1
The Case of the Learned Friend

An unarmed man shot in cold blood!

Even as Karim Baksh lay dead, two witnesses claimed that a leading Guyanese citizen, Jainarine Singh, attorney, former Minister of Agriculture, and wealthy landowner, had committed murder.

Guyana rocked with the scandal.

It all had begun with a dispute over a dam. After air, water is man's most essential need. Neighbors have feuded, murder has been committed, wars have been fought, over water rights. Hundreds of western films, the excellent to the execrable, have pounded the theme of land barons and small ranchers—or cattlemen and sheep men—struggling to obtain or retain access to a river, springs, or a dam for their animals. At a showdown, someone gets shot.

It was as if the Old West had been transplanted to Guyana. One of the prime witnesses, Yussuff, a prosperous rice farmer whose land bordered Jainarine Singh's property, related the strange sequence of events involving himself and his two sons, Shameer and Karim Baksh, and Singh.

Yussuff claimed that Jainarine Singh had ordered his workmen to bulldoze the dam between their properties—the dam to which Yussuff claimed rights of ownership. He then went to the police station to report the situation. Later, he saw Mr. Singh and a policeman come to the dam.

After the policeman left, Karim came on the scene, walking toward Mr. Singh, holding his hands in the air. Yussuff heard the discharge of a gun and saw Karim fall. Mr. Singh had a gun in his hand. Shameer rushed at the lawyer with a cutlass and chopped at his hand. The revolver fell to the ground. Yussuff ran to Karim and found him dead.

Two facts were beyond dispute. Karim had been shot dead. Jainarine Singh's left hand had been half-severed by some sharp instrument which had cut through tissue, tendon, and bone. So great was the loss of blood that doctors fought hard to save his life. Singh was arrested, put under police guard in the hospital, and, once out of danger, charged with the murder of Karim Baksh.

All professionals cleave to their own. Singh's legal brethren, sympathetic to his plight, volunteered to defend him if called upon. His tense and anxious wife insisted that he secure the best lawyer in the world to represent him, volunteering to bring back the most eminent lawyer from England.

Sick, pale, and weak, Singh smiled at her fervency and agreed with her. "I need the best lawyer in the world, but he's right here in Guyana. Get me Lionel Luckhoo."

Jainarine Singh's estimate of Sir Lionel Luckhoo, the son of Guyana's first Indian attorney, was not subjective. The *Guiness Book of Records* calls him the world's most successful lawyer. Every time he wins acquittal for a client on a murder charge, he breaks a world record—his own. Before the Singh case, Sir Lionel, who practices in most of the British Caribbean countries and the United Kingdom, had already defended more than 200 persons charged with murder, without losing a single case!

Lionel Luckhoo led a battery of seven lawyers, all eager to help defend their colleague, when the trial opened before Justice Rex McKay. Among other attorneys taking part were Lionel's cousin, B.O. Adams, and J.T. Clarke, both Queen's counsel.

Lawyers and former government ministers do not often jostle with crowds to attend a murder trial. This was the first time it had happened in Guyana. Juries everywhere tend to give credence to "I see" witnesses, as they call them in Guyana, and Jainarine Singh had both Yussuff and Shameer lined up against him.

After old Yussuff had given evidence, Lionel began to cross-examine.

"You regarded this dam as yours?"

"Yes."

"You were angry that the accused was bulldozing your dam?"

"Yes."

"Did you sign an agreement admitting that the dam belonged to the accused?"

Yussuff hesitated. "I might have done so, but it was mine."

"When the gun went off, how far was Karim from the accused?"

"About twelve feet."

"How far were you from the accused?"

"Forty-five feet."

"How far was Shameer from the accused?"

"Forty-five feet."

"Was the dam clear?"

"Yes."

"So you could all see each other?"

"Yes."

"Did Karim have to pass you to get to the accused?"

"Yes."

"Were his hands upraised?"

"Yes."

The vital admission had been made, though its significance might not have been immediately apparent.

"Was there a cutlass in either of his hands?"

"Certainly not."

"Then can you say why he had his hands upraised?"

"I don't know."

"Did the accused have anything in his hand at that time?"

"No."

"Did either of them speak to the other?"

"No."

"Did you ask your son why he was walking with his hands upraised?"

"No."

"And are you saying that in this drama of silence the accused suddenly fired a shot?"

"Yes."

"Then what happened?"

"Shameer rushed the accused."

"With his hands upraised?"

"Yes."

"And with a cutlass in his right hand?"

"Yes."

"How many shots did the accused fire?"

"One."

"Did he attempt to shoot at Shameer?"

"No."

Quietly, in the form of questions, Lionel Luckhoo put the defense version of events to the old man. Yussuff, he suggested, was angry about the bulldozing of the dam. He brought his two sons with him to stop Mr. Singh, by force if necessary, from carrying on with it. Both sons rushed at Singh with their cutlasses upraised. Not until they were within striking distance did he pull out his revolver and fire at Karim, and by then Shameer had almost severed his hand.

Yussuff made his denials. Lionel then asked, "When did you first see the revolver?"

"When it was discharged."

"This was the first time you ever saw that revolver?"

"Yes."

"Did Karim go right up to him before the accused fired?"

"No, he was about twelve feet away."

"Did the accused speak to you or to either of your sons?"

"No, he said nothing."

"Did he threaten them at any time?"

"No."

"His bulldozers were still working on the dam?"

"Yes."

"So you were the ones who were being injured? Your dam was being destroyed?"

"Yes."

"And so you were out to stop the accused? That is so, isn't it? Isn't it?"

The only answer Yussuff gave to the repeated question was to shake his head and mutter, "He killed my son."

When Shameer took the witness stand, his account differed on one important point from the tale told by his father. Yussuff claimed not to have seen the gun until it was fired. Shameer said that, about five minutes before the shooting, Jainarine Singh had three times threatened Karim and himself, on each occasion pulling out his revolver.

"How long before the shooting did the policeman leave?" Lionel questioned Shameer.

"Five minutes."

"So it was while the policeman was there that the accused threatened you?"

"Yes."

"Where was the policeman standing in relation to the accused?"

"They were standing side by side."

"Where did the accused take his revolver from?"

"His right-hand pocket."

"On each occasion?"

"Yes."

"Were you afraid?"

"Yes, I was afraid."

"So did you say to the policeman, 'Look, Officer, this man is threatening me'?"

"No."

"Why not?"

"Well, the policeman was there."

"So why did you not complain? Why? Why?" When no explanation was forthcoming, Lionel thundered at the witness, "You are lying. No policeman would stand idly by while someone produces a gun and threatens two people."

He switched his attack. "When you rushed the accused," he asked Shameer, "was your cutlass held high?"

"Yes."

"Your hand was in the air?"

"Yes."

"In like manner to your brother's?"

"Yes, but he had no cutlass."

"Why were his hands held high?"

"I don't know." It was the same answer that his father had given.

The policeman who had been at the dam prior to the shooting was called as a witness. He stated that while he was there Jainarine Singh had made no threats, neither had he pulled out a revolver. In answer to a question from Lionel Luckhoo, he said that the accused was quiet and controlled.

"If Shameer had told you he was being threatened by the accused, would you have warned him?"

"Certainly I would."

"You were near the accused?"

"Yes."

"Where were his hands?"

"At his sides."

"Did you see him push his hands in his pockets?"

"No."

Yussuff and Shameer had been battered by relentless cross-examination. They had contradicted each other, and their evidence had been shown to contain improbabilities. But on one main point they both stood firm: they insisted that Singh had shot their son and brother while he was unarmed and at a distance. Yussuff had estimated the distance to be twelve feet; Shameer had said about eighteen feet. Could this last point be disproved in the absence of other witnesses?

Lionel cross-examined the ballistics expert Eustace Kendall, who had given a technical description of the weapon and the type of ammunition that had been used.

"If this revolver were fired two feet away from a target, would the target be scorched?"

"Yes."

"If the target were a man who was wearing only a shirt, would there be powder burns on the shirt, and on the skin under the shirt?"

"I would expect to find scorching."

"From your experience, up to what distance would there be such burns?"

"I have seen burns when the gun was up to two feet away, not further."

Next came the pathologist Dr. Leslie Simon. After questioning him on his experience in conducting post-mortems on bodies bearing gun wounds, Lionel Luckhoo asked, "Did you find any burns on the body of the deceased?"

"Yes, there were signs which were indicative of burns, that is to say, powder burns."

"Have you seen burns of a similar nature before?"

"Yes, often."

"Would I be right in saying that they are consistent with the discharge of a revolver within one foot of the person?"

"Yes."

"And, if the gun were held further away than one foot, what would you find?"

"There might be very light burns."

"Am I right in saying that, if the distance were greater than two feet, there would be no burns?"

The pathologist agreed. When Lionel went on to cite passages from four textbooks on the subject of powder burns, Dr. Simon confirmed that his experience led him to support the statements made by the authors.

By his cross-examination of the prosecution's own witnesses, Lionel had shown that not much more than an arm's length could have separated Jainarine Singh and Karim Baksh when the fatal shot was fired. Now leading evidence for the defense, he put Singh on the stand to tell, on oath, his own version of what happened.

Singh testified that the two brothers Karim and Shameer, incensed by the bulldozing of the dam, both rushed at him with arms upraised, brandishing cutlasses. They were virtually on top of him when he drew his gun and fired. Simultaneously, his hand was almost completely cut through by Shameer. With the judge's permission, Lionel had his client show the jury the ghastly wound made by the cutlass.

In his final address, Lionel Luckhoo exposed the vital weaknesses in the case for the prosecution. Why did Karim approach the accused with his hands in the air? If at that time Singh had a gun in his hand, then Yussuff would have seen it. He did not. If Karim were being threatened by a gun, he would not have continued to advance unarmed on the man holding the weapon. Yussuff and Shameer had lied. There was scientific proof that Karim could not have been much more than twelve inches away from the gun when it was fired.

Neither his father nor his brother had been able to offer any reason that might explain why Karim had his hands upraised. There could be only one reason. Karim, like his brother, was holding a cutlass in his hand. They were determined to stop the destruction of what they considered to be their dam, and it was only Providence that saved the life of the accused. He drew his gun and fired even as the cutlass was descending to dismember him.

"We have heard Jainarine Singh described as a wealthy man, an expert in agriculture, an ex-member of the Cabinet, a lawyer of repute. I ask you not to think of him in these terms, but merely as a member of the community of the State of Guyana who cries out to you for justice. You, by your ready verdict, will reflect what the evidence discloses—that this man was acting in defense of his life, and was fully justified in pulling the trigger to keep off the murderous attack on his person."

In only fifteen minutes, a short retirement for a murder trial, the jury came back with the verdict for which counsel had confidently asked: not guilty. When it was read out, no fewer than fifty lawyers were in court. "A pleasing sight," was Lionel's comment on this show of fraternal solidarity, as he and Jainarine Singh walked out of the courtroom. Always ready to respond to a display of friendship and loyalty, he was as moved by it as was his client.

Fascinated with the career of Sir Lionel Luckhoo, and its degree of similarity to that of storied Perry Mason, I soon learned that fact indeed outdistances fiction; that Sir Lionel, the real-life Perry Mason, out-Masons Perry.

Erle Stanley Gardner, a lawyer and author who parented Perry Mason in print, was often accused of stretching plausibility to the breaking point by allowing Perry Mason to win every case. Literary license was the only plea his critics would consider in mitigation of his offense. Yet Gardner, in all his novels, manipulated Perry Mason through fewer than seventy courtroom triumphs. Lionel Luckhoo's unbroken string of success in murder cases runs to more than three times that number: 232.

Neither heaven nor hell issues statistics. God alone knows the number of souls His vicars on earth have sped on their upward flight, or saved from stumbling into the fiery furnace. As with priests, so with doctors: their worst mistakes are quietly buried, and to trumpet success is forbidden, by a professional ethic that makes a pretense to equality the keystone of conspiracy.

By contrast, the work of the trial lawyer is on public display. When two sides are in opposition, there must be a loser for every winner. An average trial lawyer shows a 50 percent record of success. A lawyer who wins 60 percent of his cases is good. With a 75-percent score, he becomes phenomenal. What word, then, is left to describe Sir Lionel Luckhoo, who has never lost a murder case?

How does this winner keep from losing?

I had to know, and certainly couldn't get all the answers from a few of his cases; so I looked into many, into his methods, and into the multitudinous mysteries of Sir Lionel the boy, the youth, the man, the investigator, and the attorney.

The first of my many mornings in Lionel Luckhoo's office was like plunging into the beginning of numerous Perry Mason stories. His secretary, Miss Indira Singh, cajoles him in Della Street fashion into seeing an unexpected client. A husband and wife enter, trembling in fear. The former has shot an unarmed man and is expecting to be charged with murder.

Luckhoo gives the advice Mason might offer. "Go home. If the police come and arrest you, don't make any statement. If they hurt you, even if they use a tourniquet, still say nothing. They won't kill you—and it's your neck you are saving, remember! Tell them only, 'When I have seen my lawyer, I will make a full statement.' Just keep repeating that. Nothing more."

The man looks scared and doubtful.

"Don't worry," Luckhoo reassures him. "You won't afterwards have to make the full statement. Once I am called, the onus for refusing will then be on me." He adds a last warning. "Don't tell me later you have made a statement saying how the killing took place, or how you believe it happened."

He turns to the wife. "If the police take him, let me know at once. I will find out where he is being held and go see him. Were there any witnesses?"

The wife, a handsome woman, is calmer than her shaken husband. She says there were several witnesses whom she knows.

"Give me their names. Probably the police will have taken statements from them all by now. If they have, I can't take statements. If they have not given any statements, I can inquire into their version."

There are investigators—ex-police detectives and law clerks—whom he uses part-time for legwork. Now he calls one of them and instructs him to interview the witnesses the wife of the client has named.

But, again, like Perry Mason (the repeated comparison cannot be avoided), and unlike any other practicing lawyer, Lionel Luckhoo cannot resist taking part in investigations himself. Once he walked fifteen miles to find and interview workers in the fields who might have seen a fleeing suspect. In a dozen or more murder cases, his own investigations at the scene of the crime have played a decisive part in winning a verdict.

Sure enough, he later goes to view the scene of the shooting in which his new client was involved. It is a poolroom behind a bar-restaurant. Lionel notes from the bloodstains the direction in which the body had fallen. He estimates the distances from doors and tables that might prove to be important, the width of the meshwork around the bar that obstructed the view from certain angles. When the time comes to cross-examine witnesses in court, he will know what they would or could not, should or should not, have seen.

The second client this morning is a man accused of forgery. Middle-aged, respectable, his whole career in jeopardy, he weeps and kneels before the desk as he pleads with Lionel Luckhoo to save him. Tears are not uncommon in this office, but kneeling is more than Luckhoo can stomach. "Get up!" he says, harshly. "You kneel only to God, not to me."

The third and fourth are civil cases. One concerns a dispute over a will; the other, a matter of *habeas corpus.* Apart from the last, so startlingly unusual that it could make legal history, it is all fairly typical of a morning when he is not in court. At this time, Lionel has eight murder cases pending, which is about average. Once, when the murder cases awaiting trial had shot up to twenty, he stopped taking new cases, but resumed when the number dropped to sixteen. He is vastly overworked. With seventy cases in hand altogether, half of them criminal, he decides this very week to take no more until the list is reduced.

Except for murder.

2

Lionel Luckhoo is easy to describe. He looks like Napoleon. When he was High Commissioner to the Court of St. James, the *London Press* photographers asked him to put his hat on sideways and stick a hand inside his jacket in the traditional pose. Such flummery was superfluous. Without props or make-up, he is a closer look-alike to the Emperor than Brando, Boyer, or Steiger ever achieved on film. In repose, after working until weary on a legal brief, he has the brooding look of an exiled Napoleon.

Yet, in a way, the comparison is deceptive. The stern, unyielding, and imperious Napoleonic traits are seldom in evidence, and, when apparent, are merely assumed for courtroom effect. His natural powers—a charm and gift of persuasion—are more reminiscent of Talleyrand.

When he determined to "set his cap," as he puts it, at being a great lawyer, Lionel took stock of his physical assets. They did not please him as being of the kind that could dominate a courtroom. He was five feet, five and a half inches tall. He could not forget the half foot that was lacking, not even the half inch. The commanding height of a Marshall Hall had been denied him. Neither in those days did he have a frontal bulge he could decorate with a gold watch-chain. (That touch of Napoleonic *embonpoint* has been added since.) So what had nature given him? A candid face, a ready smile, and a friendly eye. Lionel Luckhoo likes people, and he likes people to like him. His common greeting, "Hello, my friend," makes those he meets feel that it is more than a formal salute. Friendliness does not win cases in court, but it keeps judges and juries in a mood to listen.

Nonetheless, he does dominate the courtroom. Normally, with a witness he is coaxing rather than combative. Needless belligerence can rebound if a witness, made defiant, should withhold the revealing answer. Yet, when it is called for, the velvety voice can change, can pierce like a stiletto. Lionel treats judges with an old-world courtesy. Even when angered, he does not lose his temper, but he has been known to respond to blatantly bad rulings with smooth sarcasm. One judge, after much prevarication over a submission, ended by saying, "I'm afraid I must rule against you."

He was answered, "You are perfectly right to be afraid, your honor. When this matter is considered by a higher tribunal, your fears will be fully justified." They were.

One day a man came into Lionel Luckhoo's office. "Is talking to you like talking to a priest?" he asked. "Nothing I say can be repeated?"

Lionel confirmed that their conversation had absolute privilege.

"Then name your fee. I'll pay you anything. I want to get rid of my wife. Just tell me how to do it safely, and I will do it."

That was one time Sir Lionel Luckhoo did lose his temper and threaten to call the police. Usually, however, he has an even disposition and a sense of humor, sometimes tinged with the macabre. And it breaks out in unlikely places. To equate being serious with being solemn is a confusion of trivial minds. He was knighted twice—once for legal and once for diplomatic services. After the first time that Queen Elizabeth had dubbed him on both shoulders with the royal sword, she said to him, "You looked very grave, Sir Lionel."

"Yes, ma'am," he replied. "I was thinking of what would happen if you were to take a short cut from one shoulder to the other with the sword."

His most harrowing moments are while waiting for the jury to bring in a verdict. He passes the time doodling and reviewing the evidence for an appeal—just in case. Six times, Lionel has heard the death sentence pronounced on clients, and has then won the cases on appeal. Twice he has had to go before the ultimate legal tribunal, the Privy Council in London, to achieve victory. Far more often, of course, after the harrowing comes the immediate reward of hearing the foreman of the jury declare, "Not guilty."

Lionel Luckhoo has never kept a judge waiting. It upsets him if he has to rush into court at the last moment. He likes to arrive early, get his books and papers in order, and settle down for at least five minutes before the court is in session. Whether the issue is large or small, Lionel is in a state of nerves, like an actor awaiting his opening line, until the moment comes for him to rise and say, "Your honor, I represent the defendant." Then the tension vanishes, and he is completely immersed in the case—until next morning, when it starts all over again. After all the years and the hundreds of cases, "It's still an awful thing," he says, "to know that a man's whole future may be decided by your presentation of his case—no matter whether it's a question of money, imprisonment, or saving him from being hanged."

It was charged against Socrates that he made the worse case appear the better one. Demosthenes, Cicero, and every advocate in every age have had to face the accusation: "Why do you defend an unworthy cause?" Beyond all doubt, many a guilty man has owed his freedom to a clever counsel. And law-abiding citizens, who cannot imagine they will ever be in need of a defender, find this disturbing to their peace of mind.

Inevitably, the question came before Dr. Samuel Johnson. Sir William Forbes had said he thought an honest lawyer should never undertake a cause which he was satisfied was not a just one. Boswell records the blunt answer:

"Sir," said Dr. Johnson, "a lawyer has no business with the justice or injustice of the cause which he undertakes. . . . The justice or injustice of the cause is to be decided by the judge. Consider, sir, what is the purpose of courts of justice? It is that every man shall have his case fairly tried by men appointed to try causes. . . . A lawyer is not to usurp the province of the jury or the judge and determine what shall be the effect of the evidence or the result of legal argument. . . . If lawyers were to undertake no such causes until they were sure that they were just, a man might be precluded altogether from a trial of his claim, though were it judicially examined it might be found a very *just* claim."

The greatest of English advocates, Thomas Erskine, put it as plainly when he defended Tom Paine. "If the advocate refuses to defend from what he may think of the charge or the defense, he assumes the character of the judge; nay, he assumes it before the hour of judgment . . . and puts the influence of a perhaps mistaken opinion into the scale against the accused."*

Under the rule of law, a man is legally innocent until a jury has decided he is guilty. Every accused is allowed a defender, whose duty it is to say for him what he would say for himself, were he able. If the State, with all its resources pitted against a lone advocate, cannot then prove to any twelve ordinary citizens that the accused is guilty beyond a reasonable doubt, surely he is entitled to go free.

A defender should be credited with the salvation of those who, deprived of his advocacy, might have been wrongfully convicted. Under the best legal systems, there are more miscarriages of justice than most of us care to remember. Such lists would be immeasurably longer if we had to add the innocents freed through fine and fearless advocacy; conversely, they would be shorter if the best counsel had been available to all.

While admiring the art of the advocate, it is easy to lose sight of the fact that human lives and happiness depend on his every performance. Lionel Luckhoo does not forget it, nor could he if he wished. To walk down the street with him, to pass through any town or village in Guyana, is sure to bring a reminder.

A young man comes up. "You don't know me," he says, "but you got my father off a murder charge. If you hadn't, I wouldn't be here, because I wasn't born then."

Two middle-aged men come from 200 miles upcountry to bring him a gift of pawpaw, a fruit he specially likes. Years ago, they were jointly accused of murder, and his skill saved them from the rope. They still remember.

* *Lionel Luckhoo's views on how many of his clients were guilty, and the proper roles of defender, prosecutor, judge, and jury, will appear in other chapters.*

His car stops outside a country store. The group of men standing there become wildly excited. They call out to someone inside. "Come quickly, George! It's the man who got you off the murder charge. It's Lionel."

Such scenes are enacted wherever he goes. The three best-known faces in Guyana must be those of Forbes Burnham, the Prime Minister; Cheddi Jagan, the leader of the opposition; and Lionel Luckhoo. He, too, has been in politics. In the 1950s, when Burnham and Jagan were allied, he formed a party to oppose both, and met with disastrous defeat at the polls. It is a deeper and more personal recognition which he now receives than that awarded to the political figure. He is greeted as the friend of people in trouble, the defender who won freedom for them, their relatives, or their friends, when a situation seemed hopeless.

The Victoria Law Courts, scene of so many triumphs, are across the street, directly facing Lionel Luckhoo's office. But even today he will travel the breadth of the country for a preliminary inquiry into a capital charge. It is not for the money. Errol Barrow, when he was Prime Minister of Barbados, once commented to Lionel on the fees he charges, "You are not the world's most successful lawyer but the world's biggest sucker."

For a long time now, judges, lawyers, and friends have been asking Lionel Luckhoo why he does not stop, and so preserve an undefeated record. Partly, his pride will not allow him to ease up, or to weight the odds by taking only the less difficult cases—at least two of the trials now pending are likely to rank among the toughest he has faced. But the real answer is that he can resist neither the human appeal nor the challenge to his skills.

Some observers insist that Lionel's stupendous record is attributable not only to his rare ability but to a degree of good luck.

Certainly, anyone booked on a murder charge needs either luck or Luckhoo. It may be better to have both, but, given a choice . . . well, Lady Luck is an inconstant nymph, while Luckhoo is ever indomitable in the fight for victory.

Two hundred thirty-two. That number will be out of date before you read it. Will it still be rising, higher and higher? Or will the longest run of success in legal history have come to an end?

Chapter 2
The Case of the Dubious Doctor

The four-year-old boy had just met the Very Important Personage.

"Papa," he said, "people call him His Excellency and KCMG. What do they mean?"

"Oh, we call him His Excellency because he is the Governor and rules this colony. KCMG means Knight Commander of St. Michael and St. George."

The boy pondered. "Papa, it sounds nice. How can I become an Excellency and a KCMG?"

The father smiled. Wryly. "Son, you can never aspire to those heights. These people govern us from abroad, and such high honors they keep to themselves."

As things were then, in 1918, that was very true. Yet the boy's destiny was to become an "Excellency" accredited to four major countries, and probably the first Indian outside India itself to be created a KCMG.

It is with a boy slightly older that the story really begins. Lokhooa was seven when he ran away from home. His home was in India, and he ran (or, more accurately, sailed) halfway round the world to what was then British Guiana.

Guyana, as it is now known since becoming independent, was colonized by the Dutch. The first glimpse of its topography, let alone the architecture, indicates their influence.

Most of Guyana's coastal land lies below sea level. To make it habitable, the Dutch had to build seawalls and dig canals and dikes as in Holland. Only stubborn Dutchmen would have taken that much trouble. Floods are still common today, and keeping the seawall repaired is a major occupation of the Guyanese.

The country was ceded to England during the Napoleonic wars. Unlike other former British possessions in the Caribbean area, Guyana is not a small island, but a hefty wedge of the South American continent. Potentially, it is a rich country. But the interior was never developed by the colonizers, and the Guyanese themselves have lacked the means. In the nineteenth century, Guyana, from the British viewpoint, was merely a large sugar estate.

Cutting cane under a hot sun is hard work. Slaves from Africa were imported for the task. When emancipation came, the plantocracy ran into problems. Many former slaves refused to work at all; others would work only the three or four days a week that brought them enough wages to exist on. Importation of labor from other parts of the West Indies was tried without much success. Then John Gladstone, father of the future Victorian Prime Minister, investigated the possibilities of hiring labor in India. The first batch of immigrants from Calcutta sailed January 13, 1838.

Indian immigration to Guyana became firmly established during the next two decades. Doubtless, the recruiters of labor painted an overly bright picture of the future awaiting Indian men and boys in the strange land across the seas, but the reality was at least a step higher than eking out a beggarly existence in the bazaars.

The story goes that young Lokhooa and his two older brothers, Ruhoman (11) and Pahalad (13), were sightseeing at Lucknow when they met one of the recruiters. In five years, he promised, they could make their fortunes and return home rich. For Lokhooa, the promise of wealth was to come true, but he did not go back to India. He stayed and founded a dynasty.

Lokhooa learned English at a primary school in Guyana. His brother Ruhoman taught him Hindi and Urdu. Mastery of the three languages enabled him to become an interpreter in the magistrate's courts, starting a family connection with the law that has expanded up to today. No fewer than sixteen of his descendants have become lawyers, six of them taking silk. But, for Lokhooa himself, the courthouse did not offer much of a financial future. He and Ruhoman had become Christians, and were now known as Moses Luckhoo and John Ruhoman. He had married Miss Elizabeth Saywack, whose father was a merchant in the town of New Amsterdam. Moses went to work for his father-in-law, later opened his own provision store, then a dry goods store, and, in time, became one of the wealthiest merchants in town.

New Amsterdam lies along the coast, about seventy miles east of Georgetown, the capital. Here Moses and Elizabeth Luckhoo raised a family of six sons and a daughter. The eldest son, Edward Alfred, was articled to Neil Ross McKinnon, Q.C.* In 1899, he became the first Indian solicitor in British Guiana.

E.A. worked hard and earned money. When his father died, he helped to educate his brothers. Joseph Alexander went to England to qualify as a barrister. David Lawrence was sent to Canada, taking medical degrees at Toronto and, later, at Edinburgh and Glasgow.

E.A. married Evelyn Mungal Singh. Her father was a head man on the huge sugar estate at Port Mourant, and her mother kept a grocery store in the town. Evelyn was one of the great beauties of her time. Lady Davson, who, as the daughter of Elinor Glyn, had some claim to being a connoisseur, was one who rhapsodized over Evelyn Luckhoo's good looks. Their second son, Lionel Alfred, was born March 2, 1914.

Lionel Luckhoo's first memory is of celebrations that marked the end of the First World War, in 1918. Homes were decorated and the entire town was lighted and trimmed up for the coming of the Governor to New Amsterdam. That was the day Lionel's first wistful ambitions sprouted, with no seeming hope of fulfillment.

Childhood friends of the Luckhoos were the Mittelholzers, who lived next door. Edgar Mittelholzer, a few years older than Lionel, spent much of his time at the Luckhoo house.

* *Queen's Counsel.*

During the week, Lionel and his elder brother Edward Victor, and Edgar and his younger brother Mervin, would write short stories in their exercise books. On Saturdays, they read them to each other. Edgar's were much the best—perhaps not surprisingly, for he was to become the first noted West Indian novelist.

Strangely enough, Lionel's stories usually dealt with the law, often introducing court scenes, though he had never been to court. But he was familiar with the jargon, because much of his time was spent in his father's office. He knew what a brief was. It was what the chief clerk handed to his father after statements had been prepared. He knew what a mortgage was, and a conveyance. The boys played court games. "This is Ramdhani's mortgage," one of them might say, waving a bit of paper. "He can't pay, so we must take away his house and land." Another would then stand up, saying, "I am the lawyer for Ramdhani. You can't do that. It's not fair. . . ." So they became versed in legal ritual at an early age.

One mock trial, in particular, foreshadowed things to come. Lionel was the defense counsel. His schoolboy client had been seen running and, when stopped, had said, "Robin is dead in the pasture." Evidence was led of quarrels, and threats made by the accused that one day he would kill Robin. The victim had been choked, and on his neck was the clear impression of a right-handed thumbprint. Lionel had to work out his defense from this. He put his client on the stand and had him state, "I am left-handed. I bat with my left hand and I bowl with my left hand. I have little strength in my right. If I were to choke anyone it would be with my left hand. I came across the body in the pasture and I reported that Robin was dead." Lionel Luckhoo won his first acquittal in a murder trial—from a mixed jury of school children. Thirty years later, the same left-hand-versus-right-hand defense was to save a real-life client charged with murder, when he had motive, means, opportunity, and the testimony of an eyewitness stacked against him!

Edward Alfred Luckhoo gave much of his time to public service. He was Mayor of New Amsterdam no fewer than fifteen times. Despite his comment to his son on the colonial rulers "hogging" all the honors, breezes of change were beginning to blow, and he became the first Indian in British Guiana to be awarded an OBE.* In his private life, E.A. was retiring. He preferred to leave decisions about his home and children to the womenfolk. The rulers of Lionel's home life were Mummy and her sister, known to everyone as Aunty.

Mummy and Aunty were ambitious for the boys. Before Edward and Lionel had reached their teens, their futures were firmly planned. The plan was simple: first, the best schools in Guyana; then, the best universities in the world. Mummy had not had a secondary education, but she had asked advice of her English friends. Oxford and Cambridge universities were the best, she was told, unless a boy were going in for medicine, in which case London University was better. So the ladies had decided that Edward must go to Oxford and become a lawyer. For Lionel, it was to be London and the study of medicine. The third brother, Lloyd, four or five years younger than Lionel, had not yet had his future mapped out for him.

Lionel's first school, the Church of Scotland School, still stands—on five-foot-high stilts for protection against floods: a wooden-walled, whitewashed building with latticed windows and a green tin roof. From there, he went to Berbice High School, the only secondary school in town, then to Queen's College, which still has the reputation of being the best school in Guyana.

Queen's College is in Georgetown. There, outside school hours, Aunty was in charge, which meant no dodging of homework. Her strict rule was homework every day, including holidays. Just one weekday afternoon was all she allowed for games. On Saturdays, when Lionel could have played cricket, Aunty insisted that he take music lessons. This brought about a rebellion. Lionel would jump on his bicycle wearing his old "bughouse" (cork hat), wave Aunty a fond goodbye, and ride off in the direction of the music teacher's house, then turn down the first side street and be off to cricket, his gear in his music bag. Came the day when someone who saw him playing cricket informed on him to Aunty.

* *Order of the British Empire.*

He got a hiding that he still remembers. Today, with no time for practice, Lionel still gives a good amateur rendering of popular classics on the piano, so perhaps the hiding effected lasting results.

Guyana may or may not have lost another Lance Gibbs,* owing to Aunty's strictness. While Lionel insists that he was known as "Hat Trick" Luckhoo on account of his bowling performances, Sir Harold Bollers, Chief Justice of Guyana, who was one form behind him at Queen's, remembers him not for his skill at games but as a good student. His main traits would seem to have been a capacity for independent thought and the courage and energy to follow through on his ideas. By the time he reached the fourth form, Lionel had decided that the masters had too much of their own way—a viewpoint not uncommon nowadays, but unexpressed, if not unthought, in those days. As an attempted remedy, he started a magazine, the *4B Ideal Rag*, which took a look at the masters through the eyes of the boys. Alas, it achieved only one issue, partly because sales were too well organized. The 1,000 copies printed were sold at the school and on the streets of Georgetown in an hour. Within the next hour, Lionel and the other boys involved had been summoned to explain to the headmaster, E.R.D. Molder, the publication of what he regarded as a scurrilous diatribe against those in authority.

Lionel protested that no names had been mentioned. This weak defense was brushed aside.

"Who else can be *Moldy* but me?" Mr. Molder demanded. "Who else can be *Hambones* but Mr. H.A.M. Beckles? You refer to Mr. Pilgrim as *Bogus*. Everyone knows that Mr. Pilgrim is Bogus!"

Lionel said, "Sir, I agree."

The headmaster did not think that was funny, either. The press was suppressed, and its public likewise. Every boy who had a copy of the magazine was caned, and that took in most of the school.

* *Listed in the* Guiness Book of Records *as having taken the greatest number of wickets in test cricket.*

By the time he reached the fifth form, Lionel had learned better how to channel rebellion. The system had to be reformed from within; the younger boys ought to have a representative among the hierarchy. After a warlike campaign, he himself was elected, the youngest prefect ever, and the first to gain office before having reached the sixth form.

Lionel's next venture was to form a debating society. The first talking pictures had been shown in Guyana, but the sound was so poor that many people still preferred the old silent films. It was agreed that the first debate should be on the proposal that the talkies were better than the silents. Lionel spoke for the motion, his main opponent being his cousin Joseph (later to become Sir Joseph Luckhoo, Chief Justice of Guyana). When the vote was taken, all present put up their hands in favor of the motion—including the opposer, Joseph Luckhoo. After the debate, one of the masters, H.A.M. Beckles, spoke to Lionel. "I understand you are going in for medicine," he said. "Scrub the idea! You have a very persuasive manner. You should do law."

Lionel had long felt dubious about the choice of career foisted on him by Mummy and Aunty. Beckles' remark firmed him in his opposition. But his "persuasive manner" had little effect on the two determined ladies. They argued that there were too many lawyers in the family already. Uncle David was the only doctor, and, as he was getting on in years, someone should be preparing to take his place. Lionel's case was thrown out of court, and there was no way of appealing the decision.

After he had taken the Guyana Scholarship Examination (doing reasonably well overall, and coming in first in English), Lionel was shipped to London and St. Bartholomew's Hospital.

2

Up to then, Lionel Luckhoo had lived a sheltered life. At a time when few people owned private motor cars, his father had four. When asked what he intended doing with them, E.A. said that he looked upon the cars as a good investment, and the four together had not cost him more than $1,200. Of course, there was plenty of poverty to be seen in Guyana, as elsewhere in the West Indies. But it was not the harsh poverty known to colder climes.

West Indian politicians and sociologists seem to be endlessly bewildered by their people who, apparently work-shy at home, develop something akin to a Stakhanovite complex when they emigrate north. Wage differences are a factor, but the most potent reason, surely, is climate. A warm climate inhibits effort and makes living easy. If the roof leaks, it is merely a discomfort, not a hazard to health. Sitting under a mango tree and catching the fruit as it falls may not provide a satisfactory diet; but the family that has a patch of land with coconuts, oranges, or breadfruit trees, and can grow cocos, yams, sweet potatoes, and keep a few chickens, goats, and perhaps a cow, is near to self-sufficiency. Shirt, trousers, and underwear are all the clothing necessary. In the cold cities of the North, necessities must include a substantial dwelling, heating, heavy clothing, and all food must be bought.

It is hardly surprising that Lionel, like others from the colonies before and since, was shocked upon seeing the conditions people lived under in the East End of London. It seemed very wrong that in the rich mother country there should be such extreme poverty. The experience helped to form the political philosophy he holds today, somewhat left of center, a basic belief in giving fair opportunity to everyone and, by so doing, raising rather than lowering the standards of life.

For two years, Lionel struggled along at medical school, but his heart was never in it. His brother E.V. was reading law at Oxford. The closest contact Lionel had with the law during this period was to watch Sir Bernard Spilsbury do a post-mortem. Neither he nor the other students then knew enough to benefit from the experience; all they gained was the satisfaction of saying they had seen the Deity at work. And Spilsbury's dexterous dealing with a cold corpse had in no way prepared Lionel for his first sight of an operation on a living body. On this occasion, a surgeon named Knight was cutting out a cancer of the breast. When he plunged his scalpel into the woman's flesh, black blood oozed out. Lionel promptly turned an involuntary half-circle and fell to the floor in a dead faint. After this experience, the sight of blood, even his own if he cut himself while shaving, made him go weak at the knees. The Dean of the Medical School wrote to his father, saying it seemed unlikely that Lionel would be able to overcome the weakness, and suggesting that he try another profession. (The Dean was right in his prognosis. The blood phobia persists with Lionel to this day. Once, a witness had to remove a bandage in court and display a cut on his forearm. One tiny blob of blood seeped out. Lionel was so upset by the sight that he had to ask the judge for an adjournment.)

E.V. and Lionel returned together—but what a contrast in their homecomings! Although ostensibly his time had been spent in throwing lavish parties and rushing off to race meetings, E.V. had gained an honors degree in jurisprudence at Oxford and eaten his dinners at the Middle Temple. Predictably, he had a brilliant legal career ahead of him. Lionel went home a seeming failure. His father said he must do some hard work before he could go back to England for further studies. In fact, E.A. was not minded to send him back at all.

Lionel joined the Civil Service and was posted to the Deeds Registry. The unhappy conflict with medicine had not impaired his capacity for independent thought, nor lessened his zeal as a reformer. After a month, he decided that the way things were done at the Deeds Registry was all wrong. He wrote a long commentary on how matters could be improved, and was pleasantly surprised to be called to an interview with the Registrar, Edgar Mortimer Duke, the day after it was submitted. The Registrar looked on him kindly. "My boy," he said, "you have been here one month. Already you want to tell me how to run the Deeds Registry. Well, you have told me. Now, perhaps, you would like to improve the work of some other department." Lionel felt a bit hurt.

He was transferred to the Public Works Department. Here, again, he quickly saw what was wrong and how it should be remedied. For one thing, there was much too much waste. But he had learned caution. He waited two months before putting his suggestions into writing. Forthwith, the head of the department, P.H.N. Saunders, had him in for an interview. "This is progressive," Saunders said, thumbing through the screed. "But it is too progressive for us. Perhaps you would like to try another department."

Before Lionel quite knew what was happening, he found himself working in the Post Office. Here a lot of girls were employed. Lionel, a fresh flower in his buttonhole every day, became something of a masher. So apparent did it become that he found the females more interesting than the mail that his work was repeatedly checked. Curiously, the work was always up to date. Finally, the puzzled Superintendent asked him, "How do you manage to play around all the time and still do your work?" Lionel said,"I'll write you a minute on the subject." His secret was that he did the work at home, where there were no girls to distract him. The promised minute pointed out how foolish it was to have employees become so bored that they simply filled in the allotted hours till they could escape the office, taking no real interest in their work; and went on to outline some ideas for reorganization. The Superintendent read it and said, "How would you like to move to another department?"

For the third time in less than a year, Lionel was given a transfer. This time, he ended up in a District Administration far from Georgetown, acting as a sub-sub-protector of the Amerindians. The natives were badly treated. Not only did the Administration take advantage of them; they were defrauded by others through its laxity and neglect. All of this Lionel censured in an indignant diatribe. It was an indictment of his bosses, and the result was inevitable: he was asked to which other department he would wish to apply.

Four times were enough. Lionel went home and told Mummy that the Civil Service held no future for him. Looking very much to the bright side, Mummy suggested that, by moving from one department to another, he was learning what went on in all, and when he advanced to a high position such wide experience would be valuable. That argument did not appeal to Lionel. Then what, Mummy asked, did he want to do? Lionel said, "I want to go back to London and do law."

The family had not been doing so well financially. E.V.'s side studies of horseflesh and high living had made his degree-taking costly. Lionel himself had not been innocent of an interest in equine form while abroad, and the money spent on his blighted medical career had been wholly wasted. Now Lloyd was ready for university. He was a brilliant student, and it was intended he should become a lawyer. Still, Mummy decided, Lionel deserved a second chance. Somehow, she would find the money.

So Lionel and Lloyd both went to London. They romped through the first part of the law examinations. With eighteen months to go before taking finals, there was no urgent need to study. (That was what they thought.) Came September 3, the start of World War II, and, immediately, a cable: "Forget the law and return home. You are too precious to have us suffer the worry of what is happening to you from day to day."

The boys did not want to go home. Lionel had no intention of failing a second time. He went to his tutor and asked him the shortest possible time it would take to get through the finals.

"If you are brilliant and work very hard, it can be done in six or nine months."

"Do you think we can do it in three months?"

"Absolutely impossible."

"Thank you very much, sir. You are about to see the impossible happen."

Lionel and Lloyd laid out a plan of campaign. Living below them were two young men who ran a coffee shop nearby and would deliver all their meals. On the door they fixed a large notice: THE LUCKHOOS ARE OUT. Then, for three months, the two of them worked sixteen hours a day, slept for six hours, and allowed themselves two hours for meals and general purposes. Once a week, they interrupted the routine to relax at a picture show. At the end of the period, they sat their finals and passed.

Lionel went home a lawyer. He had had just one object in mind: getting through the examinations in minimal time before the family forced their return. It was done this way from necessity. Necessity is said to know no law, and Lionel knew very little.

Chapter 3
The Case of the Unexcelled Uncle

What was my ambition? My uncle had then achieved a tremendous record of fifty murder trials without a conviction. I remember setting my sights on that target and saying, "I am going to get as many acquittals as he has."

—Sir Lionel Luckhoo

The most learned lawyer is not necessarily the best advocate. If a knotty point of law arose during a trial, Marshall Hall would invariably turn to his junior and say, "You must argue this one." Today, Lionel Luckhoo is "very quick to see a legal point" (I am quoting Chief Justice Bollers), but he himself would be the last to claim that he is the best lawyer in the world, or even in the Caribbean. (In Lionel's opinion, the latter distinction belongs to E.V. While Sir Edward Luckhoo was Chancellor of the Judiciary in Guyana, all his minority judgments were upheld by the law lords in London when the cases were appealed.)

The trial lawyer needs qualities that law schools cannot teach. First, he must be a fearless fighter, unwilling to count the battle won or lost until his client is set free—or has been hanged! He must understand people, their likely motives, what makes them tick, so as to be able to bring out the best or expose the worst in witnesses. He must persistently dig, in or out of court (and many victories are won in the preparation) until he uncovers the weaknesses of his opponent's case. He must be a natural actor—persuasive, derisive, challenging, pleading, sometimes angry. The truly great defenders—Marshall Hall in England, Clarence Darrow in America, Fernand Labori in France—have had an intensity of feeling, a fierce compassion, that could wring a response from the most inert jury. When they wept, they did not weep alone.

Lionel Luckhoo has often moved juries to tears. But his own first tears in court came after the verdict. Within a week of his arrival home from England, a brief had been given him by Lloyd Cabral, one of the keenest legal minds in Guyana. The charge was attempted murder, and Cabral was plain-spoken about the neophyte's chances: "This is not just a bad case, it is a hopeless case. You cannot depend on the facts to win it; you will have to depend upon your powers of persuasion."

The trial ended with the jury voting nine to three for a conviction. One more against him, making it ten to two, and Lionel would have lost his first case before a jury. He did a better job at the retrial, and won his client an acquittal. Tears sprang to Lionel's eyes when the jury foreman read the verdict. Mr. Justice Fretz, noticing the apparent distress of the young counsel, sent his clerk to ask if he were ill and in pain. "Tell his honor," Lionel said, "that one may cry either from pain or from joy. My tears are from the latter."

Lionel's very first appearance in court had been on behalf of a man who pleaded guilty to having sold diluted milk. All that could be done was to make a plea in mitigation. Lionel rose to address the Court.

"There had been heavy rains. . . ."

A long pause, until the judge was impelled to inquire, "Well?"

"The grass was very wet. . . ."

Another pause. Another "Well?"

"The cow had been eating grass all day. . . ."

"Mr. Luckhoo, are you trying to plead that the milk came diluted from the cow?"

"No, your honor, I am appealing to the judicial sense of humor."

The farmer got off with a light sentence. Lionel received the first and smallest fee he ever collected—only ten dollars, but, jingling in his pocket, it felt like a million.

Humor is, mercifully, a feature in many trials, particularly in the lower courts, where offenses of less serious character are dealt with. The smile may be caused by the magistrate, counsel, or even the man in the dock. Lionel Luckhoo recalls hearing one of the funniest pleas ever, at New Amsterdam. Magistrate Veeraswamy said to the prisoner, "You are charged with stealing five dollars, the property of Godfrey Thomas. Are you guilty or not guilty?"

"Not guilty," said the accused. "I did steal his purse, but there were only four dollars inside it."

A magistrate before whom Lionel often appeared, Max Fitzpatrick, used humor on occasion to bring about a just decision. In a paternity case, the defendant had denied being the father. Fitzpatrick ordered that the baby be brought into court. Like every other baby, it resembled no one, except possibly Winston Churchill. The magistrate examined the baby closely. "This is one good-looking baby," was his verdict. And to the defendant: "You should be proud of him."

The supposed father looked at the child with new interest. "You think he is good-looking, sir?"

"You lucky man, of course he is."

"Well, then, sir, me the father."

There were amusing and amazing characters among the leading counsel. Lionel, appearing as junior to Sir Eustace Woolford in a fraud case, found himself conducting the defense on his own throughout a strenuous eight-day trial. Sir Eustace merely sent him the reassuring message, "Don't worry, Luckhoo. I'll be there to address."

True to his word, Sir Eustace arrived at the crucial hour, knowing little of what had taken place during the previous eight days. Lionel sat there, wondering what his leader could possibly say. "This man may be guilty," was Sir Eustace's candid opening remark to the jury. "But he is charged alone. Those above him, his superiors, are also guilty, but they are not here. Let me remind you of the famous *Punch* cartoon of Lady Castle, who was charged with larceny and was acquitted. The caption read, 'What is larceny in the kitchen is kleptomania in the Castle.' "

That was Sir Eustace's address, and it gained a verdict of not guilty.

The really outrageous character among the Guyanese lawyers was Samuel Ignatius Cyrus. To the confusion of his legal brethren, he was always late in attending court. He was the only counsel who could take three cases in three different courts on the same day and give some time to each. One Monday morning, when he was due at Berbice to defend in a murder trial, a telegram arrived from Mahaicony: "Car broken down. Coming by bicycle." Thirty miles by bicycle for a big fat advocate was no small feat! This same case went to the Privy Council in London, and Cyrus was already on the boat when he remembered that he had left his brief behind. He rushed back to collect it, but the gangway had already been taken up by the time he returned. Nothing daunted, Cyrus jumped on a baggage carrier and was hoisted aboard by crane.

In London, the Privy Council gave Cyrus a hard time with its questions, and he became slow and halting in his replies. Lord Goddard, the former Lord Chief Justice, finally said, "Mr. Cyrus, you seem to be having some language difficulties."

"Yes, m'lud, " Cyrus was quick to agree. After that, they gave him all the time he wanted. "It was their fault," he said to Lionel Luckhoo later, "if they didn't know that we spoke English in British Guiana."

Speaking English not wisely but too well gave Lionel Luckhoo his most embarrassing experience in the early years. His uncle Joseph Alexander Luckhoo was then the leading criminal lawyer in Guyana. He sent Lionel to the preliminary inquiry into a case of murder he was too busy to attend. When the car drew up outside the courthouse in the little town of Buxton, relatives of the accused crowded round, expecting to see J.A. Luckhoo emerge. Instead, it was a youthful Lionel Luckhoo. In his best British accent, not long having returned, he said, "I'm sorry my uncle finds it difficult to be present. To whom am I speaking?" The father of the accused eyed him with contempt. "To whom, to whom," he mimicked. "*Tomb* dey burial ground. Me no hire you. Tek dey car, and go back to where you come from." The very junior counsel beat a hasty retreat.

At this time, J.A. Luckhoo had won fifty murder acquittals in a row. Eventually, he was to lose just two out of seventy-one murder trials.

2

As yet, Lionel was untried in a major court battle, but his chance came quickly. Fewer than six months after having joined the Bar, he was briefed for his murder trial.

It was a heavier responsibility then than it is now, for inexperienced counsel. In those days, there was no right of appeal. The gallows operated smoothly and swiftly. Once the judge had pronounced sentence of hanging, for all practical purposes the prisoner was dead.

Lionel spent the night before the murder trial with his father, who advised him what to stress and what to avoid. "Remember one cardinal principle when you are addressing the jury," E.A. Luckhoo told his son. "Pick out two individuals. Look for one who is nodding his head and seems to be agreeing with you; then seek out another who is turning his head away because you do not convince him. Speak first to the one who is nodding. When you think you have won him over completely, move on to the one who appears dubious. Concentrate on him, look him in the eye, make him feel that you are eschewing everything else to hold his attention because the life of your client is in his hands, and that he must be convinced, as he ought to be convinced, that your man is innocent and deserves an acquittal."

Lionel made use of this advice many times, later on. But at this first murder trial, he was puzzled as to how to put it into practice. The client was pleading self-defense. Attacked by two men, he had picked up a cutlass and decapitated one of them. There was a fair chance to argue that he had been under strong provocation and in fear of his life. Lionel looked along the double row of jurors; not a head either nodded or turned away. Most of them gave the impression of being totally uninterested. One man had eased off his shoe and was playing with his toes.

"Papa!" Lionel said under his breath. "What do I do now?" Papa was not there to give advice. Lionel faced the jury and fixed his eye on the foreman.

"Mr. Foreman," he said, "let me suppose that you are on my side, that you are convinced this man was acting in self-defense. Let me further suppose that you already accept all the points and arguments I might raise which support that view of the case. Now, Mr. Juror Number Twelve," and he turned to that member of the jury, "let us suppose that you are in a state of mind where you feel that this man did too much to allow a plea of self-defense, that he exceeded the limits the law can permit. You may feel that he is guilty of having abused his rights by using a cutlass when only a stick was being used against him. So let me show you the points that, as a highly intelligent man, you should consider. Let me try to prevail on you to come to that point of view which your good foreman—as I am suggesting theoretically—has already arrived at. . . ."

His flow was interrupted by the Crown Prosecutor rising to his feet. "Your honor, I'm afraid this form of address is very novel and very new. I don't know whether it should be permitted."

The judge smiled. "Mr. Luckhoo, is this the first murder case in which you have addressed the jury?"

"That is so, if it please your honor."

"Mr. Luckhoo, you may proceed. I am very interested in your novel approach."

Lionel proceeded. Maybe because he had aroused the interest of the judge, who summed up in his favor, maybe because Juror Number Twelve really was the "Doubtful Dan" and was won over, he gained his first murder acquittal.

During the next few years, Lionel Luckhoo appeared in a dozen murder trials. Each time, he won a verdict. He was on the way, but still a long way behind J.A. Luckhoo, in achievement, when he fell into the morass of his thirteenth case.

Chapter 4
The Case of the Lucky Thirteenth

After God, I remember him. And I call upon God to give him long life and good health, that he may be able to save others also.
—*Noor Mohamed*

From the very beginning, it seemed that the thirteenth murder case would be dead unlucky—that is to say, the client dead, and Luckhoo unlucky. Lionel had never been superstitious. It was the nature of the case itself which now made him feel his luck had run dry.

The incidence of arrest and prosecution in cases of murder by poison is low. Some police authorities estimate it at no better than one in fifty. Scotland Yard, more conservative or more efficient, says one in four. Conversely, the rate of conviction is high, perhaps because juries find poisoning the most abhorrent of crimes. And Lionel's thirteenth client had lost two wives, both of whom had somehow or other imbibed a fatal dose of potassium cyanide. As the old joke has it, *sayonara* is goodbye in Japanese and *cyanide* is goodbye in any language. It is one of the quickest-acting poisons.

Noor Mohamed was a good goldsmith. After fifteen years of hard work at his craft, he had become a man of modest wealth, able to provide a comfortable home for his wife Gooriah and their daughter.

Noor was not a good husband, if judged by the standards of a jealous wife or an ardent moralist. His skill as a jeweler had the ladies flocking to his door, and Noor had a roving eye. But his "friendings" did not take a serious turn until Ayesha, the young and attractive wife of a neighbor, arrived on the scene. Gooriah's objections to this affair went unheeded. She became very unhappy.

On May 17, 1947, Gooriah, otherwise in good health, was complaining of a toothache. Allegedly, Noor was heard by a neighbor to say, "You must drink this; it will do you good." Gooriah died after drinking a glass of milk.

The doctor who was called examined the glass only superficially. He detected no smell of poison—cyanide has the characteristic odor of bitter almonds—but poison was quickly proved to have been the cause of death. At the post-mortem, two grains of potassium cyanide were found in Gooriah's stomach.

Goldsmiths use potassium cyanide in their trade. Noor Mohamed had an ample supply in his cupboard. An accident was unlikely, but suicide ranked as a very possible explanation. No doubt Gooriah had been unhappy. It could also be surmised that Noor might have wished to get rid of her. Talk and suspicion there were in plenty, but ultimately the police took no action. The file on the case was marked "Insufficient evidence to prosecute."

A few months later, Ayesha left her husband to live with Noor. Without waiting for her to be divorced, she and Noor went through a religious ceremony of marriage. For a while, they were happy. Then, so the testimony of neighbors had it, there were times when they could be overheard quarreling. One witness claimed to have heard Noor say, "Through this woman people got to say I killed my wife. She must go away now, or she will go away dead." Apparently Ayesha, like Noor himself, was afflicted with a roving eye. Occasionally he would beat her.

On the night of September 16, 1964, Noor was awakened by his young daughter. "Daddy, come quickly!" she said. "Ayesha is frothing." When Noor rushed into Ayesha's room, he saw she was foaming at the mouth. He hurriedly sent for a doctor, who came within minutes, but Ayesha was already dead when he arrived.

She, too, had drunk a glass of milk. Again, the post-mortem gave plain evidence of poisoning by potassium cyanide.

The police took prompt and serious action. Guyana's outstanding detective, Chief Superintendent Billyeald, was put in charge of the case. At the end of his investigation, Noor Mohamed was arrested and charged with the murder of Ayesha.

By itself, the evidence for Noor having murdered Ayesha was not impressive. When Lionel undertook the defense, he realized that his main effort must be directed towards keeping any reference to Gooriah's death from the knowledge of the jury. This was precisely the evidence the prosecutor was anxious to present. When it was argued in court, Lionel vigorously opposed the Crown's application that testimony to the circumstances of the earlier poisoning should be allowed. He contended that such evidence would tend to show Noor Mohamed guilty of criminal acts not covered by the indictment; and this, for the purpose of showing the likelihood, because of his previous criminal conduct or character, that he had committed the offense for which he was being tried. It was not relevant to the issue.

The submissions of prosecution and defense on this point went on for two days before the judge, Sir Donald Jackson, ruled that the evidence could be admitted.

The prosecution called as witness the neighbor living in the same yard, who said that, several hours before Ayesha's death, she had heard Noor say to Gooriah, "You must drink this. . . ." If this was said, it had no significance, Lionel argued, for any drink given her then could not have contained cyanide, or she would have died at once.

His cross-examination of the doctor who had been summoned when Ayesha was dying concentrated on extracting from him the indications for self-administration of the fatal drink.

"The deceased was lying on the bed?"

"Yes, on her back, frothing at the mouth, but she was dead."

"Potassium cyanide is one of the most formidable poisons known to chemists? You will agree it causes death rapidly?"

"Yes."

"Now, Doctor, some eight grains were found in the stomach?"

"Yes."

"The stomach was otherwise empty; death would therefore be quicker than if food were in the stomach, which would dilute the rate of absorption. Would you agree that death would be almost instantaneous?"

"Yes."

"How long after taking the poison?"

"Within a minute or two."

"Would a person taking this quantity of cyanide become unconscious at once?"

"Yes, I would expect so."

"When you saw the glass, did the trace marks indicate that it had been a full glass of milk?"

"It appeared so."

"And how much milk was left at the bottom?"

"About half an inch."

"This gave the appearance of a glass of milk having been almost wholly consumed?"

"Well, this could be so."

"Was the glass a tumbler, a large glass?"

"Yes."

"Now, potassium cyanide has a bitter taste?"

"Yes."

"Milk would not mask the taste?"

"No, it would still be bitter."

"You saw no sign of any spilt milk?"

"No."

"You saw no external marks on the throat or face to indicate pressure being used to open the mouth and force liquid in?"

"No, there were no marks."

In his address to the jury, Lionel stressed that the defense was putting forward no explanation of the deaths—because the two people who could have explained the reasons, who knew the why and the how, were the ones who were dead. If Gooriah had been unhappy, if she had felt that with poison within her reach she could commit suicide, and if she did commit suicide, there was nothing to say that Ayesha, if she were being badly treated, and if she too were unhappy, had not taken a similar course. The Crown's case was built on suspicion, but suspicion piled upon suspicion was not proof.

Nought multiplied by one was nought. Nought multiplied by a hundred was still nought. A case built on no other foundation than suspicion was bound to fail.

"Convict this man," he challenged the jury. "Convict him unhesitatingly—if the prosecution can show you the *nexus*, the connecting link between the death of Ayesha and any proven act of the accused. Let them produce evidence that he gave her the poison, or even that he gave her a glass of milk. This is the challenge I offer: let the Crown produce the evidence, let them point to the missing link."

The jury was out for six hours. One can conjecture that it was impressed by Lionel Luckhoo's argument, or it would not have taken so long. In the end, it could not accept the fact of both wives having died by the same means and in similar circumstances, leaving behind a bereaved and innocent husband, as mere coincidence. Or it may have decided that a husband who had given two wives sufficient cause to kill themselves was culpable, whether or not it was his hand that administered the poison. No one can read the collective mind of a jury. Whatever its reasoning, the jury brought in a verdict of guilty.

For the first time, Lionel Luckhoo heard the death sentence pronounced on a client.

"Noor Mohamed, the jury has found you guilty of murder. The sentence of this court is that you be taken to an approved place, there to be hanged by the neck until you are dead, and may the Lord have mercy on your soul."

The judge removed the black cap and, as was the custom, broke the quill pen with which the sentence had been written. There was a moment of somber silence in court, broken by a shrill cry from the prisoner: "Sir, I will never hang. Never!"

Lionel Luckhoo sat shaking his head, almost in disbelief. A cold shiver ran through his body. Noor Mohamed might have faith that he would not hang, but his counsel knew he was as good as dead already. The defense had no right of appeal to a higher court. Only the judge, by stating a case to go to the Court of Crown Cases reserved for consideration, could give them the chance of another hearing.

There was small hope, but Lionel rose and made his application. He was not surprised when Sir Donald Jackson turned it down immediately.

"If I had the remotest doubt that I might be wrong in admitting the evidence re Gooriah, I would state a case," he said. "I have no doubts. I am right. The application is refused."

Lionel had recovered his *sang-froid*. He bowed to the judge. "You have the last say here, your honor. I shall now endeavor to see that it is only the penultimate say."

They were bold words. All precedent made it seem certain that the case was at an end, as Noor Mohamed's life soon would be.

Lionel left Georgetown and went to Berbice. Home was the best place to go with such a problem. E.V., always his guide and mentor, was there, and so was Lloyd. It was obvious to his brothers that Lionel was deeply affected by the outcome of the Noor Mohamed case. E.V. asked him, "Do you believe in this man's innocence?"

"I do."

"Then skip the money; it makes no difference whether he has a penny or a pound. Go to England and present a petition for leave to appeal to the Privy Council." E.V. looked at Lloyd, who nodded his agreement. "We will see this thing through."

There and then, sitting around the dining-room table, they began to draft the petition. Lionel remembers it as a night of sultry heat—with mosquitoes biting relentlessly. Disregarding such comforts, the three worked until the early hours of the morning. By then, the basic outline of the petition had been sketched.

Lionel went to London to present the petition. It was fully legally based on the contention that the leading of inadmissible evidence of the earlier death was highly prejudicial. It also stressed that in British Guiana there was no Court of Appeal. Only if a trial judge were to state a case for review on a point of law could a case be taken to the West Indies Court of Appeal. Subjects of the Crown were deprived of any redress save to appeal to Her Majesty in Council. For a money debt, a case could be taken from the Supreme Court to the West Indies Federal Court, and from there to the Privy Council, as of right. Yet, where a man's life was at stake, he had no right to have his case reviewed on fact or on law. This was unjust and un-English.

Leave to appeal was granted, and, when the case came before the Judicial Committee of the Privy Council, it drew a strong court that included Lords Uthwatt, du Parcq, and Oaksey. Before these final judges, Lionel's arguments were repeated: that the facts concening Gooriah's death had no evidential or probative value; at the most, they tended to show that the accused was a man of bad character, and therefore likely to have been capable of bringing about Ayesha's death. They were strongly prejudicial. A fair trial was the basis of the English jurisprudential system. Noor Mohamed had been convicted on legally inadmissible evidence.

The argument was accepted by the law lords. They ruled that the disputed evidence should not have been admitted, and, in allowing the appeal, advised Her Majesty that Noor Mohamed should be set free.

The judgment clarified the law on similar facts, and found its place in the law books. It was also a breakthrough on appeals to the Privy Council, and hastened the setting up of a Court of Appeal. Newspapers and public meetings kept the issue alive, and the battle was won three years later. Lionel's success in saving Noor Mohamed had opened an escape hatch for many others whose cases would previously have stood no chance of review.

The day of triumph arrived when Lionel went to Georgetown Prison to witness his client's release. A huge crowd of friends and sympathizers was waiting outside the gates to mob Noor Mohamed.

"I have lived for this day," Noor greeted Lionel from his cell. "I told the world I could not hang. I am innocent." An apocryphal story, still current in Guyanese legal circles, has it that counsel and client, Christian and Mohammedan, then knelt down in the cell together and prayed.

Francis Dias, a man much respected by Lionel as a solicitor old in years and experience, was with them when they emerged from the prison. He patted Noor Mohamed on the shoulder in farewell, and said, "See you don't do this again."

"Sir," said Noor, "I promise you I will never do it again."

He may have misheard or misunderstood the admonition. After all, it was an exciting and highly emotional day.

Noor Mohamed's relatives and friends presented Lionel Luckhoo with an illuminated street address sign, not only expressing their gratitude for his restoration, but because "through the dark days of the trial, you gave us courage; when public opinion was against us, you bolstered up our morale; even when the jury brought in a verdict of guilty, you were still confident. . . . If you were not interested as an individual, you would not have suffered so many sleepless nights during the trial, and you would not have gone to England at your own expense."

There was a celebration with Lionel as the guest of honor. In keeping with tradition, Noor was to give his special guest a present and to offer him a ceremonial nonalcoholic drink.

When all was ready, a gong sounded, heralding the great moment. Noor Mohamed appeared in the doorway bearing a brass tray. As he came nearer, Lionel saw what it was he carried: a gift parcel and—a glass of milk! Lionel took up the glass, smiled and said, "Thank you." It was all the courtesy he could manage. Try as he would, he could not drink the milk, not a sip.

2

Today, Noor Mohamed, whose case did much to establish Lionel Luckhoo's reputation, is a spry seventy-year-old who looks ten years younger. Small, sallow, bald-pated, he reminds one of Mahatma Gandhi. His manner, like that of the late Dr. Crippen, might be described as "mildness itself."

Noor spent more than three years in jail. For eighteen months, he was under sentence of death. He comforted himself by studying the Koran, learning whole pages by heart. Because of the distance they had to travel from his hometown, an extra number of relatives was allowed to visit at one time. His daughter brought her husband to be introduced, before the news had reached Noor that she was married.

Six times, Noor watched condemned murderers walk across the landing to the execution shed, then heard the gallows trap fly. Each time it happened, the wooden building in which Noor occupied the Culprit's Cell would, as he put it, "shake to the very foundation."

Noor Mohamed is eternally grateful to Lionel Luckhoo that the trap did not fly open a seventh time with him standing on it. He told the writer, "After I came out of my trouble, I did not think of Mr. Luckhoo as a counsel, but as a brother of mine. Every time I come to town I must see him, just to shake his hand. Of course, I cannot do anything for him, but always in my prayers I must add his name. After God, I remember him. And I call upon God to give him long life and good health, that he may be able to save others also."

I asked Noor to tell me his version of the circumstances surrounding the deaths of his two wives. What he said—after more than thirty years, we must remember—differs somewhat from the story that emerged at the trial.

"The night before Gooriah's death I came home a bit late. I had not been feeling well that week, but three Dutch girls came across and asked me to go out with them, and I did so." (He mentions quite matter-of-factly this eye-opening testimony to his status as a local Lothario.) "Well, when I came home Gooriah didn't say anything. In the morning she prepared tea as usual. Then after lunch she told me she was going to see her mother.

"My brother-in-law Mr. Shaffeeullah was also a goldsmith. He had poison on his shelf. About a year before this, one of his brothers drank poison right there in the shop. My wife was there, in the house, when he did it." (Gooriah's mother lived in a combined house and shop.) "Anyhow, she said she was going to see her relatives, and she went.

"About an hour later I heard a scream, and I ran across the road. I saw my wife lying down, frothing at the mouth. I sent for the doctor. He came and he gave her an injection, but she died. They carried out a post-mortem. I never knew what the police got from that because they never told me."

"Were you at that time friendly with Ayesha?" I asked Noor. "If so, how did Gooriah feel about it?"

"Well, she was not happy about it. She knew that Ayesha and myself were friending. No, she was not happy about it."

"At the trial a witness claimed to have heard you say to Gooriah, 'You must drink this, it will do you good.' "

"I never said that."

"You say that didn't happen. How about the death of Ayesha?"

"The husband was not living far away. That is, the legal husband. We lived only about three rods apart. He was always telling Ayesha he was going to do her this and do her that. Whenever he passed the house and I was not at home, he would tell her he was going to kill her. She complained to me, but I told her not to worry about him."

"At the time she died, had she any reason other than that for killing herself?"

"No, she was happy with our relationship."

Two years after his release from prison, Noor Mohamed took a third wife. Their young daughter is one of the many children of thankful clients for whom Lionel Luckhoo has been asked to stand as a godfather. The marriage remains a happy one.

I asked Noor how he felt when he looked back on events leading to the tragedies of long ago.

"Well, now I do not have any friendships with other women. Since then I am trying to live a different life. When I was a goldsmith, I used to have a few girlfriends, and I used to think to myself the wife didn't appreciate it."

Noor Mohamed never went back to being a goldsmith. Should you assume, as I did at first, that this might stem from a sensitivity or a wariness about having potassium cyanide so handily within reach, you would be wrong. Like Charlie Peace, who refused to frame pictures brought by customers if he thought they had no artistic merit, Noor took an honest pride in his craftsmanship.

"I used to work very good gold. The people in the district knew that I gave them good gold, and they had confidence in me. I used to give them solid twelve-carat gold. As the price of gold went up, I could have had to give them nine-carat for twelve. I decided not to do it."

So Noor Mohamed opened a cake shop. He prospered over the years, and the cake shop has expanded to take in a restaurant. Milk is a mainstay of the menu. Cyanide is nowhere available on the premises.

Chapter 5
The Case of the King-of-All-Trades

The greatest saints and sinners have been made
The proselytes of one another's trade.
—Samuel Butler

Soon after Lionel Luckhoo started in law practice, a client came seeking a remedy for a nonlegal complaint. Jagan was an Indian driver at Plantation Port Mourant, one of the vast sugar estates. He also happened to be the father of a future Guyanese Premier, Dr. Cheddi Jagan, one of the few top Communists who genuinely can claim to have sprung from the working class.

Jagan and Lionel knew each other well as mutual devotees of the racetrack. However, it was not racehorses but human workhorses who, Jagan felt, were being unjustly treated.

"Take my own case," he said. "I have been a driver at Port Mourant for many years. I cannot read or write, but I have my own way of keeping notations. I feel that we should get the chance to become overseers. The trouble is, these white people do not want to give us the opportunity."

Lionel queries, "Do all the other drivers feel the same way?"

"Yes, they do."

There was no immediate legal answer to this kind of problem. Lionel gave the only practical advice he could think of. "My friend, what you should do is form yourselves into a union. Then you will have some bargaining strength."

Jagan agreed. "I can do that. I will get all the drivers together and we will form a union. But when we have done it, you must become president."

It was typical of Lionel Luckhoo that he did not hesitate. "All right, Mr. Jagan. You go ahead. If you succeed in getting the drivers together, I will be president, I promise you."

Wordsworth's pithy paradox is true: the child *is* father of the man. In Lionel Luckhoo's case, it was inevitable that the schoolboy who revolted against the authoritarian rule of the masters, who fought for representational rights for younger boys, would be sympathetic to the claims of disadvantaged workers as an adult. And predictable that, sooner or later, he would actively join them in their struggle.

It turned out to be sooner, for Jagan was successful in getting the other drivers to support the idea of an organization. Every sugar estate in the country, with one exception, was represented when a meeting was held to form a union. Lionel Luckhoo was elected president of what became the Headmen's Union. He invited the well-known magistrate Max Fitzpatrick to become the secretary.

Not since Billy Bennett appeared on the British music-hall stage, wearing a monkey jacket and a starched dickey, and proclaimed that he was there "on behalf of the working classes," has a less likely-looking champion of labor been seen than the suave young advocate, English-accented and bourgeois to the backbone. Yet the new president of the new union soon won the initial battle for overseers to be appointed from the ranks of the driver. Jainarine Singh, at the Diamond Estate, was the first to be given the promotion.

The next thing to happen was that the canecutters, the largest body of workers in the sugar industry, who had organized themselves into what became the biggest trade union in Guyana, said to Lionel, "Come and be our next president." For the Man-Power Citizens' Association, as the sugar workers' union was called, Lionel obtained by negotiation many benefits; among them, assurance of regular employment, incentive bonuses, and holidays with pay.

The canecutters were followed by the Sawmill Workers' Union, and they, in turn, by the Seafarers' Union, so that, in no time at all, Lionel had become the head of four trade organizations.

Since the abolition of slavery, no great strides had been made in improving conditions on the sugar plantations over the years. The workers were still enslaved in a harsh economic and social system. Management was white, expatriate, and privileged. Labor was colored, indigenous, and had small hope of redress, no matter how badly treated.

One of Lionel Luckhoo's murder cases illustrates the climate of the times.

2

History does not repeat itself in a determined design. It burps along like a drunken sailor, littering an unsteady course with undigested coincidences. Only a few years after J.A. Luckhoo won his verdict in the sensational Port Mourant murder trial, Lionel Luckhoo found himself involved in a case with the same four basic features: Plantation Port Mourant was again the locus of the crime; an estate manager was the victim; he had been shot from ambush; and estate workers were the accused.

Estate managers were as powerful then as lords of the manor in feudal times. The worst of them did not scruple to exercise what can be compared with the *droit de seigneur*. When George Wilkie, Administrative Manager at Plantation Port Mourant, rode around the canefields on his mule, he often amused himself by making sexual advances to the female workers. As a consequence, he was widely hated by their menfolk.

At Port Mourant, it was the custom for bells to be rung at eleven o'clock each morning to announce the meal break. One Friday morning, Wilkie was out on his usual rounds when a gunshot coincided with the peal of bells. Shot in the back, Wilkie died in a matter of minutes.

A hue and cry arose. The police set up a field station at Plantation Port Mourant. More than fifty detectives were rushed to the scene from Georgetown to assist with the investigation. Before it was finished, more statements than there were years on the calendar—1,960, in fact—had been taken and checked. This involved interviews with practically everybody living or working in the area. It typified the thoroughness of Stanhope Billyeald, the detective in charge. Taking a wholly negative statement, he believed, could be useful; a witness who had said he knew nothing about a crime could not afterwards appear for the defense, claiming that he did know something.

Suspicion lay heaviest upon a burly laborer named Bajoon. He was the only worker who had shown enough courage to tell Wilkie not to interfere with his wife. As a result, he found himself out of a job. With Bajoon not working, it became more than ever necessary for his wife to keep on going to the canefields, or the family would starve. Wilkie had still forced his attentions on her, and Bajoon's resentment grew. The allegation was that, having determined to kill Wilkie, Bajoon had hired a man named Jaisew Persaud to do the shooting. Persaud had the reputation of being a crackshot. Both men were arrested and charged with murder.

Samuel Cyrus, highly reputed as a defense lawyer, was engaged to represent Bajoon. Lionel Luckhoo was retained for the defense of Jaisew Persaud.

The prosecution led evidence that Persaud, who did not own a gun, had tried to borrow one. It was not proved that he had succeeded. On the day of the shooting, he had not gone to work. He and Bajoon were seen to leave Bajoon's house together, and witnesses had seen them at various points up to 10:30 A.M. Then there was a gap, and the jury was asked to infer that the two men lay waiting in ambush for half an hour. Soon after the time of the shooting, they were both seen again, but not together. Apparently, they had gone to their homes by separate routes.

An intensive effort had been made to find the murder weapon. Cane in the surrounding fields was burned down to help the search. A gunstock was found among the stubble, and other parts of the firearm came to light in a trench nearby. These finds did not advance matters, for the ownership of the gun was never established.

After Stanhope Billyeald had given evidence, he was cross-examined by Lionel Luckhoo.

"When you saw the body, how far was it from the high bridge?"

"It was a few yards from the bridge on the open dam."

"Was there a stick beside the body?"

"Yes, it was a walking stick belonging to Mr. Wilkie."

"Near to the dam there was a clump of bushes, cut back and weeded at the center?"

"Yes."

"A person could secrete himself there?"

"Yes."

"The walking stick Mr. Wilkie carried had a very sharp pointed end?"

"Yes, that is so."

"There were impressions on the ground indicating that Mr. Wilkie had dismounted his mule at the bridge and was walking towards the clump of bushes when he was shot from behind?"

"Yes, there were such impressions."

"Marks made by the ferrule of the walking stick?"

"That was my conclusion."

"A person could use that clearing in the bushes as a place for sexual intercourse and not be seen by anyone using the dam?"

"Well, one could hide away there."

Bajoon's wife was sick and stayed at home on the day of the murder. The defense theory was that Wilkie had made an assignation with another woman, and that her husband or relative could be involved.

"Did you have reports that Mr. Wilkie used to interfere with female workers at the backdam?"

"I have had no report, but I have heard people say so."

"Did you search Mr. Wilkie's clothing?"

"Yes."

"Did you find anything in his pockets?"

At this point there was an interruption from the prosecutor, Attorney General Sir Frank Holder, who objected that counsel was seeking to cast mud on the character of the deceased.

Chief Justice Sir John Vanity heard the defense submission before giving a ruling.

"Which is more important," Lionel Luckhoo contended, "to preserve the character of the dead man, or to establish the innocence of the men accused? Which is more important, to conceal from the jury the material facts the defense relies on, or to give ventilation to all the facts?"

The Chief Justice allowed the line of questioning. Lionel returned to his cross-examination of Billyeald.

"Did you find in the pocket of the deceased a little tin in which were a number of contraceptives he had carried to the backdam?"

"Yes, I did."

The tin was called for and produced, and, with the three items it contained, was admitted as an exhibit. This highlighted a point Lionel was to emphasize at a later stage: "It was not just one woman whom Wilkie interfered with; there were a number of women whom his roving eyes had selected for his favors. It was not just one husband who hated Wilkie's guts; there were a number of husbands who felt such hatred."

The weight of this argument was as much—even more—in favor of Bajoon as it was of Persaud, Lionel Luckhoo's own client. Strictly, it weighed very little in favor of the innocence of either. What it did was to make the jury aware that others might have the same motive as Bajoon to seek the death of Wilkie. And, while a revelation of the victim's character gave no legal justification for his killing, it made the jury receptive to other evidence that could be interpreted in favor of the accused.

Lionel Luckhoo is the only barrister known to me (always excepting Perry Mason!) who plays his own detective. In murder cases, especially, he has, from the earliest days, made it a practice to visit the scene of the crime. In the Wilkie case, as in a dozen others, it was what he discovered and did on a field inquiry that saved his client's life.

For once, the police had been too thorough in seeking out witnesses who had seen Jaisew Persaud before and after the time of the murder. Lionel checked all the times and distances himself. Then he got a surveyor to make certain point-to-point measurements. More than that, he took a better-than-average athlete along and had him run the vital distances. When the prosecution witnesses came to give testimony as to where and when they had seen Persaud allegedly making his escape, Lionel was well prepared.

A main witness said that, when he heard the eleven o'clock bell, he had checked his watch and found it to be accurate. Five minutes later, he had seen Jaisew Persaud hurrying along the dam. Under cross-examination, he remained certain of his times. This suited Lionel Luckhoo well. The witness could not know it, but the defender was more anxious than the prosecutor to have his evidence unshakably established.

When his turn came to lead evidence for the defense, Lionel called the qualified surveyor, who produced maps to demonstrate that the spot where the witness said he had seen Persaud at five past eleven was a mile and a half from where Wilkie was shot at eleven o'clock.

In case the maps failed to convince, a witness then testified that it had taken him twelve minutes to cover the distance, as the mile and a half were across rough country.

"Look at the accused, members of the jury," Lionel then said in his address. "He is a big man, a heavy man, a fat man. No Olympic runner, nor record holder, could have run the distance the prosecution asks you to believe he ran, in five minutes. Find against him and you will not only be declaring him guilty of murder—your verdict will be that he is the fastest man on earth!"

The jury could choose to believe that the witness who had seemed so sure was mistaken, either in his identification or in the time. Or they could accept his evidence, which, instead of helping the prosecution, now gave Persaud the strongest of alibis. They chose the latter course, and Persaud was acquitted.

Jaisew Persaud had gone on the witness stand to swear he had nothing to do with the murder and had never had a gun. Bajoon did not give evidence on oath, and, although that should not weigh against an accused with the jury, it often does.

Despite an eloquent address by his counsel which lasted a record four days, Bajoon was found guilty and sentenced to be hanged. Samuel Cyrus sought leave to appeal to the Privy

Council, but when the application was heard it was denied. Before he died, Bajoon wrote a letter to Cyrus which closed by saying, "Thank you again for all you did. I die for a good cause."

It might or might not have been an admission of guilt. If Bajoon meant that the blow struck against Wilkie had drawn attention to the conditions under which the sugar workers lived and worked, he was right. But their cause had to be fought on a much wider battlefront than he had chosen.

3

Lionel Luckhoo became proud of the fact that, in every instance, the demands of the unions he led were met without necessity for calling a strike that would hit the pockets of the workers. Neither did they ever suffer a lockout. The struggle was, nonetheless, fierce at times.

Perhaps the most dangerous negotiation Lionel entered into was with the American Cynamide Company, which had bauxite concessions up the Berbice River. When the MPCA became the first union to seek an agreement with the company, Lionel had to travel by air to a site in the hinterland to meet their officials. The danger came after the meeting.

Lionel flew in the only available aircraft, a single-engine seaplane piloted by Art Williams, a pioneer of aviation in Guyana. The ancient machine appeared to be held together by bits of string and wire. If the landing on the river at Kwakwani had been hazardous, terrifying was the word for Williams' method of departure. There was no straight stretch of river long enough for a proper takeoff. So the tail of the plane was tied to a tree by a rope. A massive Amerindian stood by with a hatchet. Williams revved the engine until the plane had sufficient power for a quick rise. At Williams' signal, the man with the hatchet severed the rope with a single stroke. If the timing was right and the Amerindian made a clean cut, the plane soared into the air with pilot and passenger, and all was well. If the operation were mistimed or the man bungled the cut, the plane dived, and all hopes of rising were postponed till the day of resurrection.

After one of these meetings with the Cynamide Company, Lionel was invited by the company doctor to go home with him for a drink. The homes of the expatriate officials were high on a hill. No natives—workers or visitors—were allowed into the area unless they had special passes. As a consequence of Lionel Luckhoo's visit, the doctor was fired—merely, it was suggested, for having invited a native into his home without permission.

"Doctor," Lionel said, when he heard, "fortune has played into your hands. Come and see me in my office tomorrow. We are going to get the biggest damages ever obtained from any company in Guyana." Taking his advice, the doctor sued the American Cynamide Company for wrongful dismissal. When the case had been settled for a very substantial amount, he asked Lionel Luckhoo to name his fee. "This is one time I want no money," Lionel said. "The result is a vindication of my union and myself."

Although he had become a king-of-all-trades (well, president!), the position had been thrust upon him. Lionel Luckhoo never agreed in principle that trades' unions should be led by professional lawyers. He believed that men should be encouraged to emerge from the ranks. They would best know and understand the problems of their fellows. The role of professionals was not to be pleased and gracious in serving the workers; it was to train them so they could serve themselves.

So, while winning benefits for workers he represented, Lionel made sure that such training was being undertaken. Three years after becoming the first driver to be made an overseer, Jainarine Singh was appointed president of his union. The MPCA, largest trade union in Guyana, was in particular need of a president who could be independent and unwilling to bend to pressures. Lionel found the man in Rupert Tello, whom he trained for six months before bowing out in his favor. It was a happy moment for Lionel when Tello was later appointed Member of the Legislative Assembly. Not only did it confirm his own judgment; it showed the workers that among them were men capable of representing them, at any level, with distinction. Within a short time, members of the Sawmill Workers' and the Seafarers' unions had been trained to take over leadership.

When Alex Perry, an old and trusted leader of the TUC, spoke at a function given in Lionel's honor, he said, "The highest tributes would be insufficient. Lionel Luckhoo, though he has walked with kings and princes, has never lost the common touch."

And, unlike those kings who hang on to their crowns at all costs, he had given his people confidence in their own democratic rule, and then abdicated.

Chapter 6

The Case of the Counterfeit Coiner

For the love of money is the root of all evil.
—Paul to Timothy

When Barnum said that a sucker is born every minute, he might have added that the majority of them migrate to the big cities. The smartest are the easy dupes of the con men and counterfeiters. Country folk may be simple, but they are also shrewd.

Paradise is a small village on the west coast of Berbice. An old lady living there, named Ella, was famous for her eschalot seeds. When Ramnarine came to her as a new customer, she asked him how many seeds he wanted to buy. Ramnarine produced four twenty-dollar notes and handed them to her. This was a large order.

Ella looked at the notes, riffling them through her fingers. "We will have to go and get the seeds weighed," she said, "so that I don't rob you or you don't rob me."

They went down the road to the shop of Mr. Mingo. The seeds were weighed out carefully. Ella then said, "Mr. Mingo, have a look at these notes."

Mr. Mingo examined the four twenty-dollar bills. "Where did you get them?" he asked.

Ramnarine said, "I sold a cow to a butcher and he gave me the money."

"H'mm. It seems right enough. But you know, you have to be very careful these days." Mr. Mingo called to his boy. "Glendon, jump on your bicycle and ride down to the police station. Tell them we want someone to come and check whether these notes are in order."

So, a little while later, Corporal Eric Douglas appeared on the scene. "What's the difficulty?" he asked.

Ramnarine said, "These are the four notes I gave this lady. She evidently thinks they are not good and wants you to look at them."

Corporal Douglas took a long look at the notes. "I think we had better go down to the station," he decided.

They went to the police station, where Ramnarine was searched. Another twenty-dollar note was found in his pocket and, like the other four, it was a fake. Ramnarine was charged with uttering forged notes.

What was wrong with the notes? Why were old Ella, Mr. Mingo, and Corporal Douglas so doubtful when they handled them? Forged currency is often, perhaps most often, detectable through faults in the paper, rather than from any flaws in the engraving process. This was such a case.

At Ramnarine's trial, old Ella was the first to explain to the court why her suspicions had been aroused. "What struck me was that the notes appeared to be of a different thickness from a good note, and too sandy, although the color seemed to be all right." By *sandy*, she meant *coarse-grained*.

Corporal Douglas gave a similar explanation, and, in cross-examination, he was asked, "Apart from the thickness, and what you call the sandiness, of the paper, it looked like ordinary money, did it not?"

"Yes," he agreed. "I thought it looked all right."

"If a single note had been handed to you, you would have accepted it?'

"Maybe I would."

"It was only when you scrutinized the notes carefully that it struck you they were forged?"

"Well, when I took a close look they seemed not genuine."

Glendon, the youngster sent to fetch the police, made his own judicial comment. "The notes were good, but not good enough," he said. Glendon admitted that, having heard others voice their doubts, he was already suspicious when he handled the notes.

When asked if the notes could have fooled a lot of people, the shopkeeper Mr. Mingo put the matter fairly.

"Yes," he said. "It was the thickness of the notes that aroused my suspicion. Maybe if someone had just handed me the notes I would have accepted them. But Ella having particularly asked me to look at them, I did so carefully, and then I found they seemed to be thicker than the normal twenty-dollar note."

Under further cross-examination, Mr. Mingo agreed that, when the police were sent for, Ramnarine could have run away. He had made no attempt to do so, but had waited without objecting until Corporal Douglas arrived.

Station Sergeant James Elcock told the court that, after examining the notes, he decided they were forgeries, and, as a result, had cautioned the accused. Ramnarine had then said he would like to make a statement, which he himself wrote. The statement was admitted in evidence, and read:

"I had a dark brown-and-white cow. A butcher from Kitty came and bought it from me for $170. Then I went to buy eschalot seeds. I had the money with me, and out of the money that had been paid I gave Ella four twenty-dollar bills. The lady suspected the money was not good enough and said she was going to send it to the police station. I said, 'Fair enough, do what you like. The money seems all right to me.' Shortly after, the policeman came, and the lady told him I gave her the money, and the policeman asked me if I had any more, and I said, 'Yes, one more,' and I produced another twenty-dollar note."

So far, the defense had succeeded in creating a favorable climate of opinion. Prosecution witnesses were ready to admit that the notes might be casually accepted as genuine. When doubts were raised, Ramnarine had not protested, nor had he attempted to run away. He had volunteered an explanation as to where he got the notes. Much now depended on the evidence of the butcher whose name Ramnarine had given to the police.

The butcher Mr. Abdul said it was true that he had bought a cow from Ramnarine and had paid him $170. "All of that is correct, but I see these exhibits here before me, and the money I gave him was not of this kind."

The choice was whom to believe—Ramnarine or Abdul? However, Abdul admitted he had not examined the money given to Ramnarine. There was no reason to do so. He had simply paid it over. This left open the possibility that both he and Ramnarine, in turn, had accepted the forgeries carelessly but innocently.

The most important witness was the last. Constable Abrahim had been sent to Ramnarine's home with a search warrant.

"The accused was not at home," Abrahim testified (this could not have been unexpected—Ramnarine was in jail). "I read the warrant to his wife and searched the premises in her presence. In the roof of the kitchen I found six twenty-dollar bills. They were between the zincs."

These six notes, admitted as exhibits, were shown to be forgeries similar to the other five in Ramnarine's possession. Two of the six had the same number as those seized at the time of his arrest.

If Constable Abrahim's evidence could not be refuted, Ramnarine was in deep trouble. The total of spurious notes that had now come to light was $220. He claimed to have received from Abdul the butcher no more than $170. Ramnarine vigorously denied all knowledge of the six notes allegedly found at his home. "No one ever searched my house," he insisted.

Admittedly, Ramnarine had been given no chance to be present at the search. His counsel drew from Constable Abrahim the admission that he had not known, of his own knowledge, the address of the accused. At the house to which he was directed, he had found a woman occupant and had asked her her name, but he had never seen her before or since.

The jury wrestled with the problem for three hours, twenty-three minutes before coming to a verdict of guilty. Ramnarine drew a seven-year sentence.

When Lionel Luckhoo was briefed for the appeal, Constable Abrahim's testimony became the main target of his attack. The evidence should not have been admitted, he contended. The officer had searched a house alleged to be Ramnarine's, and had spoken to a woman alleged to be Ramnarine's wife. But there was no evidence that it was the house of the accused he was searching, and no evidence that he was speaking to the wife of the accused. Before these facts could be admitted, there must be a link connecting them with the accused. As it now stood, a house had been searched and six counterfeit notes had been found. This had no probative value, but was merely prejudicial. Addressing the appeal judges, Lionel said:

"What clear evidence do you have in this case other than the actions of the accused himself? He let three people examine his notes without protest. He awaited the advent of the police and explained how the notes came into his possession. These actions proclaim the innocence of the accused Ramnarine. Without the other six notes allegedly found at his house, no jury would ever have convicted him."

The appeal succeeded. Ramnarine, set free, left the court swearing that, for the future, he would not even accept, let alone issue, a twenty-dollar note.

2

The Ramnarine appeal must have taken Lionel Luckhoo back in memory to his first experience of defending a client charged with counterfeiting—an unhappy experience, as it turned out, though he won the case. As with Ramnarine, it was careless police procedure which gave him the loophole.

Acting on information (as official jargon has it), the police had raided the house of Harold Ramkissoon at Bloomfield. They found a mold for making shillings, and a number of the coins it had produced. Excellent coins, but counterfeit!

Lionel was young, enthusiastic, and only a year in practice when he was retained for Ramkissoon's defense. He had been paid $150 of the $240 brief fee before going up to Corentyne for the trial. There, Ramkissoon handed him a parcel, saying, "Here is the balance." Lionel threw the parcel into his bag.

Police Constable Cato gave evidence of finding the coins and the mold in Ramkissoon's house. Lionel cross-examined.

"When you executed the search warrant the accused was absent?"

"Yes."

"This was the first time you had been into his house?"

"Yes."

"Were his wife and children present?"

"Yes, they spoke to me. . . ."

Lionel cut him short. "Since you told us the accused was not there, you cannot repeat any of the conversation. Were all the articles produced in court found in one room?"

"Yes."

"Now, officer, when you arrested the accused did you caution him?"

"Yes, he made no reply. I asked him before I cautioned him which was his bedroom and he said it was on the northern side of the house."

Constable Cato had blundered. Lionel lashed at him, why did he first ask a question and then caution the accused? Was it not his intention to charge Ramkissoon when he arrested him?

Cato, confused, could only murmur, "Yes."

"Was that the only remark made by the accused, that his bedroom was on the northern side?"

"Yes."

"Nothing else?"

"No, that was all."

As always, from the earliest days, Lionel Luckhoo had done his homework. He produced a certified plan of Ramkissoon's house, and had the witness examine it.

"There are two rooms on the northern side of the house?"

"Yes."

"The accused did not point out which of the two rooms he occupied?"

"No, he did not.'

"And he lived there with his wife and grown-up sons?"

"Yes."

The case was won. There being no clear evidence that the mold and coins had come from Ramkissoon's room, the onus of possession could not be placed upon him.

Lionel went home in high glee following his victory. He told his father how the case had gone, and E.A. then said, "Did he pay you the balance of your brief fee?"

"Oh, yes." Lionel took from his bag the somewhat heavy parcel. The exact sum owed had been paid, ninety dollars —made up entirely of shillings. E.A. picked up a few of the coins.

'What was the date on the mold?" he asked.

"Nineteen-eighteen," answered Lionel.

"Take a look at these."

Lionel was brought down to earth. All the shillings bore the same date—1918. All were counterfeit.

"Lionel," E.A. said to his son, "take them and pour them into that trench over there," pointing to an open trench opposite the house, "and bury them."

With a heavy heart, Lionel complied.

Chapter 7
The Case of the Archdemon Rum

Fifteen men on the dead man's chest,
Yo-ho-ho, and a bottle of rum!
Drink and the devil had done for the rest,
Yo-ho-ho and a bottle of rum!
—Robert Louis Stevenson

Sultan was innocent, wholly innocent of the crime with which he was charged. And this, despite the fact that Sir Kenneth Stoby, the magistrate who tried his case, believed him to be fully guilty—and said so, even in the act of setting him free. Sultan was "framed," so neatly he did not know it was happening.

The frame-up, a device very popular with writers of crime fiction, is seldom encountered in real life. There are countries where politicians in power do not scruple to manufacture charges against their opponents. Overzealous or corrupt policemen may give a slight, sometimes a hard, push to the evidence against a known criminal, or a suspect they honestly feel must be guilty. But the classic frame-up planned by an enemy to remove the victim from the scene, and using the law to do his dirty work, is a rarity. Yet it happened to Sultan.

His name was merely a name, not a title. No harem went with it. As a start towards building his harem, Sultan had, however, acquired a lady friend. Unfortunately, Lucille was married. Her husband was Jagubeer, the best cut-and-load man on the Berbice Sugar Estate, so big and strong he could earn twice as much as the other sugar workers. In contrast, Sultan was a thin and weedy type. Jagubeer, a strict monogamist, objected to the affair between his wife and Sultan, but

Lucille paid him no heed. Had it followed the usual pattern of such cases, the next step would have been for Jagubeer to take either violent action or no action at all. Evidently, he scorned to use his physical strength, or perhaps he foresaw that whatever he did unto others the law might do unto him. What he did was to get the law to help him, instead.

Solicitous governments the world over are vastly concerned with the problems of strong drink. Some will not allow their citizens to drink at all. Others are content just to make it difficult. In Australia, the determined drinker who cannot get drunk by 6:00 P.M. must stay sober, for at that time the pubs close. A Welshman who, after a week's hard work, does not have the energy to cross the English border on a Sunday cannot slake his thirst, for Welsh pubs do not open on the Sabbath. An American traveling across his own country with a bottle and a toothbrush will be, before he completes his tour, an expert on the liquor laws (no one is against toothbrushes!) or on jailhouses, for the law often changes when he crosses a state line. Strangely, except for the prohibitionists, governments do not refuse to enter into profit-sharing schemes with the demon drink. Rather, they insist upon doing so by way of duties and taxes, and, to safeguard their interest, make it as much an offense for a citizen to make his own liquor as to make his own money.

The Guyanese equivalent to moonshine is *bush rum*. This is a description with no legal definition. If the analyst gives a certificate that the liquid he has tested is bush rum, then bush rum it is, and the person found in possession of it goes to jail. In practice, it is any rum not made under license. Bush rum is commonly made in an unlawfully constructed still somewhere in the backdam.

Sultan was a moderate drinker. He bought himself a bottle of rum every Saturday. And Jagubeer happened to be a friend of the owner of the rum shop. He bribed his friend to sell to Sultan, the next time he came to the shop, a bottle of illicit *white bushy* instead of the legal white rum he normally sold. Jagubeer supplied the white bushy.

The following Saturday afternoon, Sultan called for his rum as usual. He had just settled down to an evening with the bottle, when his home was invaded by the police. When he learned that their purpose was to seize the liquor, Sultan protested that he had bought it quite legally at the rum shop. The police took him to the shop, where the owner confirmed that he had sold Sultan a bottle of rum—but what he had sold him, he said, was the genuine article. When an identical bottle taken from the shelves was opened, the contents tasted and smelled quite differently from the rum in Sultan's possession. Both bottles of rum were sent to the government analyst.

The analyst reported that the bottle from the rum shop contained legal rum, and that the rum taken from Sultan was bush rum.

Sultan sought the aid of Lionel Luckhoo. Once he had heard the facts and background of the affair, Lionel suspected that Sultan might have been framed. When the trial opened, it appeared that the only way to get an acquittal would be to prove conspiracy against him. And the only way to do that was to break down the evidence of the rum shop owner.

Under cross-examination, the man admitted that Sultan had been in the habit of buying a bottle every week, that this was known to others, and that Sultan had indeed bought a bottle of white rum on the day in question.

"Do you know that only one bottle was found at his home that evening?"

"I don't know."

"Well, would you say that the bottle which you claim you sold him was very much like the bottle seized from his home?"

"Yes."

So far, the witness had been firm but reasonable with his answers. When Lionel switched his attack, the responses were more reluctant.

"Are you friendly with Jagubeer?"

"Well, I know him."

"Have you ever discussed Sultan's drinking habits with Jagubeer?"

"No."

"Did you see Jagubeer that afternoon?"

"I don't remember."

"Come, now!" Lionel spoke sharply. "You must have seen him that afternoon. He visits your rum shop every Saturday afternoon, doesn't he?"

"Yes, he must have been there."

"Did he speak to you?"

"Everyone speaks to me."

"Did he inquire about Sultan?"

"I don't remember."

"Do you know that there is bad feeling between Jagubeer and Sultan over Jagubeer's wife?"

"I don't know that."

"Have you ever visited Jagubeer's home?"

"Yes."

"When was the last time you visited him?"

"I don't remember."

"But you visit him often?"

"Fairly often."

"And you would say he is a very good friend?"

"No, just a friend."

The witness stonewalled all through the cross-examination. He had sold the rum to Sultan, but it could not be shown that it was bush rum. He was friendly with Jagubeer, but it could not be shown that he had abetted him in a frame-up.

The policeman who had arrested Sultan was another difficult witness. He testified that, when he seized the rum, Sultan had started to fight him for it, saying, "You cannot take it."

Lionel Luckhoo asked him, "Would you agree, Constable, that the defendant said from the very beginning, 'This is my rum. I bought it from the rum shop'?"

"No. He kept saying, 'This is my rum. You cannot take it.' "

"Well, did he eventually say where he got it from?"

"Yes, but only when I asked him where he got it."

"Did you search his home?"

"Yes."

"Did you find a number of similar bottles?"

"Yes, but they were all empty."

"Did you ask him when he bought the rum from the rum shop?"

"Yes. He said he bought it an hour before."

"Had any rum been drunk out of the bottle?"

The constable hesitated. "I don't quite remember. If any had been drunk it was very little."

"I put it to you that the bottle was full. None of it had been drunk?"

"That's not true." From not being able to remember, the witness had now become positive. "I believe some had been drunk."

"About how much? One schnapps glass, would you say?"

"Well, maybe two or three schnapps glasses."

"Was the rum sealed?"

"No, it was not sealed."

"You took a bottle from the rum shop. Was that sealed?"

"No, the bottle was not sealed."

"If the defendant had bought a bottle of genuine rum, would you not expect to find it at his home?"

The prosecutor, Superintendent Chase, rose to object before the witness could answer. The constable could only say what he had found, he suggested, not what his expectations were.

The magistrate upheld the objection.

The prosecution put in evidence a statement made by the accused. Sultan had said that, after buying the rum, he visited the homes of two friends. The prosecution's theory was that Sultan and his friends drank the genuine rum together. Such an inference was not unreasonable, and the case seemed almost beyond repair. All that was required was the analyst's statement that the bottle found in Sultan's possession contained bush rum, and that would be the final clincher.

The analyst's certificate was put in as evidence. And it was when he read it that Lionel Luckhoo began to see a glimmer of light. The arresting officer had testified that he took the bottle to the analyst on November 21. The certificate stated that the bottle was received on November 22.

Lionel raised an objection to the discrepancy. The police

asked for an adjournment so that inquiries could be made as to how the difference in dates had arisen.

The point was a trivial technicality, nothing more. The bottle and certificate bore the same identification number, so there was no mixup. When the police came back with the explanation that the discrepancy in dates was due to a typing error, Lionel was not surprised. He had raised the issue merely to open another door to investigation, and had succeeded.

For, to corroborate the police on the date, they brought to court Government Analyst Neville Newson. Never before had the analyst appeared in person to give evidence in a bush rum case, and been subject to cross-examination. It gave Lionel the opportunity he was seeking.

"Mr. Newson, you are the Government Analyst?"

"Yes."

"You did this analysis?"

"Yes."

"And what was the result? What did the components of this rum prove to be?"

"I find that it was bush rum."

"Excellent!" he said, with warm approval. "And did you also analyze the contents of the other bottle, which you certify as genuine rum?"

"I did."

"Now . . ." Lionel paused, then said in measured tones, *"Will you tell me what differences there are between the one and the other that enabled you to reach your conclusions?"*

There was a long silence. Finally, the analyst said, "I cannot tell you that, it's a secret."

"Mr. Newson, you are under cross-examination. We have no secrets in court. You must answer the question. Why did you say that one exhibit was bushy and the other was genuine rum?"

"Because the analysis of the one is different from that of the other."

"That's fine. But what we want to know is, what was the difference?"

The witness turned for help to the magistrate. "It would be dangerous for me to state the differences in open court, your honor. People would then know the standards by which I adjudged the spirits to be bushy."

Lionel intervened quickly, before the magistrate could make a ruling. "Your honor, the whole principle of cross-examination would be destroyed, the full scope of justice to the defendant would be limited, if the witness were allowed to refuse to answer a question germane to the issue."

When the magistrate ruled that the question was in order, the prosecution was thrown into a panic. Superintendent Chase requested an adjournment so that he could telephone the Commissioner of Police for instructions.

When court resumed, the prosecutor stated that, rather than proceed with the case and have questions answered *which could well affect all bush rum cases in the future*, the police had decided to offer no further evidence.

The magistrate, Sir Kenneth Stoby (later to become Chief Justice of Barbados and, later still, Chancellor of the Judiciary of Guyana), regarded Sultan with a stern eye. "I believe you are guilty," he said, "but you are lucky. This is the first time the official analyst has ever been brought to court. He had to come because of some slip-up in the dates, and you are entitled to have the benefit of this advantage. The police offer no further evidence. Therefore, you are discharged."

In this case, the law gave justice unwillingly. Jagubeer's punishment, and Sultan's reward, were administered later by a lady who did not wear a blindfold. Lucille left Jagubeer and went to live with Sultan.

2

Rum, legal and bushy, was no more than a prop in the triangular tangle that led to Sultan's being landed in jeopardy. In a number of Lionel Luckhoo's murder cases, rum has triggered the crime. Days of religious significance seem to be times of special danger, almost as if rum and religion were a basic recipe for a murder cocktail.

Pagwah is a religious festival observed by Hindus. Abstinence from alcohol is called for on that day, yet not a few employ rum as their means of celebration.

On March 26, 1975, which was Pagwah Day, a man named Fagu invited a friend, Randolph Cameron, and his wife

Latchmin to go drinking. They spent a couple of hours at the Parika Restaurant, then went on to Shirley's Parlour at Philadelphia on the east bank of the Essequibo, where they stayed for four hours.

Karran Dhanpaul and a group of friends were at Shirley's Parlour, and they, too, had been drinking most of the day.

Latchmin Cameron saw Dhanpaul leave the Parlour, then return after a short interval. She had left a radio on the back seat of her husband's car and, feeling suspicious, went out to check. The radio was missing. Latchmin came back and forthwith accused Dhanpaul of having stolen it. Next moment, Randolph Cameron cuffed Dhanpaul. He struck back. Once the fight had started, Dhanpaul's friends joined in, and there was a general melee which ended with Randolph Cameron lying dead on the floor.

For once, Lionel Luckhoo had an easy case to defend. There had been fifteen men on the dead man's chest—or as near that number as human anatomy would allow. Karran Dhanpaul alone was charged with murder. He it was who had been attacked by the deceased. When his friends joined in the fray, there was no evidence that they were acting in concert, or that they had a common design to kill Cameron. None of them knew him. Randolph Cameron lost his life because reasonable people, under the influence of drink, can become madly unreasonable. With these arguments, Lionel won Karran Dhanpaul an acquittal of murder. He was convicted of manslaughter and received a one-year sentence.

Christmas Day of that same year saw another murder following a restaurant quarrel. All the rum shops in Guyana are closed on Christmas Day, but restaurants remain open, and the Dice Liquor Restaurant was doing a roaring trade. One customer, Buckman, his spirits having risen in direct ratio to the amount of spirits he had imbibed, became more than somewhat rowdy. Akai the owner made as if to put him out.

Another customer, Basil Rampersaud, filled with the Christmas and other spirits, intervened. He told Akai that this was a day for friendship and love, and a day for drinking, and he had no right to throw Buckman out. Whether or not a teetotaller, Akai was not imbued with the proper spirit. He turned on Rampersaud, who ran. Akai picked up a cutlass and gave him a whack as he was leaving. Rampersaud was cut on the hand.

Soon after this, Rampersaud was seen coming back towards the restaurant. He was carrying a cutlass. A little later, Akai was found in the roadway outside with a deep head wound, from which he died.

There were plenty of witnesses who remembered Akai firing a chop at Rampersaud inside the lighted restaurant. There were no witnesses who could be sure, under cross-examination, that it was Rampersaud who had attacked Akai in the dark roadway. Rum and the night had clouded their vision, and, doubt having been cast on the question of identification, Basil Rampersaud was acquitted.

3

The defense of Harry Singh, charged with a rum shop mur der, was, on the face of it, more difficult. Beyond doubt, it was Singh who had struck what appeared to have been the fatal blow, for no other persons were involved. And there was no problem about his proper identification.

Singh was drinking in a rum shop at Canje in Berbice when a friend, Andrew Kowlessar, came in and slapped him on the neck. Singh, who had been drinking for three hours, resented the blow. When Kowlessar refused to apologize, the two men fought. Singh got the worst of it.

He came back later in the day and started drinking again. Kowlessar came up and began to taunt him over losing their fight. Harry Singh picked up a wooden bar and swung at him. Hit on the head, Kowlessar reeled back, but did not fall. Before any further blows could be struck, friends came and separated the two men.

Kowlessar died three days later, and Harry Singh was charged with murder. The post-mortem showed a thin crack in Kowlessar's skull, and seepage of blood into the brain.

Lionel Luckhoo made a no-case submission. Before Chief Justice Bollers, he contended that the jury could not be asked to decide that the blow struck by Harry Singh had been the cause of death. All that the evidence showed was that a blow had been struck; where the blow had landed, the precise area of the head, was not in evidence. Kowlessar had not afterwards been confined and kept under observation. There was no evidence to show that, in the interval between the incident and his death, Kowlessar was not involved in an altercation with another person or an accident of some kind. His death could not be solely attributed to a blow given by the accused three days before. The Chief Justice agreed with the submission, and Harry Singh was set free.

4

The Singhs and Rampersauds are the Smiths and Robinsons of Guyana. But it is still a remarkable coincidence that the names of the accused in the last two cases—Basil Rampersaud and Harry Singh—should be shared by the accused and victim in another murder trial.

This was a simple enough case, though the weapon was somewhat unusual. There was ill feeling between Singh and Rampersaud. Meeting by chance in a rum shop, they had a quarrel, and when Rampersaud left, Singh followed him into the roadway. Rampersaud allegedly said, "You stay there. I'm gonna run you down and kill you." Singh remained where he was standing. Rampersaud climbed into his car and drove it at him. Singh was knocked down and killed.

Rampersaud crashed the car—and that was possibly the luckiest thing he ever accomplished. He woke up in the hospital, asking what happened, and the doctor who examined him was able later to testify that the content of alcohol in his blood was so extremely high as to make him virtually unconscious.

This was the basis for the original defense Lionel put forward under the McNaughten rule.* The law allows a defense on the ground of insanity if it can be proved that, at the time of the act, the accused "was laboring under such a defect of reason, from disease of the mind, as not to know the nature and quality of the act he was doing, or, if he did know it, that he did not know he was doing what was wrong."

* *The McNaughten rule is rarely invoked as a defense for acts committed while in a drunken state.*

Lionel led evidence from the rum shop owner and customers to support the medical view of Rampersaud's condition. He was a man unaccustomed to taking more than one or two drinks. On this occasion, he had been celebrating a promotion. His mind was so suffused with alcohol, Lionel contended, that he could not know that what he was doing was wrong.

It was a bold defense, but it succeeded.

Chapter 8
The Case of the Unseen Hangman

And naked to the hangman's noose
The morning clocks will ring
A neck God made for other use
Than strangling on a string.

—A.E. Housman

From the Amuku Mountains where Guyana borders on Brazil, a trickle of water becomes the Essequibo River. Ever widening, the river wriggles north to the Atlantic Ocean, bisecting Guyana into unequal parts. Where river and ocean meet, the Island of Leguan, torn in allegiance between the two, rises abruptly from the waters.

On Leguan Island, one midsummer night twenty-seven years ago, the body of a man was found hanging from a tree.

This is nearly the only firm fact there is to hold on to. Everything else, before and after the finding of the body, is muddled; there is a temptation to say *muddied*, for it is as though the waters of the Essequibo had risen to give murky cover to all that took place below the level of the tree branch holding the swinging corpse.

The dead man was Kumar Singh, also known as Bapka. The use of an alias is common in Guyana and in other parts of the West Indies, and stems from the days when a second name was given by slave owners or employers. The practice is now dying out, but slowly, and a great many still follow the custom of using, for outside activities, a "false name" having no relevance to the name by which their families know them.

An amusing consequence of this practice was that Lionel Luckhoo once found himself defending "Lionel Luckhoo." It is not unusual in country parts for the "talk man" of the village to have taken, or been given, the name "Sir Lionel" or "Lionel Luckhoo." In this instance, fortunately, at the Cove and John Court, East Coast Demerara, the offense was trivial; and, more fortunately still, the magistrate at the time was Lionel's brother E.V., which further lessened the chances of counsel being confused with his client by the court.

In the course of time, a lapse of well more than a year, four men were arrested and jointly charged with Bapka's murder. Three of the men, like Bapka himself, enjoyed the use of aliases. Dowlat Ram was also known as Tilwah and Seethalal was called James Jhagroo, while Randolph Mayers and Randolph Shepherd were one. The fourth man was Basil Henry.

What had happened was that, 395 days after the discovery of the body, the police had found an eyewitness—not a witness to the hanging, but to an incident, involving Bapka and the four accused, which took place the same day.

Nowbat was a rice farmer. That morning, he had been working in his field and, around 10:30 A.M., had heard the sound of men's voices. Looking up, he saw Bapka and Randolph Shepherd at a distance of about eighty yards. He saw Shepherd jump on Bapka. They held on to each other, and both fell to the ground. Dowlat Ram and James Jhagroo came and stood five or six yards away from the two struggling men. Nowbat heard Dowlat Ram say, "Ah, you kill the man!" Basil Henry, the last to appear, said, "At long last we got him."

Four or five minutes later, Nowbat said, he saw the four accused standing talking together. He could not hear what they said. Then Jhagroo, Shepherd, and Basil Henry walked east into the bush. Dowlat Ram ran out to the road. He did not see Bapka get up.

It was a strange story. Nowbat had seen a scuffle (a *scramble*, he called it) between two men. Three others were present who, apparently, had not taken part. There was then a four- or five-minute gap in the middle of the action sequence. During that period, Nowbat had not seen or heard a thing. What was he doing? Why had he stopped looking, at that point?

After the four men left the scene, Nowbat stayed in his rice field for two and a half hours, then made his way home through the bush. Bapka was his friend. He had not seen him get up after the fight with Shepherd. If he thought he might be lying injured or dead, why did he not go look for him during those two and a half hours?

Nowbat's subsequent behavior was no less strange. He said that, on the night of the wake, he told Bapka's widow what he had seen. This she denied. Not until 395 days after the killing did he tell the police. In the interim, Basil Henry, one of the four men he was to accuse, had stayed for a considerable time as a guest in Nowbat's home.

All the men involved were farmers except Randolph Shepherd, who sold cakes and soft drinks, and was a stranger to Leguan Island. Nowbat failed to pick out Shepherd at an identification parade.

The medical evidence was of little help. Bapka's body had been found between 7:00 and 8:00 P.M., and Bapka had last been seen alive by Nowbat at 10:30 A.M. The medical examiner was a country G.P., not a pathologist, and could offer no opinion as to the time of death that would narrow the gap between those hours. The only positive finding was that death had been caused by strangulation. Whether the strangulation had been performed manually or by the rope around Bapka's neck was not made clear, though the doctor inclined to the view that it was a case of suicide. His reasoning was that, although there were signs of minor external injuries, none of which could have contributed to Bapka's death, he would have expected to find more marks of bruising if others had attacked and hanged him.

The prosecution decided to press charges of murder. Joaquin Gonsalves-Sabola conducted the case for the Crown. Lionel Luckhoo was briefed to defend Randolph Shepherd, the only one among the accused who had been seen to lay a finger on the deceased. The other three prisoners were represented by Lloyd Luckhoo and David Karran.

Under Lionel's cross-examination at the trial, Nowbat endeavored to explain his conduct. What was he doing during those vital four or five minutes of the attack on Bapka when he closed his eyes or looked away? He was trembling with fear. Did he shout for help or seek to escape? No, he was petrified. Why had he stayed at the scene for two and a half hours? Had he come away earlier, he might have been seen and suffered whatever had been done to his close friend Bapka.

Why had he kept silence for more than a year? Because, Nowbat admitted, he was a coward. He thought only of his own safety. As the only witness, he might have been done away with, had he spoken of what he saw.

Nowbat explained his failure to recognize Randolph Shepherd at the identification parade by saying that "time had changed the man's face," and that, before, he was clean-shaven, but now he wore a beard.

There was one other important witness. Gloria Peters had at one time been the reputed wife of Basil Henry. She had given evidence at the preliminary inquiry, and again at the trial. Then the prosecution served notice that it intended to recall her to give additional testimony. Against strenuous objections from the defense, the court ruled in favor of the Crown.

The prosecution said it had only then ascertained that the witness knew more than she had stated. On her return to the stand, Gloria Peters testified to Basil Henry's having confessed to her his participation, with the other three accused, in the murder of Bapka. This alleged admission of guilt had not been mentioned in her two previous appearances.

All four defendants relied on alibis, but the lapse of time had befogged memories, and the alibis were not strong.

The entire case was a mixup, and at the end of the trial the most mixed-up person in court may well have been the judge. On no fewer than twenty-two occasions, he used expressions suggesting that Shepherd had jumped on Bapka's back, though Nowbat, in his evidence, had said nothing about Shepherd jumping on Bapka from the rear—still less, jumping on him from a tree, which was another distortion the judge seemed to have on his mind. This wrong assumption may have led the judge to introduce to the jury theories of death from causes other than strangulation, though that was the one point on which the medical evidence had been firm. Three times in his summing up, the judge put forward the possibility that Bapka might have been stunned when he fell to the ground and sustained injuries which caused his death. He advanced several alternative ways in which Bapka, if not strangled, might have been done to death in circumstances amounting to manslaughter at the hands of the accused four. While he apparently appreciated that there was no evidence at all to support any cause of death except asphyxia, instead of instructing the jury that it was impossible to find otherwise, he merely told them it was difficult to infer it from the evidence, and left it to them to decide whether they could surmount the difficulty.

When it came to the question of murder, the judge's directions were unequivocal: he related the possibility that the victim was strangled by Randolph Shepherd, assisted by Basil Henry.

The jury was sufficiently confused by it all to bring in a verdict of manslaughter against all four defendants. Each of them was sentenced to five years' imprisonment.

There had to be an appeal. Mr. Justice Archer as president, Sir Donald Jackson, and Sir Kenneth Stoby comprised the British Caribbean Court of Appeal which took the hearing. The prosecutor at the trial, Joaquin Gonsalves-Sabola, contended before the court that the verdict of the jury could be supported on the basis of strangulation without intent to kill or to do grievous bodily harm.

But, Lionel Luckhoo pointed out, the judge had never put this to the jury as a circumstance in which they could find the appellants guilty of manslaughter, though he had suggested several alternative ways in which manslaughter could have been committed.

Lionel was addressing the court on behalf of all four appellants, as he had at the trial where they were held to have acted in concert. He went on to argue instances of misdirection and nondirection by the judge. The evidence of Nowbat and Gloria Peters, he maintained, was extremely unsatisfactory. The part which Basil Henry played in Gloria Peters's account was inconsistent with Nowbat's description of the incident between Shepherd and Bapka. Her motive for incriminating Basil Henry was apparent, and should have excited the suspicion of the jury. Yet the judge had paid no particular attention to the improbabilities in the evidence of either of these two witnesses, leaving it to the jury with no helpful comment. Moreover, he had not told the jury that Peters's evidence concerning Basil Henry's alleged confession could not be used against the other accused.

The circumstantial evidence, Lionel submitted, was exceedingly weak, if not completely valueless. Nowbat had stated that Basil Henry was not present when Shepherd jumped Bapka. Dowlat Ram and James Jhagroo did not come up till several minutes later. None of the three took part in the scramble. After the scramble, all four appellants left the scene. From other witnesses, the prosecution had elicited that the four men were seen at various places, all considerable distances away from where the scramble took place, during the remainder of the day. On the other hand, Nowbat remained on the spot for two and a half hours, by his own testimony. He could see the tree from which Bapka's body was subsequently found hanging. But he gave no further evidence, either about Bapka or about the appellants doing anything to Bapka. *So it must be taken that, up to the time Nowbat left the scene, Bapka had not yet been strung up.* That was what the prosecution was saying. The judge's direction to the jury—that the circumstantial evidence could be considered along with the other evidence—must have led them to think that in some way it strengthened that evidence. In fact, being valueless in itself, it could not add a thing.

The Appeal Court agreed with Lionel Luckhoo that the circumstantial evidence did not strengthen the other evidence, and, without it, the case against the appellants had hardly any foundation at all. Their judgment was that the evidence against the appellants was unsatisfactory, and that there were serious misdirections concerning it. For these reasons, the court allowed the appeals.

With the convictions quashed and the sentences set aside, a victory had been won. But the mystery remained unsolved: who was the unseen hangman? Did Bapka die at the time of the scramble? And was he strung up to the tree to make it look like suicide? If so, when, and by whom?

Did Bapka, by an improbable but not impossible coincidence, encounter another enemy that day who knew about the earlier incident, and who hanged him in that place to cast suspicion on others?

Or was the medical examiner right in thinking that Bapka hanged himself? If this last possibility is the truth, then the unseen hangman remained at the scene of the crime as the most visible object in view.

2

Sometimes the trouble is not to know what has happened, but to whom. It can become quite a problem when the body has no head.

The murderer who is anxious to conceal his crime completely faces a grave difficulty—that of finding a grave. Corpses are not easily got rid of, though Henri Desire Landru did it so successfully that, even today, no one quite knows how. John George Haigh thought to remove all traces of his victims by dropping them into drums of acid, but learned that gallstones do not readily dissolve. James Camb pushed Gay Gibson's body through a ship's porthole into the Atlantic Ocean, and she was never found. Mrs. Urban Napoleon Stanger, we can be almost certain, turned her husband into twopenny meat pies.

With the exception of the ingenious lady, all were found guilty of murder, their efforts wasted. Yet many people still believe that, unless a corpse is present and (more or less) correct, the charge cannot be brought against them. Accordingly, they will go to any lengths to conceal a body or destroy it.

The murderers of Harry Hussain must have been thinking on these lines when they decapitated him and flung his headless body into the sea. The sea let them down—as it did Donald Hume, when he dropped neatly parceled sections of Stanley Setty from an airplane into the English Channel.

Chapter 9
The Case of the Mining Millions

I sprang to the stirrup, and Joris, and he;
I galloped, Dirck galloped, we galloped
all three.

—Robert Browning

The Luckhoo brothers began and ended the biggest financial case of their careers, a $10 million wrangle, by flinging away their chance for a fortune.

The American Cyanamid Company was the first United States industrial concern to set up a large-scale operation in Guyana. Their bauxite mines at Kwakwani produced high-grade ore, but to get it out was a problem. Only flat-bottomed punts could pass the Berbice Bar and bring the bauxite downriver from the interior. The Berbice Company, as the local organization was known, began to lose money.

In his role of trade union leader, Lionel had negotiated agreements with the Americans and had several confrontations with them. It was no surprise when, one day in November, 1952, the manager David Logan telephoned and asked to see him. But Lionel was surprised when he learned the reason for the meeting: Logan was offering to sell him the company, lock, stock, and barrel.

The asking price was 400 grand for buildings, equipment and stockpiled bauxite, and Lionel knew that the stockpiled bauxite alone was worth that amount. He could not understand why a company he had so recently been fighting on the industrial front should now be willing to sell him a concern worth at least $10 million, for less than one-twentieth of its value. The only catch seemed to be that an answer was required within forty-eight hours. Logan explained that, if the sale were made before the end of December, the company would be able to claim several millions for losses incurred in their operations abroad.

Lionel had a conference with E.V. and Lloyd. Raising 400 grand would not be difficult, because of the tremendous assets which could be proved to exist at Kwakwani. But, being lawyers and not businessmen, they kept on looking for the catch. Why should the American company be willing to drop millions in their laps when, at ten times the price being asked, it would still be a gift? Lionel went back and asked David Logan, who again went into long details about his organization being able to reclaim their substantial losses over the years, and their preference for selling out to Guyanese rather than to Americans. To the Luckhoos, it still did not add up, and, with only forty-eight hours to decide, they turned down the offer.

Forthwith, American Cyanamid offered the Berbice Company to Harvey Aluminum in America. Now the price had doubled. Instead of being 400 grand (equivalent to about 200 grand U.S.), it was nearer to 500 grand U.S. Pending their investigation of the property, Harvey Aluminum posted the necessary money in escrow in the States.

In the meantime, another U.S. giant, Reynolds Metals, heard about this gem waiting to be picked up in far-off Guyana. One of its engineers, Ralph Roley, flew in with a colleague. An aerial survey was enough to convince him that the gem was priceless. Roley asked to be put in touch with the leading firm of lawyers in Guyana. So the Luckhoos were retained to act for Reynolds in acquiring mines which they themselves could have owned.

"Bad businessmen make good lawyers" might be a moral for the rest of the story. The Luckhoos advised Reynolds that, since the land belonged to the government, the Berbice Company could not transfer their leases without the government's authority. Immediate steps should be taken to get the consent of the government for transfer of the leases from the Berbice Company to Reynolds Metals, if the latter purchased the former's assets.

The three Luckhoos approached the then Governor of British Guiana, Sir John Gutch, and asked for a letter of intent. Aware that the Berbice Company was about to close down, and that thousands would be out of employment, the Governor was happy to learn that Reynolds was interested. He did not then know that Harvey Aluminum already had engineers doing surveys and making estimates. Nevertheless, when Lionel asked for the letter he immediately stalled. He wanted to consult his Executive Council.

Finally, under Lionel's persuasion, Sir John there and then did dictate a letter. When the draft was completed, E.V. looked at it, then shook his head. "Sir," he said, "you are saying here that the government of British Guiana will favorably consider transferring the leases. We are dealing with American businessmen who do not have the old-school-tie traditions of the English, who do not fully appreciate that an Englishman's word is his bond. I'm afraid that the words *favorably consider transferring* will stall the entire undertaking."

The Governor said, "Well, give me a little time." But, with all three Luckhoos pressing him for an immediate change, he gave in. The phrase "favorably consider transferring" was removed, and a positive "will transfer" was substituted.

Events began to move swiftly. Reynolds paid over the money—a little less than half a million dollars—to buy up the assets of the Berbice Company. Next, the Luckhoos put in for the transfer of the Crown leases from the Berbice Company to Reynolds. After that, the Harvey Aluminum Company claimed that its purchase of the assets had taken place at the time the money was posted in escrow, and that it was entitled to the transfer of the leases. The opening shots had been fired in a legal war which was to be waged for two years in Guyanese and American courts, and to be dubbed by the newspapers as "The Ten Million Dollar Suit."

Harvey went into action by seeking a declaration from the Guyanese courts that their opposition to the transfer to Reynolds Metal of the leases was just, legal, and well founded, and sought an injunction restraining the Berbice Company from effecting any transfer of lands, buildings, mines, or equipment to Reynolds. Soon the tussle had spread to the

American courts, and the Luckhoo brothers had to go to New York and swear affidavits as to the state of land law in British Guiana. The American courts decided to await the determination of the issues by British Guiana before passing judgment. The case went through some forty legal applications, appearances, and hearings before Chief Justice Fred Boland gave the lasting verdict.

Judgment was that the opposition by the plaintiff Harvey Aluminum Company was unjust, illegal, and ill founded. The action was dismissed out of court, with an order that costs be paid both defendants.

It was a triumph for the Luckhoos, and a classic illustration of the adage which tells us that, although "twice-armed is he who hath his quarrel just, thrice-armed is he who gets his blow in fust." What won the case was the firm assurance, given in writing to Reynolds, that the government would transfer the leases to them. The Chief Justice stated that, if there had been only an expression of intention to favorably consider, then other consideration might well arise, but he regarded the unequivocal statement as binding on the government, making it obligatory that the transfer would go through.

This killed the main actions, both in Guyana and New York, which claimed that a purchase had taken place when Harvey Aluminum posted the money in escrow. If the Guyanese courts had held that the government was not obligated to transfer the leases to Reynolds, then it would have had to be determined legally, before transfer took place, who was the buyer having the rightful claim. Reynolds was unlikely to win, as Harvey had contracts already drawn up. But Harvey could not buy what the government had agreed to transfer to Reynolds.

After the case was won, Richard Reynolds, Sr., turned to the Luckhoos and said, "Let me give you boys the best holiday you ever had." Knowing that all three were avid racegoers, he took them to the Kentucky Derby, one of the three American classics, and treated them royally. Then he offered them fees far higher than they had bargained for; or, as an alternative, he said, they could take stock of the same value in his company. With legal caution, the Luckhoos plumped for cash. And, as at the beginning of the case, they picked a losing bet. If they had taken the stock, they would all be millionaires today.

Chapter 10
The Case of the Galloping Mayor

Time travels in divers paces with divers persons. I'll tell you who Time ambles withal, who Time trots withal, who Time gallops withal. . . .

—*As You Like It*

Newton was up for sale—the entire village. Six hundred families were about to lose their homes. Lionel Luckhoo, member of the Legislative Council, went to Governor Sir Patrick Renison and pleaded with him, "Stop the sale. I will get the bank to put up the money to buy the village. Then I will sell it back to the villagers at cost."

The Governor eyed him doubtfully. "Lionel, what is there for you in this scheme?"

"Nothing. I want to help these people to save their homes."

"Very well," Renison decided. "If you can do it solely to help them, why shouldn't I help you do it?"

As early as 1947, the Governor of what was then British Guiana had invited Lionel Luckhoo to join the Legislative Council. Such bodies, there and elsewhere in the British West Indies, had a purely advisory role. Members were permitted to have their say, but the final say always rested with the Governor. Harsh or humane, despot or democrat, his power within the law was vast, so long as he did not create too many ripples at Westminster. Council members were commonly chosen from the ranks of the commercial and land barons, who could be counted upon to be props of the establishment, save in minor affairs that might affect their sectional interests. The system was, perhaps, slightly more democratic than England B.C. (*Before Cromwell*)—slightly less so than England following the Restoration.

Sir Charles Wooley, who preceded Sir Patrick Renison, was a liberal-minded governor. He told Lionel that he wanted to appoint someone young, with vitality, as counterweight to all the greybeards who dominated the Council. Lionel saw the drawbacks of the system, but accepted the appointment with the intention of turning the advantages to account. The main advantage was that the Governor had the power to circumvent any sectional interests if he could be so persuaded. Rescuing the village of Newton from forced sale was Lionel's first notable success in this direction.

During the forties and fifties, the question of whether capital punishment should be the penalty for murder was guaranteed to arouse murderous passions, as it still does, in the most civilized communities. Having already saved half a hundred clients from experiencing the final "turn off," as the *Newgate Calendar* liked to term it, Lionel Luckhoo had come to have firm views on the subject. He gave notice of a motion he wished to bring before the Legislative Council, calling for a select committee to inquire into aboliton, and to recommend changes in the law as applying to murder. It took two and a half years to get it debated.

The most logical argument against hanging is that you cannot bring a dead man back to life and apologize for your mistake. This was stressed by Lionel Luckhoo in his speech to the Council. "We have the right to go to appeal, and after the Appeal Court we also have the right to go to the Privy Council, and finally to approach the Governor for a reprieve. Nonetheless, it is still possible, and it will remain possible, for mistakes to be made, so long as human judgment remains fallible, and so long as the death penalty is irrevocable."

He referred to well-known instances of prisoners who were almost certainly hanged in error, and of two recent near-misses which were stopped only at the Privy Council stage. In the Woolmington case, a man was convicted at his second trial, after the first jury had disagreed. In summing up, the judge had said, "It is incumbent on the accused to prove death was as the result of accident." The verdict was quashed by the House of Lords, on the grounds that the onus of proof remained with the prosecution and did not shift—it was not incumbent on the accused to prove anything.

The second instance was Lionel's own Noor Mohamed case. In refusing leave to appeal, the trial judge had said, "If I had one single shade of doubt in this matter—if I could possibly be wrong about it—I would readily grant your request to have a case stated for review by the West Indian Court of Appeal." Despite the judge saying that he could not possibly be wrong, the Privy Council ultimately decided he was quite wrong.

Lionel reviewed the history of capital punishment under English law, from the days when "hanging was regarded as much of a public event as a classic football match is today. Customs, habits, prejudices die very hard, indeed. The British system of jurisprudence is the finest in the world, but an unhappy relic is the penalty of capital punishment which still persists. What are the main objections to reform? The first is that the classification of murder is not practicable; the second, fear of the consequences."

Answering these objections, he cited the reform of the Indian Penal Code in 1837 by Lord Macaulay. He allowed the judges the right to say that a particular offense, although murder, need not have the death penalty associated with it, but the prisoner could be sent to penal servitude for life. That system worked. We find that Sir Charles Metcalfe actually suspended capital punishment in Bengal with success—success, in the sense that there were fewer cases of murder subsequent to the suspension. . . . In Scotland, from the year 1929 to the year 1944, there was no execution. During those years, there were fewer cases of murder than for the previous fifteen years. In no country has the abolition of capital punishment increased the murder rate. The existence of the death penalty makes no difference to the security of life. You cannot teach people the sanctity of life by hanging.

"It seems to me that that sanctity would be observed and respected only when those in responsible positions set the example. The acceptance of this motion could make this Colony an example in its practice of the criminal law relating to murder. Why should we wait on the inhabitants of England?

Surely we have men in this Colony who are capable of formulating these changes and putting them on the statute book. Why can't we be progressive enough to move forward in a matter which affects the lives of the people?"

The motion was accepted by the House.

That was a quarter of a century ago. In his appeal to the Legislative Council, Lionel had referred to his personal experiences of having seen men in the death cell, waiting the final day. "It is not a pleasant thing even to recall. I have seen human beings behave worse than subhumans, groveling there with broken spirits. It is tragic to feel that we are perpetuating it." Since then, he has been involved with murder most of the days of his life.

How does he now feel about capital punishment?

"I feel I was wrong," he told the writer. "I feel that certain people have forfeited the right to remain in the society of their fellows. But I don't mean in every case of murder. I don't mean cases of a sudden rush of blood to the head, that kind of thing. I might get into a fight, lose my temper, and pick up a gun and shoot someone. It is not premeditated, but it happens. I am thinking of cases where there is preparation. The poisoner, for example, has to procure the poison, carry out acts of preparation, of patience, of contemplation, before the final act of administering the poison. I think a poisoner is a desperate character, and can well be removed from society.

"And, definitely, policemen, warders, watchmen, people who are protecting the interests of the public at large, should be so protected that their murderer goes to the gallows. If I were advocating a change of policy, I would suggest that judges be allowed to review sentences, when the act of murder might be regarded as premeditated, to decide whether, in their view—or, alternatively, in the view of a committee not necessarily formed of judges—the extreme penalty should be used. I know this would provide difficulties, but it deserves consideration."

One criterion, I suggested, might be the wantonness of the crime. A policeman may be killed because he bars a robber's way of escape; even a poisoner may have been pushed to extreme limits by the victim. In such cases, the killer feels menaced and reacts under stress. In that state of mind, the act, however wrong, has become an act of necessity. But the criminal who shoots a policeman merely because of his uniform, who, after robbing a harmless victim, batters him to death, who poisons out of greed for money, who blows up a planeload of innocent people, shows a disregard for human life that—if it should ever be said of anybody—makes him not worth the effort of redeeming.

"Anyone who shows a wanton disregard for human life forfeits, in my view, the right to have his own life preserved," Lionel agreed. "The outstanding defect in the law of murder is that it provides a single penalty for a crime widely varying in culpability. Lord Denning has said that the ultimate justification of any punishment is that it is the emphatic denunciation by the community of a crime. It is difficult to establish with any degree of certainty how far the death penalty acts as a deterrent more powerful than such punishments as imprisonment. When a murder is committed, the deterrent obviously has failed. We can number these failures, but we cannot number the successes.

"Impulsive murders, sex murders, and murders committed by the mentally abnormal, are unlikely to be much affected by any sanction. But then there is the professional criminal. If we were to abolish the death penalty for the murder of a police officer, we might well have to take the stand that the police should be armed. It would change the attitude of the professional criminal who does not now arm himself because of what might ensue. In the final analysis, the question is whether the repulsive features of the penalty are outweighed by its force as a deterrent."

Then what about mistakes? What he himself had referred to as "the relentless finality inseparable from the capital penalty" remains a valid argument for its suspension. Was Lionel Luckhoo now prepared to take the risk that justice might miscarry?

"My main objection to capital punishment is its finality. Once it has been carried out, there is no room for correcting an error, and it cannot be argued that, of all human activities, a murder trial is the only one free from fallibility. Mistakes have been made. We have cases like Oscar Slater's, whose innocence was subsequently established. Timothy Evans was convicted on the evidence of Christie, who, when giving evidence, was regarded as an irreproachable character, but who later was himself convicted and hanged for murder. Lloyd Harris is the one man who I am convinced was innocent, yet the girl who was raped identified him as one of the men who killed her boyfriend, and he was convicted.*

"All this is one reason why I advocate that judges or committees should be allowed to review sentences before the death penalty is invoked, and peruse the evidence so as to reduce the chances of error. But I confess that mistakes could still be made. That is why I feel that it is only in the clearest cases, which fall into the categories I have suggested, that there should be hanging."

2

Prime Minister Forbes Burnham often refers to Lionel Luckhoo as the man who beat him in an election. Lionel did —by one vote! It was when they were competing for office as Mayor of Georgetown.

Lionel Luckhoo takes life at a gallop. Always overstretched himself, he yet stretches time as though it were elastic. Full though his days were with law and racing, he could not resist the challenge of politics.

His entry into municipal affairs came about by chance, when he joined a meeting where citizens were discussing a motion the city councilors had just passed to pay themselves for their services. Lionel took the view that this was a luxury which local government could not afford, and said so. Elections were due, and the group asked him if he would be willing to contest a seat. Lionel stood, and was elected for the Laceytown Division.

At that time, Georgetown's most influential citizen was Percy Claude Wight, a stockbroker and realtor. When an issue of municipal bonds was offered to the public, Wight was allowed to take up the unsubscribed bonds at a price below par. Lionel's objections to this deal were regarded by a majority of his council colleagues as a prime act of impertinence. The courts took another view when Lionel brought the matter before them. Mr. Justice Boland ruled that he was right in

* *See Chapter 20, "The Case of the Disappearing Double."*

his stand, and ordered that the bonds be re-advertised, to give the public an opportunity to bid. This affair made Lionel popular with the populace, very unpopular within the council chamber.

From the date of his first election in 1950, Lionel remained for fifteen years the member for Laceytown. In 1954, he was elected Mayor of Georgetown. Even for Lionel Luckhoo, that was a busy year, for he also became Minister without Portfolio in the Interim Government. Again in 1955, and for two further terms in 1960 and 1961, he was to serve as Mayor.

The mayoral office enabled him to put a number of progressive ideas into practice. One innovation was to hold regular monthly meetings, to which the people could come and bring their problems to the Mayor with the hope of getting them resolved. Georgetown is a city after the Dutch pattern, well laid out, with canals running down the middle of its broad thoroughfares. Lionel Luckhoo beautified the city by planting hundreds of trees and flowering shrubs along the grass verges of the canals. He did not neglect practical needs. He built car parks, which were strongly criticized at first as being unnecessary; but more and more cars were coming into the country, and soon he was being praised for his foresight.

There was no public swimming pool. When Lionel proposed that the Council should provide one, the idea fell flat. "Where is the money coming from?" he was asked. It was the $64,000 question. Lionel answered, "I won't ask the Council for a single penny. I will raise the money myself." He got together a steel band, and led them around the streets of Georgetown. He walked fifteen miles, collecting pennies, shillings, here and there a few dollars. This raised enough to get the fund off to a good start. The rest he collected from commercial firms, telling them they were making a contribution to posterity. Soon the total had reached $65,000—a neat response to the original question!

With the help of the City Engineer and the Water Supervisor, Lionel then designed the pool. A rocky piece of parkland was chosen as the site. The rock provided a solid foundation which only needed to be concreted over. With one rock face utilized as a wall, only the three remaining sides needed to be built. Before it was completed, students and other intending users had suggested calling it the "Luckhoo Park Swimming Pool"—and so it was named. At the opening, the Mayor, for the first time in his life, delivered a written address. E.V. told Lionel afterwards that it was the worst speech he ever made.

When Lionel became Mayor, he spent some time going through the archives of the municipality, which were "in a hell of a mess," as he thought. But an old janitor told him, "You should have been here last year. You'd have found the place in a lot worse mess than this."

Lionel said, "Impossible! It couldn't be worse than this."

"It was," the janitor said. "We had a tremendous collection of old letters still in their envelopes, going back to the time we became a city and the postal service started."

Lionel's heart skipped a beat. Georgetown became a chartered city in 1840. A British Guiana penny stamp of 1856 is the most valuable stamp in the world.* There is said to be only one in existence. It was then owned by a man named Vaughan, who lived opposite the Luckhoos in Georgetown.

"You mean letters from the 1840s and 1850s?" he asked the janitor.

"Yes," the man nodded. "All those years."

Lionel licked dry lips. "What did you do with them?"

"Oh, they were only gathering cobwebs and dust. I took them to the rubbish heap and put a match to them."

He had likely sent a fortune up in flames.

This nondiscovery was followed by a discovery, among the old papers in the vaults, which had a more pleasant result. Lionel came upon the original letter from Queen Victoria, duly signed and sealed, that created Georgetown a cathedral city in the 1840s. It appeared that, for all those years, the civic head of Georgetown had been entitled to the appellation "Lord Mayor." Forthwith, Mayor Luckhoo created a flurry in the dovecotes of Whitehall by asking to have the position

* *The British Guiana 1856 one-cent stamp was sold at auction in New York April 5, 1980, for $850,000, the highest price ever paid for a postage stamp—thus, breaking its own record of $280,000, which had stood for ten years.*

clarified—and Georgetown became the second city in the Commonwealth, outside Britain, to have its Lord Mayor.

During his years as Mayor, Lionel gave up most of his law practice. He did manage to improve and streamline the civic police force in certain ways. And one achievement that gave him real satisfaction was that he settled by negotiation all the labor disputes which arose while he was in office. There were rumors of strikes among the municipal workers, some near misses, but never a strike!

Early on, he had set up a small committee of councilors and workers to meet every week, to discuss and resolve problems as they arose. Major problems, he firmly believed, usually start in microscopic manner, then time adds to their dimensions. On one occasion when a strike was threatened, the Mayor called all the workers to the Municipal Compound, explained the Council's side of the dispute, and offered to meet an enlarged committee of their representatives. He called to the front the two workers who had been most vociferous at the meeting, and asked them to join the committee as *his* advisers. They were proud to be chosen, and the crisis was averted. Lionel's experience had taught him that to give a troublemaker responsibility is often the best way of producing a valuable ally. Or, to put it another way, if you can't beat them, have them join you.

3

The grip of colonial rule was beginning to slacken on all the larger territories of the British West Indies. Politicians of all hues were agitating for constitutional changes that would give their countries a greater measure of self-rule. One of the ideas being strongly touted in the 1950s was for a federation inclusive of Jamaica, Trinidad, Barbados, a number of smaller islands—and Guyana. The issue came before the State Council twice, and Lionel Luckhoo took part in both debates.

His attitude was that caution should be exercised. "Those who advance the proposition that we should accept federation are in the nature of prosecutors in a court of criminal jurisdiction urging the case on behalf of the Crown, *which has to be established beyond reasonable doubt.*" He did not feel that the time was ripe, if it ever would be, for British Guiana to join in a federation.

Some of Lionel's doubts centered upon the proposed distribution of seats in the projected Federal Parliament. The balance was overwhelmingly in favor of Jamaica and Trinidad. True, they were more populous, but, in size and untapped resources, British Guiana had much greater scope for development.

This "basic bias," as Lionel Luckhoo described it, was the main reason for the motion being rejected. When the subject came up again three years later, he was once more in opposition.

"If ever there was cause for righteous indignation, it is when one sees six seats allotted to British Guiana in the Rance Report, as against sixteen for Jamaica and nine for Trinidad! On what basis? An arbitrary determination. And yet . . . they seem to feel it is more than we should get." (Five seats had, at first, been proposed for British Guiana at a preliminary conference set up by the Colonial Office; a sixth was added after the threat of a walkout.)

Although the terms and conditions of entry into the Federation were still unclear, the motion before the State Council was that British Guiana should join. Lionel proposed, in an amendment, that the question of participation should be re-examined.

"The point is: should we, first of all, put our heads into the noose and express an opinion which is unnecessary now, and say that British Guiana should join the Federation? Or should we make representations, obtain all the conditions, and then express an opinion? That is the point. . . . We must wait until the cards are before us, and then express an opinion which will reflect mature judgment upon factors we know about."

He was also concerned as to whether the body of which he was a member had any right to take the final decision.

"Who are we? We are all nominateds, put here in this Council. It was very necessary, because of the times, but can any of us rise and say that our views necessarily reflect the body of opinion of the people of this country, without first going to the people?"

The amendment was carried. British Guiana never joined the West Indies Federation. Lionel was informed that his stand on the issue had been the biggest obstacle in the way. A federal government was formed, but his prognostication that it would not last quickly came true. From its inception in 1958, there was conflict between the federal government and its members, and between the members themselves. Jamaica's withdrawal, after an anti-federation vote, cast in a 1961 referendum, led to the final demise.

Under its own steam, British Guiana was moving towards self-rule. The dominant political faction was the very left-wing People's Progressive Party, led by Cheddi Jagan and Forbes Burnham. With the coming of universal adult suffrage, Lionel Luckhoo felt there was a real danger of the country going Communist. And communism, he considered, would be bad for Guyana. So he formed a political party, the National Labour Front.

The new party received no support from large organizations or public associations. Lionel was joined by some old-timers, middle-of-the-road politicans, but the Jagan-Burnham combination had a firm hold on the grassroots voters. When the election came in 1957, the National Labour Front won only a single seat. Lionel Luckhoo, contesting a Georgetown constituency, lost by 220 votes—perhaps largely because of the intervention of another moderate, P.A. Cummings, a former judge, who took away several hundred votes.

The overwhelming defeat of his party was a bitter blow to Lionel. Not less so was his own failure to win a seat. He declined the offer of Steven Campbell, an Amerindian who was the only NLF candidate to be elected, to resign, so that Lionel could contest his seat at a by-election. By now, he could lay reasonable claim to having done more for the people than any other native politician had succeeded in doing. The National Labour Front disbanded, ending Lionel Luckhoo's first, and last, venture into front-line politics.

Chapter 11
The Case of the Angry Amazon

Ophelia: 'Tis brief, my lord.
Hamlet: As woman's love.

—Hamlet

Love is where you find it. The Greeks depicted Eros as indulging himself with innumerable childish diversions; and divine whimsy can be as deadly as devilish humor in the outcome. No one cares to imagine Romeo as a lank-haired, pimply-faced teenager; or Juliet, cross-eyed, and running to puppy fat. Yet tall, short, lardy, bony, fuzzy, bald, clever, numbskull, sweet or sour, the arrows fly where Eros listeth.

So the romance of John and Doris should have surprised no one. Yet, it did.

John was a bit heftier than a seven-stone weakling. He stood five feet four, if wearing thick soles, and, wringing wet, weighed 130 pounds. Doris was six feet tall without high heels, and muscular. But, though Doris had worked as a *chucker-out* (a bouncer) in Georgetown bars, the muscles did not show so as to mar her beauty of face and figure. In younger days, she had been singled out to be introduced to the Prince of Wales (later to become Edward VIII, and afterwards Duke of Windsor), and it was not her conversation alone that delighted him.

John was a Barbadian. Although slight, he was adventurous, and had come to Guyana because of the dazzling stories he had heard about gold and diamond finds in the unexplored interior. He went into the jungle of the Upper Mazaruni, staked out a few claims, and eventually struck lucky in diamonds. He returned to Georgetown to splash around his money and to purchase supplies. When he went back, Doris formed part of his extra baggage.

No doubt, Doris was aware that diamonds are a girl's best friend. On the other hand, remembering the Prince of Wales, who was no giant, she may have had a natural yen for smallish men. At forty, her charms were a little tarnished, but she still had the looks and vitality to overwhelm the shy and romantic John. Often she treated him roughly. Once, in a temper, she picked him up by the scruff of the neck, held him out of a second-floor window, and dropped him to the ground below. It did not lessen his love for her.

Mining for precious stones is a hard and unrewarding task, until a big strike is made. Then the money floods in, and it often floods out again as quickly, for the bad times that went before are easily forgotten. John lavished diamonds on Doris, and fine clothes to go with them. He built her a house. Everything was "hunky," until his claims began to peter out; then Doris cooled towards him. She began to bring men friends to the house when John was away. Inevitably, the night came when John returned home and found Doris in bed with a man. The man leaped out of a window and ran. Only John knew for certain what happened next.

When the police came, they found Doris lying on the bed. There were twenty-four slashes, made by a cutlass, on her body. She had been literally cut to ribbons. John was immediately charged with murder.

John was popular with all the diamond miners. Many remembered his generosity to them when they had been down on their luck. They clubbed together to provide for his defense, and sought the aid of Lionel Luckhoo. There was plenty of public sympathy for the little man, but sympathy is not evidence. It was a difficult case to defend.

John's story was that, when he went into the room and the man ran out, Doris leaped out of bed and advanced towards him, yelling, "I'll kill you with my bare hands!" He knew she was capable of doing it. There was a cutlass in the room. John knew where it was, and he dived for it. He then slashed about in front of him, in fear of his life. He felt the cutlass connect, but in the dark room could not be sure what was happening. When the attack on him seemed to have subsided, he ran out of the room and went for the police.

The weakness of John's case was that Doris was unarmed, and he had no injuries to show. She had received multiple wounds, and was carved up so horribly that she must have died within minutes.

The police sergeant for the district, giving evidence for the prosecution, testified that most of the blood was on the bed. Only a few drops had spattered over the rest of the room. The prosecution intended to imply that John had attacked Doris where she lay.

Lionel, cross-examining the witness on this point, said, "Sergeant, was the room in a mess, tables and chairs lying all over the place?"

"Yes."

That reply gave strong indication that there had been a chase or a struggle in the darkened room.

"Where was Doris?"

"She was on the bed."

"Was she on her back, lying across the bed?"

"Yes."

"Then that would explain the blood on the bed?" He did not wait for an answer.

Struggle or no, the only hope for John was the reduction of the offense of murder to one of manslaughter. The cross-examination of the sergeant had helped, but Lionel felt that what was most needed was a favorable summing up from the judge. He knew Mr. Justice Ward to be not only learned in the law, but a humane man, with an understanding of people. And the judge, like the prisoner, came from Barbados. Barbadians were the people he knew best.

Lionel advised little John to go into the witness box and give evidence under oath. "Don't try to talk like a Guyanese," he warned him. "Use your own Barbadian accent."

When John had taken the oath, Lionel's first question was, "Where were you born?"

John answered, in the inimitable style of a true Barbadian, "Oi come from Black Rock in Barbados."

Mr. Justice Ward raised his eyebrows, looked at John, but made no comment. John went on to tell his story, how he had loved Doris, how she had appeared to love him in return, until his fortune dwindled, and, finally, the events of that last fatal night.

The prosecutor, acting Attorney General Gilbert McRae Farnum, cross-examined. "You knew Doris was unarmed?"

"Yes."

"You knew that your first blow had connected?"

"Yes."

"Why did you continue to lash at her with the cutlass?"

This was the all-important question, and the trial might hinge on whether John had an answer the court could accept.

"Because, sir," he said, "she was so very strong. If I had stopped, I would have been dead. You see, sir, she used to be a chucker-out at a Georgetown hotel, and on one occasion I saw her lift up two men together and throw them out."

Addressing the jury, Lionel said, "This unfortunate man does not seek to invoke your sympathy. He asks for your understanding." He went on to paint a vivid picture of the setting of the crime—the brooding forest of the Mazaruni, the lonely house, darkness all around, no help within earshot. Then, the confined space of the bedroom, Doris, angry at John's intrusion, and screaming at him, "I will kill you with my bare hands!"—a threat she could carry out very easily. Doris had taken the best John could offer—in fact, all he had—and then rejected him. That night, the frail little man had one chance only of saving his life—to reach the cutlass. Fear and despair lent strength to his arm as he slashed blindly before him, for he knew it was his life or hers.

"The question may well lie between a complete acquittal and a verdict of manslaughter," Lionel ended. "What it is not is murder. There was no murder, *no murder*, NO MURDER!"

Mr. Justice Ward analyzed the evidence, directed the jury on the law as it related to provocation and self-defense, then went as far as a judge properly may, in his last comment. "I rarely express my own opinion," he said, "and if I do, you are not bound by it, but I think there is sufficient evidence on which you may well find yourselves prepared to bring in a verdict of manslaughter."

It was the summation Lionel Luckhoo had been hoping for, all along.

If a woman kills a man, it is relatively easy for a jury to believe that, at the time, she was in fear of her life, and panic-stricken. She is assumed to have been physically the weaker. When a man kills a woman, no matter how much the normal contrast of strength and weakness might be reversed, an effort of the imagination is needed to accept that his danger, and consequent fright, could have been as real. Even the aggressive women's liberation proponents have done little to alter this embedded belief in one sort of male superiority.

The jury took three hours to reach a verdict. When it declared that John was not guilty of murder, but guilty of manslaughter, a loud cheer went up from the miners who thronged the court. After order was restored, Mr. Justice Ward turned to the prisoner.

"Man from Black Rock," the judge said, "you are fortunate, very fortunate. When you have served your sentence, you would do well to return to Black Rock. The sentence of this court is that you be imprisoned for four years."

Only a quirk of fate prevented John, and Doris, too, from coming to a far happier ending. Hardly had the prison gates closed behind him than a rich yield of diamonds was discovered in the area where John had been working. A little sooner, and the tragedy might never have happened. Or, human nature being what it is, would it merely have been postponed?

2

There was never any doubt or denial that John was responsible for the death of Doris. The only approach open to his defender was to hammer the question: was it murder? When Sujit died with a neat bullet hole driven through his forehead, there was no doubt about its being murder. The only question was the identity of the killer. And the police appeared to have a cast-iron case against Lionel Luckhoo's client—motive, means, opportunity, and an independent eyewitness who had watched him do it.

Baldeo, twenty-four, was an outdoor man, tall and muscular, a farmer and a hunter. Sujit, thirty, was the sedentary type, a cake shop owner. Despite the contrast, the men were close friends until Sujit took a fancy to Baldeo's wife, which witnesses were, afterwards, to suggest she had encouraged. However it be, the fancy turned to love, and, perhaps, obsession. For, when Baldeo threatened Sujit with what would happen if he did not leave his wife alone, the warning was disregarded.

And Baldeo was a man to be feared. He was acclaimed as being the best shot on the west coast of Demerara. Once he had brought down a cattle-stealing tiger with a bullet through its forehead, at a distance not much short of 100 yards. Friends told him he ought to be representing Guyana at Bisley, but Baldeo was content with his local fame as marksman.

Little wonder that Baldeo was the prime suspect when Sujit was shot. Baldeo had a motive. Baldeo had a gun. And, as a target, Sujit was far less fearsome than a tiger. The clinching factor was an eyewitness, a forest ranger named Alfred Grant. His testimony led to Baldeo's arrest.

At the trial, a police sergeant gave evidence of going to Baldeo's home and seizing his gun. Lionel Luckhoo, defending, asked him what condition the gun was in when he saw it.

"Well, when I found the gun it was oiled."

"So you could not tell whether it had been used recently or not?"

"No, I could not tell. But it was strange that it was oiled."

Lionel lifted an eyebrow. "Why strange, sergeant?"

"Well, it was broken and oiled."

A lame response. Lionel said sharply, "Baldeo was a regular hunter. Would it not be advantageous to him to keep his gun in good order?"

"Well, perhaps," the sergeant admitted reluctantly.

So far, so good. But the condition of the gun did not weigh heavily, either way. It was the ranger's evidence that had to be demolished before there could be the slightest chance of an acquittal.

Alfred Grant said he had first seen the accused at a distance of sixty or seventy yards. Baldeo was creeping along as if he might be stalking a deer. Grant stood still, watching his movements. He saw him take aim. He heard the report of the gun, and, away in the distance, he saw a man fall. Baldeo ran.

Grant quickly covered the hundred yards or more to reach the man who had fallen. It was Sujit, and he was dead.

Grant had told an apparently straightforward story. The prosecution must have thought their case already won, as Lionel Luckhoo embarked on a rigorous cross-examination that was to last a full day.

"Mr. Grant, you say that when you first saw Baldeo he was about sixty yards away from you. Did you at that time see Sujit?"

"No."

"Did you see Sujit at any time before the firing of the gun?"

"Yes."

"How long before?"

"I saw Sujit, but I didn't recognize him at first. He was still some fifty yards away from Baldeo."

"Did you see Baldeo aiming at him?"

"Yes."

"Did it strike you he was going to fire the gun?"

"Yes."

"Did you shout a warning?"

"No."

"Why didn't you shout?"

"I was confused."

"After the man fell, did you shout?"

"No."

"Why not, Mr. Grant? Why not?"

"Well, I was stunned."

"The first time, you failed to shout because you were confused; now you are stunned. Is it not the truth that you never saw Baldeo fire?"

"Oh, yes, I saw him fire."

"You saw him take aim?"

"Yes, I saw him take aim."

"How did he hold the gun?"

"He held it to his shoulder."

"Show us."

The line of questioning had made the witness anxious to offer proof. He was handed Baldeo's gun, which was an exhibit. He demonstrated by holding the weapon with the butt to his shoulder and sighting along the barrel at an imaginary target.

"Thank you. Now, did you recognize the man with the gun as being Baldeo?"

"Yes."

"Then why didn't you call out to him?"

"I told you I was confused."

"Had you ever seen Baldeo fire a gun before?"

"No."

"Do you yourself have any experience of firing guns?"

"No, I do not have a gun."

"Have you ever been shooting?"

"No!" Grant's voice rose, as his nerves became worn with the inquisition.

"Mr. Grant, you are swearing on oath that this is how Baldeo held the gun?" Lionel imitated the way Grant had held the weapon a few minutes before, and, in a more controlled voice, the witness murmured his assent.

"You were standing to the north of him; he was to the south of you?"

"Yes."

"And the gun was being aimed towards the west?"

"Yes."

"So you had a clear view of the gunman's profile?"

"Yes."

Lionel Luckhoo's voice had been calm, even coaxing. Now, it became stern and accusing. "Witness, you are lying! Baldeo is a left-handed shot. The gun would be to his left shoulder. He was firing to the west. You were to the north of him. You could not see his profile."

Grant was as confused as he claimed to have been at the time of the shooting. "I don't know anything about that," he muttered. "I saw him shoot the man."

"No, Mr. Grant, you don't get away with it as easily as that. You saw him shoot the man, you say. When you saw him take aim, he had the gun at his right shoulder?"

"Yes."

"All right, let's take another aspect." The witness was so relieved to escape further pressure, he scarcely realized he had made the vital admission the defender was seeking. "You could see the gun clearly. Could the gunman see you?"

"He could have done, had he looked in my direction."

"When the gun went off, what happened? Did you see a flash?"

"Yes."

"Which came first, the flash or the sound?"

Alfred Grant hesitated. "They came together."

Lionel Luckhoo smiled. "Witness, you are lying again. Flash and sound do not come together. The flash comes first. The speed of light is faster than the speed of sound. You never saw this incident at all."

Grant said resentfully, "If I didn't see it, how did I go up and see the man lying dead and report it to the police?"

"Quite right, you did do those things. But you did them after you had heard the report of the gun. You didn't see what happened prior to the report."

Witness after witness was led by the prosecution to testify to the bad blood that existed between the dead man and the prisoner, and the threats Baldeo had made. Of the fifteen witnesses called, the most important, apart from Grant, was Sujit's brother Byah. He had heard Baldeo threaten his brother, and knew how accurate he was as a marksman.

Lionel's cross-examination centered on this point. "Byah, you say the accused is an excellent gunman?"

"Yes, sir."

"You have seen him bring down birds from a great distance?"

"Yes, sir."

"You have seen him shoot alligators?"

"Yes, sir."

"And every time you see him shoot, does he use his left hand to pull the trigger?"

"Yes, sir."

"Do you know that his friends call him Lefty?"

"Yes, sir."

"Is that because he is a left-handed man?"

"Yes, sir."

By the simple affirmative answers he had given to every question, the prosecution witness, Sujit's own brother, had been of enormous help to the defense. As if he were beginning to realize it, Byah now protested, "But he killed my brother."

"Well," Lionel said benignly, "that is a matter for the jury. Tell me, Byah, are there other good marksmen on the west coast?"

"Yes, sir, plenty of good marksmen."

"And you have seen others bring down birds and shoot wild animals?"

"Yes, sir, but they are not as good as he is."

"Almost as good, but not as good?"

"Well, some of them are good."

"But Baldeo is the only one who shoots left-handed?"

"Yes, sir."

Baldeo did not give evidence on oath, but he was allowed to demonstrate how he normally held a gun to his left shoulder when firing.

When Lionel Luckhoo came to address the jury, he was able to put the case before them as a choice between simple alternatives. If they believed that Alfred Grant had seen the shooting, then his evidence was that it was a right-handed man he saw, and, plainly, that could not have been the accused. If they did not believe that Grant saw the shooting, then there was no direct evidence at all against the accused, and therefore the prosecution had no case.

"You must act on the evidence. It is not for you to play God. You were not there." And, again, Lionel hammered home the point: "You must act on the evidence, and on evidence alone."

The jury took only thirty-five minutes before coming back to pronounce the accused not guilty. It was a quick verdict for a murder trial.

Once sympathy has been aroused for a prisoner, a jury will often ask themselves two questions: "Is the accused guilty?" and then, "If guilty, do we want to punish him?"—though this second question might never be put into so many words. Baldeo's case was a classic example of the opposite, solely legal, approach. Probably every person in court thought he was guilty, but the jury, acting strictly in accordance with their oath, set aside all considerations other than the evidence they had heard, and set him free.

In discussing his murder cases, Lionel Luckhoo says, "People who ask how a guilty man can escape the rope are wearing blinkers. They are thinking of a strictly moral approach. The courts are not concerned with morality. For a conviction to be brought in, the jury must be certain beyond reasonable doubt, *on the evidence led within the court*, that it was the accused who committed the crime. They may have a strong feeling that the crime was committed by the accused, but, under their oath as jurors, they must find solely on the evidence led in court that he is guilty. Or else acquit him."

Chapter 12
The Case of the Unloving Neighbors

Thou shalt love thy neighbor as thyself.
—St. Mark 12:31

What's in a word? How many changes of meaning can be conveyed in just a single syllable? There is the instance of a murder suspect in Guyana who, while being interrogated by the police, said, "Me kill Mary." His counsel, S.E. Wills, shaped a defense from the seeming confession. A change of emphasis on a syllable, and it became an expostulation: "*Me* kill Mary!"

When it was alleged that Subedar had said to his son, "Me too old. You kill 'em, one-one. Me got money. Me take Lionel for you," it appeared to be a direct incitement to murder.

The Subedar and Juman families, both very wealthy, owned adjoining estates. There were frequent disputes and much ill-feeling between them, arising out of cattle trespass. On September 26, 1953, there was a series of worsening quarrels. On the morning of the 27th, fighting broke out between the two clans. It was after this that Karamat, nicknamed Bengal Tiger, went home and collected a twelve-bore shotgun and two cartridges. Later in the day, members of the Juman family converged on the cattle pen where the Subedars were gathered. Karamat fired, encouraged, it was alleged, by his father and four brothers. His shots killed Haniff Juman and Juman's mother. All six Subedars present at the time were arrested and charged with murder.

Old Subedar briefed not only Lionel but all three Luckhoo brothers to defend them. The consequence was that the luck of the draw, literally speaking, prevented Karamat from having Lionel as his defender. For this was the occasion when Lloyd suggested that they each defend two, and pull straws to see who would represent which of the accused. E.V. and Lionel agreed. Lionel drew Subedar as one of his pair. Lloyd himself drew Karamat, whose defense was likely to prove the most difficult.

In defending Subedar, Lionel was able to produce witnesses who gave the old man an alibi for the time of the shooting. He had gone to visit his rice cultivation, and workers could attest to his presence there. But this did not make him innocent of having incited the killings. It hinged on whether he had said to Karamat the exact words witnesses claimed to have heard.

The defense strategy was to agree that Subedar had said, if not then, on other occasions, "Me got money. Me take Lionel." He had said it to members of his family whenever trouble arose. He had said it before bringing civil cases for trespass against the Jumans. What the prosecution witnesses had done, in order to involve the old man, Lionel urged the jury to believe, was to adopt his usual expression and add to it the three vital words,"You kill 'em." This he had never said.

The jury acquitted Subedar and four of his sons. Karamat was found guilty and sentenced to hang.

Lloyd Luckhoo took the case to the Privy Council. One strong argument which he put to a court that included Lord Goddard, Lord Tucker, and Lord Somervell was that a visit had been made to the scene of the crime without the accused being present. Witnesses had been allowed to help reconstruct what had happened and to point out their positions. Lloyd contended that this was a part of the trial, and the fact of its having taken place in the absence of the accused had vitiated the trial.

The Privy Council dismissed the appeal. But, in so doing, they made strong comment on the witnesses being taken to the *locus* when the accused was not present, and expressed the view that it called for executive action. The Governor and Executive Council acted on this opinion, and granted a reprieve.

2

Feuding was the fashion with the Baksh family. Lionel found himself defending Mohamed Baksh, who was accused of having shot a neighbor in the middle of the night.

The neighbor, Ali, was going to the outhouse at the back of his own yard when, allegedly, Mohamed shot at him from his window. The ill will between the families made Mohamed the first suspect, and he was charged with murder. It was his good fortune that the circumstantial evidence did not point unremittingly to him. Lionel Luckhoo was able to win him an acquittal.

There was nothing clandestine about the Persaud-Maraj feud. The two families were related by marriage, and lived on opposite sides of Mahaicony Creek. Their habit of potting away at each other across the creek escalated into a small-scale war. One day, four members of the Maraj family were killed in action.

Gobin Persaud's family had set up what amounted to an independent republic on their side of the creek. The police were afraid to go in and make arrests. Eventually, it required a military operation to surround the Persaud property and bring about a surrender. All the family were hauled away to the police station, where Gobin and his three sons were charged with murder.

There was widespread prejudice against them before the trial. This was intensified when surviving members of the Maraj family identified the accused Persauds as the men who had guns and were shooting at them from various points. But their reconstruction of events did not stand up under Lionel Luckhoo's cross-examination. With conflicting evidence, the jury found it impossible to decide beyond a reasonable doubt which of the Gobin clan were responsible for the fatal shootings, and acquitted all four.

Quarrels between neighbors usually have their origin in small matters of little consequence. Often, the trouble starts with the children, who complain to their parents, who take up the cause of their offspring; matters worsen, and time brings a deepening embitterment.

Lionel Luckhoo recalls a number of such cases, though only one of these led to a murder charge.

It began with children who were, respectively, eight and nine years of age. It culminated with the mother of one, Sanicharie, her husband, and their two grown-up sons, taking on what Guyanese call the *fire rage*. One Saturday morning, in full view of a large crowd, they held a pitched battle with the other child's family, the Doorgas. Two youths, eighteen and nineteen years old, of the Doorgas family, were hacked to death.

Sanicharie, her husband, and sons were charged with murder. At the trial, Lionel Luckhoo won an acquittal for Sanicharie on a plea of self-defense. The Doorgas had brought the fight to Sanicharie's yard, and were armed with sticks. All that could be achieved for the men was a hung jury.

At the retrial, Lionel was unable to appear for them. He was in London, representing Guyana at the Independence Conference. The three men were convicted and hanged.

3

Loving and lovable neighbors are in short supply in the criminal courts. A year, a month, even a day, spent watching human nature at its rawest might do much to shake the optimism of the most fervent Panglossian philosopher. Lionel Luckhoo had been practising in the courts for eighteen years before he took the first, and only, purely holiday trip of his life. It was not so much the legal work that had made a holiday necessary. His intensive and unsuccessful efforts before and during the election, when he fought the Jagan-Burnham combination at the polls, had physically exhausted him. When his doctor advised a long rest, he took the advice, and a sea voyage to England. Little did he know, as the saying goes (they never explain how anybody could know), that on board ship he would, very literally, come to love his neighbor.

Sheila Chamberlin, a beautiful English girl, joined the ship at Curacao. Her father worked on the island as insurance manager with Dutch Shell. She was placed at Lionel's table. No one on board knew that, at night, Lionel liked to sit by himself beneath the crow's nest, where it was quiet. Sheila, too, went looking for solitude, her first night aboard, and they found themselves sitting alone near each other. The third chance circumstance was that, of the 700 deck chairs put out for passengers, theirs had been placed side by side.

Lionel was wholly in love with this constant neighbor before the end of the voyage. "No one could have been more in love than I was," he still says, in recollection.

They were married a year later.

Chapter 13
The Case of the Murderous Malady

Diseases desperate grown,
By desperate appliance are reliev'd,
Or not at all.

—*Hamlet*

Although Lionel Luckhoo is wont to overmodestly attribute his success to having been Fortune's favorite in the law courts, luck does not win many murder cases. Miracles are in even shorter supply. Once, on a lecture tour in England, he was asked, "Sir Lionel, have you ever witnessed a miracle?"

Lionel hesitated a moment, then said, "Yes, in one of my court cases there were *two* miracles."

A miracle entails the suspension of natural laws. Whatever else it did, or how, the case of Jules Pereira outraged the laws of ballistics and common sense. It was not a murder case. And that, in itself, seemed like a miracle.

Jules Pereira was a wealthy businessman living on the east coast of Demerera, a good man, a kindly man, but a man with an ungovernable temper when aroused.

Jules bought himself a huge combine harvester, a labor-saving device guaranteed to do most of the work for the rice farmer, so long as it worked. Jules soon discovered that his machine did not work; at least, not for long, and not very well. It developed all kinds of trouble, and Jules's pride in his new acquisition turned to fury. When he complained to the manufacturer's agents, they sent mechanics to attend to the machine, but, after repeated efforts at cure, it still gave trouble.

One day, Jules decided he had had enough. He slipped a revolver into his pocket and went to Georgetown. He walked into the large hardware concern which had sold him the harvester, and demanded to see the managing director.

"What about?" he was asked.

"A personal matter concerning a machine I bought."

After a few minutes' wait, he was shown into the office of John Jardim, the managing director. Heated words were spoken. Then Jules Pereira pulled out his revolver, and, at point-blank range, pulled the trigger.

Nothing happened.

Jules looked unbelievingly at the gun in his hand, that had failed to fire. He threw the weapon to the floor. Then he rushed at Mr. Jardim, held him fast by both arms . . . *and bit a chunk of flesh out of his chest!*

Jardim yelled, and, before Jules could do further damage, members of the staff ran into the room and overpowered him. He was charged with attempted murder.

When the trial took place at the Victoria Law Courts before Mr. Justice Miller, the case presented for the prosecution by Gilbert Farnum, Q.C., was simple and straightforward. As counsel for the defense, Lionel Luckhoo took a most unusual course of inaction that must have puzzled everyone in court. For the first time in an important trial, he did not cross-examine any of the prosecution witnesses. Not a single question!

The ballistics expert who gave evidence stated that he had examined Pereira's gun, and could not account for its having failed to go off when the trigger was pulled.

"I have never before encountered a matter like this," he said. "There is no explanation as to why this live bullet in the chamber was not discharged."

This was what Lionel Luckhoo, afterwards, referred to as the first miracle. It had saved his client from being indicted for murder. Now a second miracle was required, to free him from the charge on which he was arraigned. Yet the case seemed hopeless. What defense could there be to an attempt to kill with a revolver, the disgust at the failure of the gun to fire, followed by a ferocious attack with hands and teeth? Intent had been shown, unmistakably.

What Lionel did was to put his client into the witness box and have him give evidence on oath. Jules Pereira told how, on that fateful day, he became enraged at the sight of his expensive piece of machinery, lying idle and incapable of use. He recalled going into Georgetown and starting to have a row with Mr. Jardim. Beyond that point, he remembered nothing of what had taken place until he found himself in a police cell. Jules was cross-examined at great length by Gilbert Farnum, but he stuck to his story.

A police sergeant called by the defense testified that Pereira's revolver was a licensed firearm, and he was permitted to travel with the gun, as he often carried large sums of money to buy goods or to pay workers. Pereira had a clean record, and was regarded as a responsible individual. This helped as a character reference, but said nothing about the offense with which he was charged.

To plead loss of memory is often the last resort of the guilty, when all else fails. In the dock and in the witness box, Jules Pereira appeared to be in full possession of his faculties. So he had seemed when he first told his story to Lionel Luckhoo. Was there anything, apart from his own statement, that could corroborate, or at least give plausibility to, his claim?

Digging into his client's history, Lionel discovered that Jules had long suffered from a skin ailment. He had been receiving treatment from a medical specialist in Georgetown. The disease was very painful, and it affected the nervous system. Could this have affected his conduct under stress?

Lionel called as a witness the doctor who had treated Pereira—Dr. Bettencourt Gomes, skin specialist at St. Joseph's Hospital. Dr. Gomes reviewed the medical history of the accused. He then gave it as his opinion that a person with that history, suffering from the particular ailment, could, under very great stress, go into a state of *fugue*, so that he did not know what he was doing and would not, afterwards, remember what he had done.

The defense contention was that the offense committed was not a voluntary act on the part of the accused. Lionel Luckhoo addressed the jury for three hours, stressing that, although science had made great progress, although mankind had developed in so many directions, yet human knowledge of the mind and its mechanism was still *jejeune.*

"Most of us," he said, "have never had the unfortunate experience of suffering a mental blackout, but most of us are not afflicted with the ailment which affects Jules Pereira, and which is evidenced by the markings on his skin. We are not the experts. The doctor who is a specialist in such diseases is the expert, and he has said that a person suffering from this malady could, under extreme stress, experience a mental blackout and do things of which he was not conscious. The accused said he was under extreme stress. The accused and the doctor have said that he was suffering from this malady. Why, then, should we not accept that he had this mental aberration?"

Lionel ended on a note of appeal. "Let us not play God to determine what has happened. Let us accept the evidence of the medical testimony; let us accept what this medical expert of the highest integrity has told you."

It was not one of Lionel Luckhoo's strongest appeals, nor was the basis on which it rested of the strongest.

Gilbert Farnum, in his closing speech for the prosecution, did not fail to point out that *anything* was possible. "The doctor did not say this *had* happened; he said this *could* happen. Such a defense has never been raised before in the courts of our country, and it would be a dangerous precedent to give it any credence. It is a desperate effort on the part of the defense to seek to exculpate a man who was clearly out to do murder."

The judge's summing up was fair, but did not go in favor of the accused. "If this man only recovered his conscious self when he was in the lockup," Mr. Justice Miller said, "why did he not ask then what had happened? Or ask how he came to be there? Instead of which, so he told us, he remained silent. It is a far-fetched defense," he told the jury, "but that is a matter for you to decide."

The jury retired to consider its verdict. Lionel, less confident than he had ever been before at the end of a trial, turned to his client and said, "I'm afraid we must expect the worst."

Pereira nodded his head despondently. "How can I get anyone to believe I was speaking the truth?" he said. Then he looked across the courtroom to where his wife was sitting.

She had been there all through the trial. She had not spoken a word. Her hands held a rosary, and all the time she silently prayed.

Lionel went over to try to give her a word of comfort. She smiled at him and said, "You don't have any hope, do you?" It was only too true. There was no comfort in anything he could honestly say. Mrs. Pereira went on fingering her rosary, the same sad smile on her face. As Lionel was about to move away, she said, very softly, "You see, with God all things are possible. It is for Him to decide, not us."

After half an hour, the jury was still out. A quick return of the jury, more often than not, signifies an acquittal. If it takes longer than twenty minutes, but less than an hour, a verdict of guilty can be expected. When the jury came back after fifty minutes, the last flicker of hope died in Lionel.

"Mr. Foreman, are you agreed on a verdict?"

"We are."

"Is that verdict unanimous?"

"It is."

"How say you, is the prisoner at the bar guilty or not guilty of attempted murder?"

"Not guilty."

In the relief of that moment, Lionel Luckhoo did not look at Jules Pereira. He looked at Jules's wife, who, with head bowed, still held her rosary and was moving her lips in prayer. The verdict, he considered, was the second miracle in the Pereira case. What on earth (if the expression was appropriate) had influenced the jury to flout common sense and decide that the true verdict was not guilty?

Lionel will say, even now, "This is one case I did not win. Pereira's case was won by the prayers of a loyal and good woman, his wife."

2

"You will never believe it, but I can never be hanged!" Nurse Mildred McAllister was in the dock, charged with murder, but there was quiet jubilation in her voice when she spoke to Lionel Luckhoo. She was not, like Jules Pereira's wife, a woman of great faith hoping for a miracle. She had four solid reasons for her belief—though whether it was luck or a small miracle that vouchsafed them to her, who can say?

At her first appearance on trial, Nurse McAllister had been far from confident. She was near to collapse when the charge was read and she was asked, "How say you, are you guilty or not guilty?"

The middle-aged, matronly prisoner swayed slightly, and clutched at the rail of the dock. Her counsel, Lionel Luckhoo, had to urge her, "Nurse, answer the charge."

She shook her head to clear it, then, in a low voice, said, "Your honor, I am innocent. I plead not guilty."

The female is less homicidal than the male. Ladies may kill when they have a drastic desire to be rid of a husband or a lover. Seldom do they murder for other motives, though a very few lady killers have been among the worst.

Mildred McAllister was a well-known figure in Georgetown. She had the reputation of being a skillful nurse and midwife. She was accused of having caused the death of a young girl by performing a criminal abortion. Death as a sequel to abortion can be defined as murder, manslaughter, or misadventure, depending upon who was the operator and what were the circumstances.

Nurse McAllister had used her home as a nursing home, and there had attended a number of young girls who found themselves in the plight of an unwelcome pregnancy. This was the evidence the prosecution wanted to lead. Lionel leaped to his feet immediately and objected. It was "highly prejudicial," he said. Mr. Justice Camacho agreed with him.

The first witness for the Crown was an aunt of the girl who had died. She testified that, early in her pregnancy, Miss A had sworn that she would not stand the disgrace of bearing a child while she was unmarried. Lionel cross-examined.

"Did the young lady actually say that she preferred to die rather than to be an unwed mother?"

"Yes."

"In other words, she was willing to go to any extreme to get rid of the child?"

"Yes."

"Did she say she would commit suicide?"

"No. She wanted to be free of the child, but she never said she would kill herself."

"Do you know that she visited midwives other than the accused?"

"She may have done so. I don't know."

"Did she suggest that she would have to get help since she didn't know what to do?"

"Yes, she said something to that effect."

"How long was this before her death?"

"About one week."

The case for the prosecution was that, on the day of her death, Miss A had gone by car to the home of Nurse McAllister. The driver gave evidence that she walked like a strong and healthy woman when she went into the house. The cross-examination was brief.

"As a hire driver, your profits depend on a quick turn-around?"

"Yes."

"After the fare is paid, you move on quickly?"

"Yes."

"She walked out of the car, and you paid no special attention?"

"Yes."

Three hours later, passersby saw Miss A coming out of the house. She was being propped up by Nurse McAllister and another woman. She was put in a hire car and taken to her own home, and was found to be dead on arrival. Her relatives rushed her to the hospital, but it was too late for anything except to get confirmation of death.

The pathologist who did the post-mortem, Dr. B.B.G. Nehaul, stated that there was evidence of criminal abortion, and that Miss A had died from shock and loss of blood. For a whole day, he was cross-examined by Lionel Luckhoo. The most crucial questions came near the end.

"Doctor, it would be impossible for you to say when this interference took place?"

"Well, I cannot be precise."

"It could have taken place the day before you saw the girl's body?"

"Yes, that is possible."

"You cannot say when the bleeding began, and for how long a period of time it lasted?"

"No."

There was evidence before the court that various surgical instruments had been found in Nurse McAllister's home. The police corporal who executed the search warrant had admitted, when cross-examined, that the house was clean and neat, no bloodstains were to be found anywhere, and there were no sheets or pillows bearing traces of blood. Lionel now asked the pathologist, "Can you tell precisely what kind of instrument was used to produce the effects you describe?"

"No, not precisely."

"Would you agree that the effects you saw could have been the result of something done by the girl herself?"

"Yes, although it is not likely."

"Doctor, we are concerned with the question I asked. Could the girl have done this harm to herself? Is there anything to prevent her from having done so?"

"No, nothing."

"Did you find anything to show that the injury was not self-inflicted?"

"No, nothing."

Lionel had asked Nurse McAllister if she wished to give sworn evidence on which she could be cross-examined.

"If I go into the box," she answered, "those who feel I am guilty will not change, and all I could say would, in their eyes, confirm it. If they believe I am innocent, nothing I say will change their opinion, either. I will make a statement from the dock, and not go to the witness stand."

In her statement, she admitted that Miss A had come to her. She had found the girl to be in a shocking condition. She gave her first aid and told her to go at once to the hospital. After Miss A had rested for a while, she assisted her into a hire car. She denied having any knowledge of any criminal act.

Addressing the jury, Lionel pointed out that the Crown's case was built on circumstantial evidence. The prosecution was saying that an apparently healthy girl goes into the home of a midwife; she comes out in poor condition, or maybe she is dead; surgical instruments have, at some time, been used on her; some surgical instruments are found in the midwife's home; *ergo*, these are the instruments that have been used illegally on the girl, thereby causing her death.

Suspicion was all there was in the case. Suspicion was not proof. The chain of circumstances was only as strong as the weakest link, and the weakest link was the failure of the prosecution to connect the accused with the commission of the crime.

The suggestion that the girl died while in the home of the nurse was no more than a suggestion. This was not believed by the hire car driver, who saw her walk to the car, although she was assisted. He thought only that she looked ill.

Lionel concluded by again emphasizing the absence of a nexus between the cause of death and any act of the accused which would inculpate her, and appealed to the jury:

"The case against Nurse McAllister was tissue-thin from the beginning. It has been torn to shreds by the answers given in cross-examination. Only prejudice can convict the accused. You, members of the jury, are not concerned with prejudice, but with proof which would point to her as having committed the crime. There is no proof."

The prosecutor closed his case by telling the jury that there was evidence of a healthy girl walking into a house, and a dying or dead girl being led out of it by the accused. "She knows what took place," he declared. "Has she told you the truth of what took place? This is a simple case of unadulterated murder."

The jury did not find it a simple case. After an objective and fair summing up by the judge, it retired and deliberated for five hours, then returned to inform the court that its members could not agree on a verdict. They did not wish to receive any further help or directions; after trying their best, they had agreed that no agreement on a verdict was possible. The judge discharged them.

Nerve-ridden from the beginning, by the end of the trial Nurse McAllister had become a quivering wreck of a woman. Now she had to face up to the ordeal a second time.

The day arrived. Once more, she was arraigned before an all-male jury. Again, she was asked the question, "How say you, are you guilty or not guilty?" And this time she did not falter. To Lionel Luckhoo's astonishment, his client's voice rang out firm and clear: "Not guilty."

At the first opportunity, he turned to her. "Why, nurse," he said, "what has changed you so? You look positively happy."

"Sir Lionel," she said, smiling, "you will never believe it, but I can never be hanged."

"Why, what has happened?"

"Sir," she replied, "four of the twelve jurors hearing my case are my clients."

"Clients?"

"Yes, I have been of some assistance to them."

She was right to be confident that she would not hang. The second trial was very much a repeat performance of the first—the same evidence, same cross-examinations, same type of addresses from prosecution and defense. But it had a different ending. Nurse McAllister was acquitted, by a jury unanimous in her favor. She left the court a free woman. With luck and Luckhoo in combination, how could she lose?

3

The jury system is very nearly as old as the law itself. Like democracy, it is not a perfect system. Perhaps the crucial thing to be said in favor of both is that contemplation of the known alternatives makes one shudder. If Talleyrand was right (and he was!) in declaring that war was too serious a matter to be left to the general, it can be similarly argued that law should not be left to the lawyers, when life and liberty are at stake.

A main reason against putting the expert in sole charge is that, the more a man grows accustomed to anything, the less he sees its significance. After having had the experience of serving on a jury, G.K. Chesterton wrote:

"And the horrible thing about all legal officials, even the best, about all judges, magistrates, barristers, detectives, and policemen, is not that they are wicked (some of them are good), not that they are stupid (several of them are quite intelligent), it is simply that they have got used to it.

"Strictly, they do not see the prisoner in the dock; all they see is the usual man in the usual place. They do not see the awful court of judgment; they only see their own workshop.

Therefore, the instinct of Christian civilisation has most wisely declared that into their judgments there shall upon every occasion be infused fresh blood and fresh thoughts from the streets."

Most judges and lawyers themselves are strongly in favor of the jury system. Sir Travers Humphreys, that most experienced and dispassionate of English criminal judges, wrote, "The correctness of a jury's verdict has almost come to be an axiom with me." Other judges are agreed that juries seldom make mistakes, and, when justice miscarries, it is not often the fault of the jury. Even prisoners found to be guilty share these views, in Lionel Luckhoo's experience. "When an accused is convicted," Lionel says, "he may blame a witness or the prosecutor or the judge, and sometimes his own lawyer. But he never blames the jury, for he knows that they seek to do justice on the evidence led in court."

The cases of Jules Pereira and Nurse Mildred McAllister are, of course, exceptional. The Pereira jury brought in an unexpected verdict, which is not to say that it was not a just one. As for the four "clients" of Nurse McAllister who served on her second jury, there is no means of knowing whether, or to what extent, they influenced the verdict. At best (or worst), they had the power to prevent a conviction, but could not have secured an acquittal unless the other eight members of the jury were ready to accept the arguments of the defense.

Under English law, jury selection is not the long, drawn-out process it often becomes with the American system, where examination and challenge of jury candidates by attorneys for both sides can go on for days, or even weeks. The names of the panel go into a box, the Clerk of the Court gives it a shake and pulls out slips, one at a time, and the first twelve to emerge form the jury to try the next case.

Today in Guyana, both prosecution and defense have a right of challenge—three peremptory challenges, and others for cause—but the right is seldom exercised. "I find the juries in Guyana understanding, and with good, sound common sense," is Lionel Luckhoo's verdict. "They ask few questions, but these are always relevant. In a society in which one of six races, or an admixture of six races, appears in the dock, it is good to find that the jury is a mixed one, truly representing the 'peers' of the accused. The jury system has stood the test of time. It is not perfect, but, until another system can be evolved to surpass it, I remain a firm advocate of its continuation."

The right to challenge without cause was introduced in the late fifties. Before this, there was one occasion when Lionel thought he would be forced to raise an objection to two particular jurors, however difficult it might be to show cause. Both the jurors were white expatriates; one, an estate overseer; the other, the manager of a large department store. Their names had come up for three successive trials. Each had resulted in a verdict of guilty going against the weight of the evidence. By the hostile attitude they showed, Lionel had a strong feeling that the two men adjudged any local person guilty as soon as he stepped into the dock, and that they were influencing the other jurors.

He went to the Clerk of Court and said, "You know, I think the defense is not getting a square deal in these cases."

The Clerk (who shall be nameless, for reasons that will become apparent) said, "I think you are right. I've been listening to the cases, and I have an idea that even his honor feels that the jury is taking too much of a pro-prosecution stand."

"Do me a favor," Lionel requested. "I don't want to do it myself, but I'd like you to ask one of the other jurors who appeared in the last case whether those two are using some form of compulsion on them."

Next day, the Clerk told him, "I have spoken to two of the jurors. Both of them said that these two men just simply bully them."

Lionel's next case on the list was a serious felony. He debated with himself what form of challenge he could make, if the same two jurors should be picked. Officially, at least, everything that takes place in the jury room is secret, and a member of the previous juries could not be brought forward to say undue pressure had been put on him to convict. He mentioned his dilemma to the Clerk, who was sympathetic. "All right, don't make any objection," he said. "I don't think you will have them on the next jury."

The names of the jurors called for service went into the box. The Clerk dipped in his hand and began the draw. Neither of the two expatriates were among the twelve whose names came out, and they seemed quite upset about it. The Clerk, too, had visibly winced at one stage, Lionel noticed, but thought no more about it.

The trial began, and, at the end, Lionel gained an acquittal for his client. Afterwards, the Clerk of Court came to him and said, "You haven't thanked me."

Lionel said, surprised, "Thanked you for what?"

"I kept the two men who would surely have knocked down your client off the jury."

"Oh!" said Lionel. "How did you do it? You kept their names out of the box?"

"No, I didn't do that," said the Clerk. "It would have been highly improper."

"Then what did you do?"

The Clerk grinned. "Maybe you didn't notice, but when I pushed my hand into the box after the third or fourth draw, I pulled it out again quickly."

Lionel said, "Yes, I did see it. What had happened?"

"Well," said the Clerk, "I pinned the two names together . . . and the damn pin stuck in my finger!"

Chapter 14
The Case of the Cagey Communist

Confound their politics
Frustrate their knavish tricks
—*Henry Carey, "God Save the King"*

And Liberty plucks Justice by the nose.
—*Measure for Measure*

When pirates ravaged the Spanish Main, their favorite ruse was to creep up on a victim in the guise of an innocent merchant vessel. Not until they were close enough to throw out grappling irons did they show their true colors. Then the Jolly Roger was unfurled, and it was "Ho-ho, my hearties! and at 'em!"

The ploy has not been lost to the twentieth century. Caribbean politicians at both ends of the spectrum have learned a lesson from the sea rovers. In many of the Latin countries, governments are overthrown or undermined—deservedly so, in most cases—and the new regimes win support, with promises of free elections, free speech, and even free lunches. The party boys or the army boys (as the case may be) get the free lunches, anyone may speak freely in praise of the government, and the promise of free elections is not forgotten, just postponed. Why hurry? The ship of state has been captured, dissenters may be made to walk the gangplank, and, as always, the sharks are waiting below for *their* free lunches. Only the skull and crossbones has gone out of fashion. Right-wing dictators seldom bother to run up a flag. Not by their ideology, but by their misdeeds, do we know them.

On the other hand, the extreme left-wingers tend to be both proud and shy: proud of their flag, but shy of revealing it in its exact shade of coloring. The best-known example is Dr. Fidel Castro. Everyone with the slightest liberal leanings was eager to cheer when he did the necessary job of ridding Cuba of Batista. His denials that he was a Communist—when refuting what appeared to be, and often were, the prejudiced attacks of reactionaries—gained him much support. Some faces were as red as his flag, when it suited him to proclaim that he had been a Communist all along.

In the British colonies, the roots of democracy ran deep, even though the people had not been allowed to take an active part in democratic forms. During the stages to full independence, Communist parties were not banned. While, in the United States, under the cloud of McCarthyism, anyone who had paid to see a Charlie Chaplin film or bought a Paul Robeson record would do well to keep quiet about it, the only reason a colonial politician might have for hiding his true colors was the unwillingness of voters to rally round the red flag. A delicate pink, yes! A pleasing rose madder, maybe. But the blood-red of repression, *no*!

After the disastrous defeat of Lionel Luckhoo and other moderates in the 1957 elections, the People's Progressive Party, led by Dr. Cheddi Jagan and Forbes Burnham, held undisputed political sway in Guyana. Then there was a split. Burnham formed the People's National Congress Party, and became Jagan's strongest opposition. Both parties were well to the left. Their supporters were divided more on racial than on ideological lines. Most of the Indian population favored Jagan's PPP, while the Africans went with Burnham's PNC. Racism is founded on fear. In Guyana, the Africans feared the Indians because they were in the majority; the Indians feared the Africans because the security services were largely under their control.

A crisis came in 1962. The PNC and the trade unions called a general strike which lasted eighty-five days. There were riots and race murder. Such was the state of national upheaval that the Colonial Office in London sent out a High Court Judge, Mr. Justice Wynn-Parry, to hold an inquiry. When it became known that the Premier, Dr. Jagan, would take the witness stand, the Chamber of Commerce came to Lionel

Luckhoo and said, "We would like to retain you to appear and cross-examine Dr. Jagan."

It was widely suspected that Dr. Jagan was a Communist. He had never acknowledged such a belief. The Chamber hoped that Lionel Luckhoo, who was allied with no party, could get him to admit it while he was under oath. An unprecedented opportunity, from their point of view!

The Premier of British Guiana took the witness stand. Lionel Luckhoo rose to engage him in a duel that was to last two and a half hours on the first day. He called Dr. Jagan's attention to a *Los Angeles Times* report that alleged he was one of the twelve top Communists in the world. Jagan said he had been neither flattered nor hurt by its reproduction in the local *Daily Chronicle*. He had made no attempt to get withdrawals or apologies from either the *Chronicle* or the *Times*.

"Would you agree with me, Dr. Jagan, that the people of the country are entitled to know the political policy of the government they are under?"

"Of course."

"And entitled to know the individual political policy of the individuals who are in charge of them?"

"Not necessarily. The government is elected at elections, and in these days of party politics one goes to the electors with party manifestos explaining this, so individual issues do not matter."

"You have your own political beliefs?"

"I am leader of the government and the People's Progressive Party."

"Are you ashamed of your political beliefs, Dr. Jagan?"

"I am not ashamed."

"Are you a Communist, Dr. Jagan?"

"You will first have to explain what you mean by Communist."

"Do you have any idea of what I mean by my question?"

"No."

"You have heard of Dr. Fidel Castro?"

"Yes."

"Do you know his policies?"

"I know some of them."

"Would you say Fidel Castro is a Communist?"

"I cannot say; that is for him to say."

"Are your policies the same as his?"

"As leader of the government, my policies are reflected in my party's manifesto."

"You know him quite well, and have studied his policies. Are your policies akin to his?"

"My policies have already been enunciated. That is all I want to say."

The Commissioner, Sir Henry Wynn-Parry, intervened: "You must answer yes or no."

Dr. Jagan replied, "I am not aware of all of Dr. Fidel Castro's policies, and therefore I cannot compare them with my own."

The Commissioner said, "You were asked if they were akin."

"I cannot say."

Lionel Luckhoo persisted. "The policies of which you are aware, and know that Fidel Castro pursues—are these policies which you yourself pursue? Do you believe in state ownership, for instance?"

"Yes."

"Abolition of private property?"

"My party does not believe in this," Dr. Jagan answered, evading a statement of personal belief.

"What does your party believe in, which Fidel Castro does not have, or which the Communists do not have?"

"My party believes in free and fair elections, democratically held at regular intervals."

"Did you say when you returned from Tanganyika* that you admired their system of a one-party government?"

"No, I did not say that. I said there was a form of coalition government where almost all of the members of the Legislature belonged to one party, but this did not mean a denial of democracy. I would like to see this, here."

"What are your views on communism? Do you know what it is? Are you aware of its tenets?"

"Are *you* aware of them?"

* *Now Tanzania.*

"Dr. Jagan, if you want to ask questions you will have to come here." Lionel Luckhoo indicated a place behind the bar table. "While you are on the witness stand, you must answer."

Again, the Commissioner spoke. "Will you say yes or no, whether you are aware of the tenets of communism?"

The Attorney General of Dr. Jagan's government, Dr. Fenton Ramsahoye, protested, "If the witness is to answer yes or no, my lord, it will mean that he is going to answer a question in relation to communism which he may understand differently from my learned friend Mr. Luckhoo."

The Commissioner said, "He has been asked to say whether he is aware of the tenets of communism. If he continues to be silent on this issue, the Commission will be forced to take note that the witness has avoided answering this vital question."

Dr. Jagan then answered, "I believe the tenets of communism to mean, *inter alia*, from each according to his ability, and to each according to his need. I believe that represents the Communist belief, and I accept it."

"Dr. Jagan," Lionel Luckhoo said, "you have a clear idea of the tenets of communism. Do you accept these tenets of communism?"

"I do."

"Then, Dr. Jagan, according to your own acceptance of these tenets, you are a Communist?"

"I am a Communist," Dr. Jagan said, finally; then he added quietly, "in accordance with my own views of communism."

This was the first time in his career that Jagan had ever made such a public pronouncement. Always before, when asked, he had said, "No comment." For the first time, the Guyanese public had heard his ideology stated.

Lionel Luckhoo resumed by asking, "Are you an admirer of Fidel Castro?"

"Yes."

"Would you endeavor to pattern your own government after his style and manner?"

"Not necessarily, but I do admire him."

There were questions about scholarships given through the PPP for young people to be sent to Cuba as well as Russia. Dr. Jagan said he did not know if they would receive military training.

Then came the issues of press and individual freedom.

"Dr. Jagan, you believe in freedom of expression, and you do not believe in suppression?"

"I believe in freedom of expression."

"And you do not believe in control or muzzling?"

Dr. Jagan's answer was to repeat, "I believe in freedom of expression."

"But did you not ban the *Daily Chronicle* from government offices?"

"Yes."

"Why did you ban it? Were you, perhaps, seeking means to see if the *Daily Chronicle* would be forced to close down?"

"No. I am not interested in closing it down."

In response to further questions, the Premier admitted that a proposal had been made to set up a Press Council. But it was not with the intention of controlling what was published and what was not published, he said. The idea merely was to maintain and preserve the ethics of journalism.

"When certain well-known Communists were prevented from coming into this country, you said you believed in freedom of movement for everyone?"

"Yes."

Why, then, Lionel Luckhoo asked, had the Jagan government banned two men from entering the country? Dr. Jagan answered that it was because the men were known to be associating with others who were trying to overthrow the government by force and violence. He had evidence.

Then why had he not disclosed such information to the Commission, which was there to inquire into the disturbances?

Dr. Jagan said his Ministers had made a collective decision on the matter.

"If people came to British Guiana and were participating in, or engineering, riots and other disturbances, don't you think it would be in the interest of the public to make that information known?"

"It is in the interest of the public to see that these people do not do these things."

When the Premier said he could not divulge all the sources of his information to the Commissioner, his cross-examiner suggested that he was not speaking the truth.

The duel went on. Dr. Jagan admitted that the government was considering validating a by-election result that the court had ruled void. Lionel Luckhoo put it to him that this was not a democratic approach.

Was the last budget a good budget, was another question, and was it for the benefit of the people?

Dr. Jagan replied, "Certainly."

"Must the leader of a country be strong, even to decide against the popular wish, if it is to the benefit of the country?"

"Yes."

"Then why did you agree to amend the budget?"

"Because of misrepresentations and representations."

"Could misrepresentations be removed by informing the people?"

"Yes."

"And do you agree that the representations should not have had effect if the original budget were sound and good?"

Dr. Jagan had tied himself up by his previous answer. Now, he could only give a series of conflicting replies. Altogether, he had been under cross-examination for some five hours. Years before, it is said, he had advised the public, "When you have a murder case, take it to Lionel Luckhoo; but when you have a vote, don't vote for him." So limp did he look now, he might well have been wishing that his cross-examiner were a better politician and a worse lawyer. It is said that he has never forgotten nor forgiven Lionel.

Certainly, the country had a clearer idea of Dr. Jagan's beliefs when he left the witness stand than when he stepped to it. Seven years later, while on a visit to Moscow, Dr. Jagan was reported by the *Guyana Graphic* as having formally enlisted his party in the international Communist movement. Some members of his party were surprised!

The Wynn-Parry Commission did not bring peace to Guyana. Riots, arson, and racial murders persisted in various areas of the country for the next two years. Here, a crowd of

Indians would descend on a minority of Africans, and there would be one or two fatalities; there, it would be the Indians who were beaten and would have to run away. From 1962 to 1964, and in the aftermath, Lionel Luckhoo defended about forty clients (some Indian, some African) charged with killings that had their origin in racial strife.

On the anniversary of his cross-examination of Dr. Jagan, two attempts to bomb Lionel Luckhoo's home were made in one day. First, a smoldering bomb was discovered and thrown into a trench. The second attempt gave him a narrower escape. A bomb was hurled at the house and struck a wire mesh. It did not explode. The policeman who picked it up had never seen a live bomb before, and he shook it—in Lionel's presence. The bomb expert who dismantled it said, later, that only divine providence had saved them both. No one was charged as a result of either incident.

2

So far, no one has succeeded in bringing communism to any part of the English-speaking Caribbean. While Russia can be counted upon to give limited encouragement to such antics (as constituting a minor nuisance to the United States in its own duckpond, so to speak), in Highgate Cemetery the bust of Karl Marx must weep; for his doctrine no more considers underdeveloped agrarian economies to be ready for communism than an empty purse can be made into a sow's ear.

It is not likely that Dr. Cheddi Jagan ever sang "God Save the Queen" with much fervor or enthusiasm. But, like the schoolboy who, when asked what he knew about Appius Claudius, answered, "Well, sir, he comes into the National Anthem," he should have taken care to learn the words correctly. Then he would have been better prepared to cope with the lesson in *realpolitik*, as played by the big powers, that was given him the year following his appearance before the Riot Commission.

At that time, Jagan's PPP, Burnham's PNC, and the United Force (a third Guyanese party, formed of an alliance of conservative elements ranging from Portugese and Indian businessmen to Amerindian tribesmen) were holding talks in

London with the British government, preparatory to the granting of independence.

Officially, Lionel Luckhoo was there as adviser to Peter D'Aguiar, leader of the United Force. But he had also become the link between D'Aguiar and Forbes Burnham. After Lionel's cross-examination of Jagan, Burnham had said to him, "I know you don't have any wish to go into politics, but I would like you to be associated with me, working together for the progress of our country. My aim is to lift the living standard of our peoples, and provide equal opportunity for all." This, too, was Lionel's aim.

Owing to the preponderance of Indian voters, Jagan's party was assured of a majority of seats under the system of single-member constituencies. Lionel Luckhoo felt that, if Burnham and D'Aguiar could be brought together, they could beat Jagan, provided elections were held under a new system of proportional representation.

In London, each party was to put forward its ideas as to what form the future constitution of their country should take. Lionel knew and was on friendly terms with the then Colonial Secretary Duncan Sandys and his Under Secretary Sir Nigel Fisher, and he spoke with both. Their attitude was that the British government could not impose a system unless all parties agreed that they should.

The talks were then at a stalemate; Jagan, standing firm on single-member constituency voting; Burnham and D'Aguiar, demanding a change to proportional representation. Lionel advised Burnham and D'Aguiar to consent to the resolution of the issue being decided by Duncan Sandys. Obviously, Lionel was not the man who could sell that idea to Jagan.

It was a Permanent Secretary of the Colonial Office who went to the Premier and said, "Dr. Jagan, we British play cricket. We have always played with a straight bat. Leave it to us to decide. We have never had anything like proportional representation for any of our colonies when they have been granted independence."

Dr. Jagan may have missed the ambiguity of the last remark. He said, "All right. I agree."

When all the parties had agreed, Duncan Sandys said,

"That's fine. I want you all three to sign a letter to that effect, so we have it in writing."

It was decided that the letter-signing should be done at a meeting to be held next day. That night, Lionel met, by chance, a Senior Parliamentarian, and was told something. He passed on the information to D'Aguiar and Burnham.

When the letter was laid on the table next day, Peter D'Aguiar signed without hesitation. Lionel had advised Burnham, "Don't be in too much of a hurry to sign, or Jagan is going to take up the opposite attitude." Burnham had agreed that that made sense. So, when the letter was passed to him, he said,"I'm afraid I have to give this a little more time."

Jagan said, "I would like to have more time, too."

Neither of them signed. For about fifteen minutes, there was a tense silence.

Then Burnham said,"You know, I'm not sure I could place the future of my country in the hands of the British, for them to determine what should be the procedure for electing the members of our Parliament." He sounded so reluctant that Lionel wondered if he was overplaying his hand.

But Jagan said, "Well, I will show you. I am going to sign, because I feel all will be well." And Jagan signed the letter.

Then Burnham signed.

When Duncan Sandys announced that the decision was for proportional representation, Jagan hit the sky. He went on British television and claimed he had never read the letter.

The end of the story is that, in the elections held the following year (1964), the Burnham and D'Aguiar parties collected more seats between them than the PPP. Burnham became Premier, and eventually led the country into full independence.

There is an addendum. Some time after the decision was made, and the matter became history, Lionel and Sheila were lunching with Duncan Sandys and his wife. Lionel said, "Duncan, tell me, how were you ever able to convince your Cabinet that you should introduce proportional representation in Guyana?"

Sandys laughed. "My dear Lionel, whatever in the name of creation makes you think I ever went to Cabinet with it? If I had gone to Cabinet, I could never have got it through. I decided it myself, unilaterally. I only informed the Cabinet of the result, and the deed was done."

How proportional representation came to Guyana is a tale that bristles with morals. You may picture an innocent Premier Jagan, being confounded by the knavish tricks of wilier politicians—or the plucking of Justice by the nose, to the end that Liberty be maintained. Dr. Jagan probably took small comfort from the thought that his friends in other countries would have had no hesitation in playing worse tricks, if it were to their advantage. After being asked by Lionel Luckhoo, while he was on the witness stand, what he knew of the tenets of communism, he should have borne in mind that the one widely practiced is that the end justifies the means.

And, whatever judgment history may pass upon the means, the immediate end was achieved: preventing a party led by an admitted Communist from taking power over a nation just emerging into independence.

Lionel's admiration for Burnham's intellect and drive has often been expressed. He maintains that, in a mixed community of six peoples, only Burnham could bring about peace for the nation. This has been significantly fulfilled with the coming of Burnham into power. Lionel foresees, under the Burnham aegis, prosperity for Guyana.

Chapter 15
The Case of the Candid Commissioner

> *The first of all earthly blessings, independence.*
>
> —*Edward Gibbon*

Voting in the December 7, 1964, election in British Guiana, under the new system of proportional representation, resulted in Jagan's PPP winning twenty-four seats; Burnham's PNC, twenty-two; and D'Aguiar's UF, seven. This gave the PNC and the UF, in alliance, a majority of five in the fifty-three-member House of Assembly. Burnham became Prime Minister; D'Aguiar, Minister of Finance. Their major task—certainly, the one that lay nearest their hearts—was to bring their country to full independence.

Early in 1965, Lionel Luckhoo was named Commissioner-designate, and sent to London to pave the way for talks with the British government which would settle the date self-rule would be granted. His own prediction to the press, not long after his arrival, was that Independence Day for the new Guyana would be celebrated in March, the following year. The forecast turned out to be only slightly optimistic.

Commissioner Luckhoo's appointment was described by the *Sunday Guardian* as having "created a more favorable impression among London's hard-bitten Commonwealth correspondents than any Guianese measure of the past two years." Journalists who interviewed him appreciated quickly, in the words of one writer, his "total lack of prickliness, pomposity, and protocolitis." Already, he was the world's most successful criminal lawyer, with 149 murder defenses to his credit.* And reporters were amused by the irony of his last case as a private lawyer, which had been to force the government of the country he now represented to disgorge $7,000,000 of compulsory savings taken from salary-earners.

Lionel had fought the case of *Lilleyman and Others v. the Inland Revenue Commissioner and the Attorney General of British Guiana*, and won it before the High Court, then before the Appeal Court of British Guiana, and, finally, before the British Caribbean Court of Appeal. All three courts had decided that the levy was unconstitutional.

Britain also had undergone a change of government. The Tories had lost an election to the Labour Party. Harold Wilson had replaced Harold Macmillan as Prime Minister. Lionel still had a friend in the high place formerly occupied by Duncan Sandys. He had known the new Colonial Secretary, Tony Greenwood, as a friend of E.V. at Oxford. Lionel was able to assure Greenwood that, since the previous year's elections, there had been no racial or other troubles in British Guiana. The indications were that peace and stability would be maintained.

The new Commissioner was also emphasizing to everyone that the quickest way of achieving economic means for development was immediate independence. Unlike other Caribbean colonies, British Guiana had plenty of land—an area of 83,000 square miles, with a population averaging only seven to the square mile. Forbes Burnham planned to attract Guianese immigrants to Britain back home. Within weeks of this being announced, Lionel Luckhoo had received 3,500 applications from the 25,000 Guianese then in Britain. He was advising them to register and await the offer of jobs. But expansion could come only through acceleration of development aid to exploit the country's untapped resources. The government, ambitious and hopeful, estimated an economic potential to absorb 2,500,000 people. After opportunity had been given to Guianese immigrants to return, the next step, Lionel Luckhoo suggested, might be to encourage immigrants from overpopulated and underemployed areas of the

* *Judge Samuel Leibowitz of New York achieved 139 victories as defense lawyer in murder trials before losing a client to the electric chair.*

British Caribbean. This would take the edge off Britain's immigration problem.

Dangling this carrot before the Labour Government, the Commissioner added the spur, "History has evidenced the marked rise and growth in undeveloped and underdeveloped territories which follow naturally and quickly the grant of independence." An immediate example was Jamaica, whose economic expansion, not more than 2 percent before becoming independent in 1962, had since risen to between 5 and 6 percent. Although Guiana still had a serious unemployment problem, with independence only in the offing, aid had already started to flow in.

On meeting Harold Wilson, the Commissioner stated the situation with undiplomatic candor. Colonies, he suggested, were now becoming an embarrassment to Britain. They were costly. They created headaches. It was better to win a friend by the grant of independence than to earn enmity by refusal. "Better that you jump to a decision than have us push you."

But, either way, Harold Wilson had a headache. His own Left Wingers had become the champions of Cheddi Jagan over the proportional representation issue, and could be counted on to oppose immediate independence being given to a Burnham government. Among them was Michael Foot, the most articulate voice in the Commons, who happened to be a particularly close friend, from E.V.'s undergraduate days. The opposition Lionel faced within the now-ruling party was formidable.

On June 2, the House of Commons held a debate on Commonwealth and Colonial affairs. A lively report of the proceedings from David Smithers appeared in the *Barbados Advocate*. A visitor from Mars, Smithers said, would have supposed that British Guiana's affairs were the only Commonwealth and Colonial affairs that mattered. British Guiana's fitness for independence, and the dire possibility that Prime Minister Forbes Burnham would become a disillusioned man if it were not quickly granted, was the subject which seemed to make Conservative voices grow hoarse with anguish.

Commonwealth Relations Secretary Arthur Bottomly, "with apparently calculated imprecision, seemed determined to be as vague as possible about when a British Guiana constitutional conference would be called; or, when it was called, whether it would be empowered to fix the date that will transform British Guiana into the Sovereign State of Guyana."

Curiously, thought Smithers, Colonial Secretary Anthony Greenwood sat impassively on the Front Bench throughout the debate, and uttered not a word. Not even when former Colonial Under Secretary Nigel Fisher "sternly rebuked the government for apparent breach of faith. Not even when the normally aloof and magisterial Duncan Sandys himself leaped to his feet with unaccustomed passion to preach a sermon on political morality," declaring that the promise by one British government—that a conference fixing a date of independence would follow the proportional representation elections—was no less binding on a succeeding government. Sandys demanded that Prime Minister Harold Wilson should state without qualification that he would honor the freedom pledge given to the people of Guiana.

Hours later, at the end of the debate, Harold Wilson said he would keep Sandys's promise. It came as a surprise to everyone, from the Tory Front Benches to the Left Wingers on the Labour Back Benches. "Only Lionel Luckhoo," wrote Smithers, "watching the proceedings from the Distinguished Strangers Gallery, seemed to wear a secret, knowing smile. Without hesitation or exaggeration, I can truthfully report that, in the days preceding this debate, Commissioner Luckhoo literally took the Conservative Party in the palm of his hand and squeezed it to conform to the shape he desired."

Smithers believed that Harold Wilson more readily accepted the Tories' urgings for a constitutional conference and early independence in order to stamp on the toes of his rebellious Left Wing and show them who was boss. "All this was grist to Luckhoo's mill. It does not in any way diminish the credit—or, depending on your political viewpoint, the opprobrium—he deserves, for what must be the most successful one-man lobbying campaign that has been conducted in the House of Commons for many years. Without Luckhoo's frantic buttonholing, in the preceding week, of almost every Tory who matters, I am certain Harold Wilson would not have been prompted into committing himself so firmly on British Guiana's Constitutional Conference."

Lionel had lobbied not only the Tories but also his Labour friends. He had spoken to Members individually, and had also addressed them in groups. One card he had played was to suggest to many Members who esteemed Sir Patrick Renison, the former Governor of British Guiana, in whose Cabinet he had served as Minister without Portfolio, that they inquire of him about Jagan and Burnham. He knew Renison's views, and learned afterwards that some MP's did check, and heard his opinion that independence under Burnham was highly preferable. Before the day of the debate, Lionel knew that indications for a successful outcome were excellent. He had reason to smile.

The conference date was fixed for November 2. Lionel now concentrated, in his lobbying, on members of the government and the Labour Party. He was the only Colonial or Commonwealth Commissioner to attend the Labour Party Conference that year. Outside the conference hall, pickets from the U.K. Committee of Guyanese Progressives—the London arm of Dr. Jagan's PPP—were holding a "symbolic vigil." The protest, they told Labour delegates, was against "the British government's further maneuvers to bamboozle the Guyanese working people, by sending Queen Elizabeth and her husband to British Guiana next year to cover up for the unprincipled act of the former Tory government in changing the electoral system to remove Dr. Cheddi Jagan's party from office, so as to be able to maintain colonialism and neocolonialism in our country."

Dr. Jagan still smarted, and, when offered equal representation for the PPP at the November conference, he refused to attend. He had accused the Burnham government of making a mockery of Parliamentary democracy by ignoring the Legislature and having the Governor sign an emergency order allowing arbitrary detention of suspects for eight days without trial. When the issue reached the correspondence columns of the *Times*, Lionel Luckhoo wrote to point out that the emergency regulations were originally imposed under Dr.

Jagan's administration, and that, while there were twenty-four detainees when the Burnham government took office, there were now only seventeen.

Burnham had strengthened his hand before the conference by inviting the International Commission of Jurists to send a team to study the racial problem in British Guiana. An Irish judge, Mr. Justice Henchy, and two professors of law from Austria and Greece were sent to investigate. Their report appeared just before the constitutional conference was held, and it emphasized that "the racial disharmony in British Guiana is due in no small degree to the uncertainties and tensions of a community passing from colonial tutelage to full independence." Only when independence was achieved would the country find "the national self-reliance, the common purpose, and the cohesion of nationhood necessary for the pursuit of a racially integrated society." They recommended that, as a means of redressing the preponderance of Africans in the security forces, recruitment for the next five years should be 75 percent Indian and 25 percent other races; that an ombudsman should be appointed to deal with complaints of racial discrimination in the public service; and that, in case of another emergency, arrangements should be made for providing a military force from outside British Guiana until the country had an adequate force of its own.

But, by then, the Burnham government and its Commissioner in London had a graver danger to contend with than problems of internal dissension. Venezuela, bordering on British Guiana to the west, had chosen at this time to revive a claim to more than half of Guianese territory. The Venezuelans considered 46,000 square miles of Guiana to be rightfully theirs. Uncompromisingly, Burnham said that they would not get one square inch.

The dispute had its origins in the nineteenth century, when British mining and timber companies pushed westward in search of gold, diamonds, and hardwoods. Ignoring Venezuelan protests, they extended the border of British Guiana to the mouth of the Orinoco River. The United States invoked the Monroe Doctrine in 1895, and demanded that Britain accept arbitration. President Cleveland went so far as to threaten war. A tribunal, under U.S. Supreme Court Justice

Melville Fuller, drew a fresh border line, giving Venezuela control over the mouth of the Orinoco, but leaving in British hands 53,000 square miles of land claimed by Venezuela. Both Britain and Venezuela accepted this as a "full, perfect, and final settlement."

Judgment was delivered in Paris in 1899. Exactly fifty years later (in 1949), a statement was published which questioned the award, claiming that Britain had gained land "over which she had not the shadow of a right." The statement had been made by a New York lawyer, Mr. Severo Mallet-Provost, who had helped Justice Melville Fuller to reach the lauded "full, perfect, and final" settlement. Unfortunately, all the members of the tribunal were dead by then, including Mr. Mallet-Provost, who had died in 1944. This did not make checking easy.

Now, in 1965, the Venezuelan Foreign Minister, Ignacio Iribarren Borges, was telling the United Nations General Assembly that he regarded British Guiana not as a colony but as "occupied territory." In London, the Ambassador, Dr. Hector Santaella, distributed a new map, dated 1965, on which all of British Guiana west of the Essequibo River, from the Atlantic Ocean to the border of Brazil, was marked "Zone of Reclamation." Lionel Luckhoo was meeting with Dr. Santaella and officials from the British Foreign Office and the Colonial Office to frame an agenda for talks on the border issue, to take place on November 9. The meetings were secret, but correspondent David Smithers gathered from Venezuelan sources that they "have been taken aback to discover that in the Commissioner they are confronted with a highly tuned legal mind, which does not hesitate to take the initiative for the British side when necessary, and is more than a match for the best brains the Venezuelans can call upon in London."

The Guianese fear was that the British might be prepared to compromise the issue and allow the border question to go to the World Court, resulting in long legal battles and years of uncertainty. Britain was trying to extend her influence in Latin America and open up new markets there. Opposition from Venezuela could weaken their position with other members of the Organization of American States.

These were the circumstances in which Lionel Luckhoo told the Venezuelans that, in his view, there was no border dispute. Such firmness may have been welcomed by the British Foreign Office, so long as they could not be held responsible. Although taken by surprise at the Guianese attitude, they were impressed by the Commissioner's candor and clear thinking. The Venezuelans hurriedly canceled the next meeting, and urgently contacted Caracas for fresh advice.

The United States, as well as Britain, had at first supported Burnham's stand on the border being kept where it was. In July, the two governments were considering giving a joint guarantee, to be incorporated in the Constitution under which independence would be granted. By October, the U.S. had backed away from any undertaking to help repel a possible aggression. The State Department felt that its popularity was at a low ebb following its embroilment in the affairs of the Dominican Republic. A treaty obligation to resist border claims against British Guiana would have brought a protest to the OAS from Venezuela, accusing the U.S. of breaching Pan-American agreements. Canada, not being a member of the OAS, was being mooted by the United States and Britain for the role of protector of an independent Guyana. Such an arrangement, it was thought, could be linked with the recommendation made by the International Commission of Jurists, that a military force from outside the country should be at hand to keep the peace in an emergency. Now, it appeared more likely that an armed force would be needed as a defense against invaders than to quell disturbances arising within.

Not only was there the threat from Venezuela. October brought more trouble, in the form of a claim to another chunk of British Guianese territory from Surinam, formerly Dutch Guiana, the neighbor to the east. Surinam wanted the claim settled before independence, and had asked the Dutch government to take up the matter with Britain.

In the midst of these contentions, Lionel suffered a grievous personal loss, through the bizarre and tragic death of the novelist Edgar Mittelholzer, his friend since boyhood. As West Indian writers must, in order to survive, Mittelholzer had emigrated, years before. At home, people had laughed at his writings. He offered his remarkable watercolor paintings at five shillings each, and could not sell. Twice Lionel had talked him out of committing suicide. Finally Lionel stole a typewriter from his father's office to give him, and helped him to get to Trinidad. He was living in England and had become a successful novelist when Lionel took up his appointment as Commissioner.

One day Lionel received a letter from Edgar, saying that he needed his help, and would he go down and see him. Official meetings at Whitehall prevented Lionel from going immediately, so he replied that he would go down the following weekend. Before the end of the week, Edgar Mittelholzer was dead. He died by his own hand, and in gruesome fashion. After pouring petrol all over himself, he lay down on his back with his hands and feet in the air, and set himself afire.

Edgar Mittelholzer was Lionel's oldest and dearest friend. "He was a most unusual person," he recalls. "He always said that when he was going to die he would like to portray his death and live through it before it happened. Macabre, you might say, but that was Edgar. Why he died, I don't really know, but it was one of the experiences he looked forward to. He often said, 'Death must be a glorious experience, if it means opening a door and going through to another realm. If it just means going into darkness and nothing, well, there's no point in continuing to live.' Edgar was a very restless sort of person. He always struck me as being in search of something which he could not find. I never knew him to admit defeat. So perhaps his death was a part of the search."

The constitutional talks started as scheduled, on November 2. Dr. Jagan had refused invitations to attend both from the British and Forbes Burnham. In his absence, discussions went smoothly, a draft constitution was prepared, and May 26 of the following year was agreed upon as the day when British Guiana would become independent.

When border talks with Venezuela finally took place in December, it was on British Guiana's terms. Lionel Luckhoo had insisted, with Burnham's full support, that they were willing only to examine the historical documents relating to the issue, not to discuss the redrawing of the border. And when Burnham arrived, he won a battle with the British Foreign Office to have the Guiana team recognized as a separate entity not tied to the British line. So the talks became tripartite.

The Venezuelans faced an outstanding legal team in Forbes Burnham, Attorney General Sonny Ramphal (now Secretary General of the Commonwealth), and Lionel Luckhoo. And they insisted on arguing the case from legal grounds. The Venezuelans claimed that they had never accepted the settlement made in 1899. Then why, the Guianese wanted to know, had they participated in the joint commission set up to demarcate the boundary as decided by the tribunal? And why had they signed the final report of the Demarcation Commission in 1905?

The Venezuelans contended that they were not represented on the tribunal. But that, the Guianese answered, was because they had declined offers to be represented, and, instead, had put their faith in the United States.

The Guianese argued that the Mallet-Provost memorandum, alleging that the 1899 decision was corrupt, was self-serving evidence relying solely on the memory of an old man, writing forty years after the event, when any possible corroborating witnesses were dead. As legal evidence, it was worse than useless. The overwhelming evidence was that there was no defect in the manner by which the 1899 tribunal reached its decision. There were neither grounds nor machinery for an appeal from its award.

The matter was left for the parties to report to the special political committee of the United Nations, where Venezuela had first brought up the issue. The Guianese insisted that it not be raised until their country was independent and had become a member of the United Nations, able to present its own case.

Both the Venezuelan and the Surinam disputes were to drag on for years. Lionel Luckhoo was to continue to play a part in attempts to resolve them. In the meantime, British Guiana was preparing to celebrate its long-sought freedom from colonial rule.

It was widely expected that Lionel Luckhoo would become the first Governor General of the new Guyana. The post called for a Guyanese of forty years or older, able to command the confidence of the broad masses of the people. Neither his age (fifty-one) nor his ability to command the people's confidence were in much doubt. Politically, he stood right of the PNC, to the left of the United Force, the two parties forming the government. Since they came to power, he had spent more than a year waging a battle against all obstacles placed in the path to final independence. Forbes Burnham, it was believed, had already spoken to him about the appointment. Strangely, it was Peter D'Aguiar, who had first brought Lionel into the constitutional talks as his legal adviser, who now seemed to object to the choice. Whatever the reason, Lionel was not appointed, and a compromise candidate was selected.

Chapter 16
The Case of the Duplicate Diplomat

Which hat are you wearing today, Sir Lionel?
—Queen Elizabeth II

Commemorating the euphoria of Guyana's Independence Day celebrations is a photograph of Forbes Burnham and Cheddi Jagan, wrapped in close embrace. Beaming upon the present and former Chief Ministers, one-time friends who had become bitter political foes, is Lionel Luckhoo, once an opponent of both, and a sorry failure at wielding the political bludgeon against them. But his finesse with the diplomatic rapier had done much to bring about this magic moment.

After the flag-raising ceremony, it was back to Britain for Lionel. Burnham had invited him to become the country's first High Commissioner to the Court of St. James, as well as Ambassador to Paris, Bonn, and the Hague. London was still the most vital of diplomatic posts, the hub of the Commonwealth of which Guyana was the newest member. Also, Britain sheltered thousands of Guyanese immigrants.

The new High Commissioner struck an arpeggio of informal notes upon his assumption of office. The first was when he had his initial meeting with Queen Elizabeth. Her enthusiasm for racing is well known; indeed, she is considered to be an authority on racehorse breeding. The Queen remembered Lionel from her visit to Georgetown, while he was president of the Turf Club, and now talked to him about her current crop of two-year-olds. When the audience had overrun by a good ten minutes, there came a gentle tap at the door. "My goodness!" said Her Majesty, "I'm sorry I kept you so long." Lionel said impulsively, "Think nothing of it, dear," as he would to any woman. At his lapse from the formal "Ma'am," he apologized and the Queen gave him her widest grin.

The first job of any ambassador from a newborn state is to put his country on the map. Sometimes this has to be done literally as well as metaphorically, for it is no pun to say that ignorance of simple geography has no geographical bounds. The proud citizens of small countries, when they go abroad, are astonished to find that the natives they meet appear never to have opened an atlas. A dinner to honor Lionel was arranged by Lord Sorensen at the House of Lords. After Lionel had spoken to the guests about the role of a small country, Yehudi Menuhin rose to give the main toast of the evening. Menuhin said he had listened to a magnificent speech by a great orator; that, having heard what Lionel had said about his country, he could hardly wait to pay it a visit. Lionel felt himself grow taller and taller as the great violinist went on to lavish more compliments. His head was touching the chandelier by the time Menuhin picked up his glass and said, "Let us now drink to this wonderful country we have been hearing about, and of which we know so little. I ask you to charge your glasses and drink to . . . Guinea!"

Lionel lost height so quickly that his chin almost hit the table. He had failed to put across the basic sales point, the name of the product. It was not Guinea, not Ghana, but *Guyana* he was selling—and Menuhin had not been properly sold. The appalling thought was that everyone else at the table might have been left with a firm grip on the wrong handle.

Lionel Luckhoo provided good copy for the newspapers. Their reporters had never met a diplomat quite like him before. One writer, throwing a bouquet of alliterative adjectives, described him as "dapper, dignified, dynamic—and on occasions (especially legal occasions) diabolical," and went on: "Nine months ago he burst on to the London scene like a bundle of fireworks and in that short time has completely transformed the British image of Guyana. Sir Lionel Luckhoo the diplomatist at work is like nothing so much as a bottle of vintage champagne: mature (with his courtly manners, even old-fashioned)—yet potentially explosive; civilized, smooth and stimulating—yet liable to intoxicate if taken in large doses. . . . I am the least of a great company of admirers in Britain—politicians and judges, diplomats and lawyers, doctors and civil servants, Guyanese immigrants and wealthy industrialists."

All these groups had felt the impact of the High Commissioner. His own profession was one of the first to have the experience. Lionel burst in on the Commonwealth Legal Conference, and urged that a postfinals course in professional ethics be instituted for young lawyers, and that they should read in chambers in their home countries before entering practice. Both suggestions were accepted. He arranged informal gatherings at his home for West Indian law students and invited leaders of the profession to attend. In this way, the students met the Lord Chancellor, the Lord Chief Justice, the Master of the Rolls—the three highest legal officers under the Crown—and a number of High Court judges.

Neither did he neglect that profession at which he describes himself as having been an inglorious failure. British medical schools were then receiving 30 applications for every available position. Lionel went to the Commonwealth Medical Conference in Scotland to urge other developed members to open their doors wider to Guyanese students. Canada, Australia, and New Zealand all gave a favorable response. Like the law students, medical students were invited to meet leaders of the profession at the High Commissioner's residence. Soon Lionel had the idea that lawyers and doctors at home might benefit from an extension of this program, and he asked Prime Minister Harold Wilson if the British government would pay for trips by eminent professional people to Guyana during the Christmas vacations. They would get away from the cold, he pointed out, and at the same time would be warming the hearts and enlivening the minds of brethren and colleagues overseas. Harold Wilson agreed, and, as a start to the scheme, the Lord Chief Justice and Lady Parker spent the next Christmas in Guyana as guests of Lionel's brother E.V., who was then Chancellor of the Judiciary.

On the legal and domestic fronts, the High Commissioner made himself readily available to help his people with their problems. He secured the release of a Guyanese woman who was being wrongfully detained in a mental hospital. He forced an apology from the police to Guyanese girls who had been unjustly arrested and charged with soliciting. He traced husbands who had gone away and left their families without support, found jobs for those in search of employment, gave counsel to warring wives and husbands, and attended weddings of the fatherless.

Lionel Luckhoo was vicar, in all but name, of a very large parish. And soon the Duke of Edinburgh would be referring to him, appropriately, as the man with *two* parishes.

2

Premier Errol Barrow of Barbados had noted the effective part Lionel Luckhoo had played as Commissioner in the negotiations for Guyanese independence. He asked Forbes Burnham if Lionel's services could be directed towards obtaining the same independence for Barbados. Burnham agreed, and Lionel acted as legal adviser to Barrow throughout the talks. As the *Barbados Daily News* expressed it, "he was of great assistance to the government of Barbados in obtaining a date for independence when all might have seemed lost." Barbados celebrated its independence less than a year after Guyana.

This was the only connection Lionel had had up to that time with the country. So it was something of a surprise when Prime Minister Barrow invited him to become the first High Commissioner for Barbados in Britain, and Ambassador to the capitals of France, West Germany, and Holland—the identical posts in which he was serving Guyana. The government of Guyana raised no objection. Although, politically, Burnham was well to the left of center and Barrow slightly to the right, the two men were personally friendly, and, as West Indian members of the Commonwealth, their countries had many interests in common.

The dual appointment created a furor in diplomatic circles. It was the first time that a man had undertaken to represent two countries at such a high level. And of one of them he was not a citizen. Reactions ranged through the ABC of emotions—amazement, bemusement, cynicism! How could it possibly work? Errol Barrow was to say, later, of Lionel that he was not the world's most successful lawyer, but the world's biggest sucker. This was a comment on the moderate fees he charged clients who could have paid fabulous sums, but, in the minds of many, it could have applied as justly to his acceptance of this dichotomic task.

Lionel Luckhoo's own approach to the situation was more lighthearted. "The biggest problem," he told the press, "is how I can show myself as a representative of two countries in one car. It sounds facetious, I know, but it is amazing how seriously some people take such things."

Queen Elizabeth took it with her usual sense of humor. Lionel had the Barbadian coat of arms on one door of his car, Guyana's on the other. He flew two national pennants on the bonnet, which he thought was "just a little bit showy." But what to do about the number plates? The Queen tried to help him by suggesting he get both GUY 1 and BAR 1.

"But which should I put in front?" asked Lionel.

"Ah, yes," said Her Majesty. "That raises another problem."

In the end, he had to stick to the number already in use, which was GYA 1. Even acting on the Queen's advice, he could not contravene police regulations, which allow a car only one registration number.

After he became a duplicate diplomat, the Queen would always ask with twinkling eye when he met her, "Which hat are you wearing today, Sir Lionel?"

In an independence issue, a Barbadian newspaper heralded Lionel's new appointment by declaring, "If a High Commissioner's prime task is to see that the country he represents is not overlooked in the diplomatic, financial, social, cultural, sporting, or business worlds of the country to which he is accredited, then Sir Lionel is a success in his new job even before he starts it. His appointment to the double office aroused more interest, and occasioned more publicity, in London than any diplomatic appointment since Napoleon was made First Consul."

Lionel's Napoleonic look may have done something to inspire the comparison. As was to be expected, *The Times* of London welcomed him in more stately fashion: "Sir Lionel is well informed on Caribbean, British and Afro-Asian affairs and has a wider range of British political acquaintance than most Commonwealth diplomatists. . . . He will not only be setting an interesting precedent for the smaller and less wealthy countries, he will be adding plenty of work to his own desk."

Lionel coped with the doubled work by reaching one or another of the High Commissions by seven every morning. At the Guyana office in Cockspur Street, he had a staff of about forty. Barbados, a more prosperous though smaller country, provided seventy-five to man the Kensington High Street office. Colleagues in the Diplomatic Corps never stopped asking, "Don't you have trouble representing two countries, with two Prime Ministers giving you different, perhaps contrary, instructions?"

"None at all," Lionel would answer. "Firstly, my Prime Ministers understand each other; secondly, they both understand me; and, thirdly, I understand them. I usually know what they are thinking, what they will tell me to do, and can act responsively, almost automatically."

His Prime Ministers did have what appeared to be conflicting points of view on one occasion. The three small Caribbean islands of St. Kitts, Nevis, and Anguilla were under one government. When Anguilla sought to break away, the Commonwealth countries, especially those in the Caribbean, were concerned and wanted to have a say in the dispute. On arriving at the Guyana office one morning, Lionel found a cable from Burnham saying that Guyana supported the established government of Robert Bradshaw. When he reached the Barbados office, there was a cable from Barrow, setting out a more favorable stand towards the separatist movement led by Ronald Webster, without supporting it.

Lionel went to see Fred Lee, Minister for Commonwealth Relations. "Mr. Lee," he said, " in the name of Guyana I bid you good morning. I wish to tell you the views of my Prime Minister. Forbes Burnham supports Mr. Bradshaw and his regime in this impasse." There was a suitable pause, then: "Mr. Lee, I bid you good morning in the name of Barbados. I wish to tell you the views expressed to me by Prime Minister Barrow on the Anguillan question." This he then recounted.

The Minister then discussed with him how to get Bradshaw and Webster to enter into some form of resolution. Lionel knew the pride and passion aroused by political issues in small West Indian territories. He said, "We may try, you may try, but only one thing will provide a solution."

The Minister said, "Tell me what that is."

"Time," said Lionel.

At times, the double representation brought diplomatic advantage. When a World Sugar Conference was held in Geneva, both Guyana and Barbados wanted a particular delegate to be elected chairman. As soon as the floor was open, Lionel stood up and, in the name of Guyana, nominated the individual. Then he said, "And in the name of Barbados, I beg to second the nomination."

There was consternation. Could the same person be allowed to nominate, and then to second his own nomination? The protocol experts started a lengthy discussion of the pros and cons. Lionel Luckhoo interrupted them to ask, "Are there two places here, one for Guyana and one for Barbados?"

He was told that there were.

"Very well. I am seated in the Guyana place. I beg to nominate from here. Now, could you show me where the Barbados place is?"

When an empty seat was pointed out to him, Lionel got to his feet and marched round the table. He seated himself, then rose, bowed, and said, "In the name of Barbados, I beg to second the nomination." That, apparently, resolved the problem satisfactorily. The particular delegate was elected chairman—helped by *two* votes from the High Commissioner for Guyana and Barbados.

People he met were startled and intrigued to learn that one man could represent two countries. Both countries benefited from the extra emphasis it gave to establishing their identities, when, wherever he appeared, Lionel was introduced as speaking on behalf of both territories. He received twice the usual number of invitations to Wembley finals, Lords' Tests, and other formal and informal events.

On one occasion only did he suffer defeat in the role of a double diplomat. At a dinner given by the La Rue Company, he discovered that two plates had been set for him. He told his host that he could wear two hats, fly two flags, make two speeches, if necessary—but he was not going to eat two dinners!

He was invited to Buckingham Palace on many occasions. At one dinner there, Lionel found himself seated beside Sir Joseph Simpson, Commissioner of the Metropolitan Police. He remarked on the lavish display of gold plate and silver cutlery. "Pray tell me," he said, "do you have people counting and checking to see that all is correct?"

"Do you know, the remarkable thing is that in my time nothing has ever been missed from the royal table." Simpson chuckled as he added, "One cannot say that about the Mansion House—bits of silver have been lost or gone missing from there."

Buckingham Palace is within the metropolitan area, not much more than a stone's throw from Scotland Yard. The Mansion House comes under protection of the City of London Police.

Lionel was slated to address the Victoria League at a Mansion House dinner. Before going to the rostrum, he was asked about his script. He said he had no script, and was told that he must have, because they wanted to publish it afterwards. Lionel explained that he never used a script; the only time he had was at the opening of a swimming pool, when he had made the worst speech of his life. After he had spoken for an hour without notes, he was told it was the best speech ever heard at a Victoria League meeting. A man who was about to become president of the national bank of a rich Middle East country complimented him on the content and fluency, and said, "I will pay you twice what you are getting now, to become my speech writer." Lionel said, as seriously, "I could do with the money, but I could not do with the honor."

Reading speeches had always made him hot and bothered. At his first audience with President de Gaulle, he had, as was customary, sent a copy of his speech beforehand to the Chef de Protocol, so that de Gaulle could prepare his reply. But when Lionel met the President, he pushed the speech into his pocket and spoke without notes. At first de Gaulle looked annoyed, then appreciative, when Lionel touched on the subject of the European Economic Community, which had not been mentioned in the original address de Gaulle had already read. The EEC was a matter of deep concern, both to France and the British Caribbean countries, as at that time Britain was negotiating for membership.

Lionel understood French tolerably well, and de Gaulle understood English much better, but, even at less formal sessions, the President always insisted on using an interpreter. One reason for his unwillingness to speak the language was his animosity towards England since the wartime disagreements with Churchill. But whenever the translation of his French did not please him, de Gaulle would sharply interrupt, "I did not say that. What I said was . . . ," and give his own version in impeccable English.

While arguing the case for West Indian interests not being overlooked in the negotiations between Britain and the Common Market countries, Lionel pointed to a statistic that had gone unrecognized. The Caribbean nations were among Britain's best customers. In 1966, they had bought British exports to the value of $100.80 per capita. This was only slightly below Australia at $105.60 per capita. It was higher than the European Free Trade Area, to which Britain belonged, at $81.60, and much higher than the expenditure of the European Common Market countries, at only $24.00.

The flood of immigrants to Britain had become a continual contentious issue. The loudest voice in favor of damming, and even reversing, the tide was that of Enoch Powell, a former Conservative Minister of Government. He advocated that colored immigrants should be sent home, passage paid, to save Britain's towns from Afro-Asian domination in the future. The High Commissioner for Guyana and Barbados made retort that, if Britain were denuded of Asians and West Indians, the health and transport services would grind to a standstill. He also presented a plan to ease the problem.

Guyana was a part of Sir Walter Raleigh's fabled El Dorado. On a modern and practical level, the United Nations had just completed a geophysical, geological, and geochemical survey, which indicated that diamonds, nickel, copper, zinc, molybdenum, and other riches in untold quantities were there for the digging. There were a million acres of land available for crops and cattle.

So: "Quit Britain and come to live in my country" was Lionel Luckhoo's message to the unwanted immigrants. Guyana was nearly as big as Britain, but had a population of only 640,000. It was as much a challenge to the British government as it was to West Indians, for mass immigration to Guyana would be possible only if Britain was prepared to finance it. Large-scale development would be necessary, and the cost would run into millions. But, even if it were several hundred millions, that would compare favorably with the amount of money Britain spent every year on welfare and integration schemes for the immigrants. So Britain would not be making a charity donation to Guyana. In return for development aid, Guyana would be relieving Britain of what was declared to be its biggest social and political problem.

"Guyana is an Aladdin's cave of forest and mineral wealth," said the High Commissioner. "In the face of all this potential for a happy and reasonably prosperous people in a warm climate, it seems criminal to keep Caribbean people here as second-class citizens, made bitter by what seems to be increasing social hostility. I'm not attacking Britain when I say all this. You have your own climate, temperament, cultural background, and way of life. Our Caribbean people have theirs. You don't want them. We want them."

The offer was open to all Caribbean immigrants, Lionel Luckhoo promised, regardless of race or nationality. When they were absorbed, Guyana would open its doors to immigrants from other areas.

Even before independence was granted, Forbes Burnham had suggested that the sensible thing would be to direct the flow of West Indian immigrants to Guyana, and thereby reduce the pressures building up in Britain. Guyana provided an answer to the problem, he said, and was willing to play its full part, with the assistance of other countries which were involved.

The issue of immigration to Guyana had often been raised in the past. At one period, the question of Jews, displaced by Hitler's persecutions, being allowed to settle there was under consideration. Although Britain's immigration problem has been talked about endlessly at all levels, no serious effort has been made by Britain or any West Indian government to investigate or help implement the solution proposed by Forbes Burnham and Lionel Luckhoo. The West Indians appear to have taken the line that Guyana must first develop its interior to attract them, rather than invite them to be pioneers.

What Burnham and Luckhoo could do for their own immigrants to Britain was to give them a say in the affairs of their home country. When Guyanese nationals were enabled to vote in the 1968 election, it was the first experiment in non-resident voting ever attempted by a West Indian territory. In any West Indian election, the losers can be expected to shout fraud—justifiably, in some instances. An elaborate procedure had been devised as a safeguard against such accusations. Anyone in England who claimed he was Guyanese could submit a registration claim, giving particulars of his residence in Guyana, the names of his parents, and other details. The claims were then checked, and a voting list compiled. When ballot papers were sent by post to those listed, a slip of paper was enclosed for signature, which could afterwards be compared with the signature on the original registration form. Securicor, a leading British security organization, guarded the drum into which the votes were placed at the High Commissioner's office. But, as always, the challenges and charges of malpractice were aimed. When a newspaper made the snide remark that the High Commissioner had taken the overseas votes to Guyana in his overcoat pocket, Lionel sued, and settled for damages, which he gave to charity.

Cricket, the only game that compares with politics for rousing West Indian ire, caused another crack in the High Commissioner's normally smooth relationship with the communications media. A BBC television commentator, at the conclusion of a Test match being played in Jamaica, had made the remark, "It is a pity that the West Indians have not yet learned how to lose." Lionel Luckhoo went to bat for the whole Caribbean. In a letter to the *Times*, he demanded to know: "What did he mean by West Indians? Was he referring to the team? The team had surely not taken part in the disgraceful exhibition of ill manners (for this is what it was, rather than the flamboyant use of the word *riot*). If, by the expression *West Indians*, the commentator was referring to a section of the Jamaican crowd, then one would expect him to say, when there are similar football incidents in England (and there are many), 'It is a pity that Europeans have not yet learned how to lose.' "

Racing was still the sport to which Lionel was wholly devoted. He had six racehorses in training in England, during his diplomatic years. The best of them, Philodendron, won on four successive outings. One trophy he collected was the Liverpool Summer Cup.

On one occasion, the Luckhoos were on the way to Ascot in the impressively large and immaculate car belonging to the Mission. Suddenly, there was a grating noise and the car stopped—the engine had dropped out! Standing in the middle of the road, Sheila beautifully gowned, Lionel in morning dress with grey top hat and silk umbrella, they felt they must be a comical sight as the stream of racegoers drove by, laughing at them. Lionel did not much mind the laughter. His worry was how to arrive in time for the first race. He had a tip from a friend, an owner. A small, rackety-looking baby Austin drew up alongside them. The smiling driver leaned out and said, "Do me the honor of sharing my car." Lionel handed Sheila into the rattletrap, jumped in after her with alacrity, and off they drove to Ascot in a style to which they had become unaccustomed. The owner-friend proved to be more knowledgeable than most friends (or most owners), for the horse he had tipped was a winner.

It was at Ascot that Lionel was once greeted by Prince Charles, who, like his parents, has a sense of humor. Knowing he had just come back from abroad, Lionel asked the Prince where he had been, and was told, "Malta." Lionel said, "They have the most magnificent women there. What shapes! What wonderful forms!"

Prince Charles nodded. "Yes," he agreed. "I take it you're referring to the girls and not their mothers."

Living a double life, so to speak, did not always allow time for going to race meetings. To the amusement and interest of the newspapers, Lionel took up the very British sport of greyhound racing, and bought a two-year-old Irish greyhound named Healthex. Most dog racing takes place in the evening, and Lionel told the press he found a visit to the Wimbledon track "wonderfully relaxing after a hard day."

The days were hard, indeed, for Guyana was still being threatened by the border claims of its neighbors. A joint commission was discussing the Venezuelan claim, and had been allowed four years—1966 to 1970—in which to report. Then, in 1968, Venezuela occupied the island of Anakoko in the Cuyuni River, transgressing the border set up by the 1899 agreement. Venezuela had also extended the twelve-mile limit, claiming that her territorial waters extended to the mouth of the Essequibo River at Georgetown, Guyana's capital. Her naval craft, in violation of international law, were sent to patrol to within three miles of Guyanese shores. Protest notes over both these actions were rejected. Forbes Burnham then took Guyana's complaints to U.S. President Lyndon Johnson and United Nations' Secretary General U Thant. But the Americans did not want to become involved, and the Venezuelans, after having appealed themselves to the United Nations in 1965, now insisted that the U.N. was not competent to discuss the matter.

In London, the High Commissioner found most of his time taken up by the Venezuelan and Surinam disputes. At dinners and luncheons, he kept his Commonwealth colleagues informed, and made special efforts to bring the ambassadors of South American countries, particularly Brazil—Guyana's third neighbor—into the picture. He represented his country at meetings in London, Geneva, and the Hague.

The Dutch Foreign Minister, Dr. Luns, told Lionel, "If disputes cannot be settled around the table, then there is no dispute." At a conference with Dutch newspaper editors, Lionel was asked, "Is the friendship of Surinam not worth a few thousand square miles of disputed territory?" "Yes," he replied, "it is worth it. In like manner, the friendship of Venezuela is worth many thousand more square miles; also, in the name of friendship, we may let Brazil take our land to the south, and perhaps, to appease the sea gods, we should allow the Atlantic to erode away our northern shores! Then we will be friends with everyone, but with no country of our own."

Surinam eased off its claim to 6,000 square miles of Guyana, but it could be predicted that, if Venezuela sought a military solution, Surinam might then invade from her side. Brazil, too, it was suggested, had hinted that it would seize a slice of Guyana, to which it considered it had a claim, should Venezuela attack.

When strained relations over the border issue had almost reached breaking point, it was suggested that Lionel Luckhoo should be sent as Guyana's emissary to Venezuela. A leading newspaper voiced a widely held opinion: "If there is one man in Guyana capable of averting catastrophe through the sheer brilliance and energy of diplomatic approach, it is he."

Chapter 17
The Case of the Faithful Father

Daddy, you are the best father and mother anyone could ever have.

—*Luckhoo Children*

Although he was in greater demand as a public speaker than any other member of the Diplomatic Corps in London, Lionel Luckhoo's most successful speech was shorter than many a postal address.

It was delivered at the House of Commons, where he had been invited as chief speaker at a dinner of the . . . perhaps it is kinder not to include the name of the society, as they suffered embarrassment enough at the time. The preliminary speeches had been timeless and tedious. At a late, late hour, the toastmaster announced the main speaker: "My lords, ladies and gentlemen, pray for the silence of his excellency." Lionel rose to the introduction and to the occasion. He smiled sweetly at the toastmaster (how often does a member of the efficient red-coated brigade fluff his lines!) and said, "My lords, ladies and gentlemen, your prayers are answered." And he sat down—to deafening applause.

In a small way, the incident was a portent, for in the parlors of diplomacy the voice of Lionel Luckhoo was soon to be stilled.

Like his father and, indeed, his grandfather before him, Lionel has always been a strong believer in the family unit. His own family life seemed anchored in secure foundations. He and Sheila had been deeply in love when they married. Sheila was beautiful, charming, and she shone as a twin star in the hectic glamor of diplomatic life.

The Luckhoos entertained lavishly. At some of the dinner parties, gifts of gold-filigree jewelry were given to the ladies, a costly way of promoting Guyanese products at Lionel's own expense. Monthly luncheons were inaugurated for Commonwealth High Commissioners, where they could let down their hair and discuss openly what was happening in their countries and the world at large. The nationals of Guyana and Barbados were invited every month, up to 800 at a time, to cook-ups of West Indian foods—peas and rice and pig tail—and rum punch provided by the Luckhoos. There they met their friends, and Lionel gave them the news from home. The British press was entertained and, in a sales pitch for Guyanese rice and rum, Lionel, donning an apron for the benefit of the photographers, introduced them to the idea that (as one subsequent headline put it) *Rice Has Other Uses than Rice Pudding.*

Perhaps every book would do well to offer food for the stomach as well as for thought (at least, it gives the tentative author an each-way bet). Any voracious reader who wishes to try the High Commissioner's recipe for what he calls "a kind of pilau" should:

> *Fry onions until they are brown. Mix with fresh tomatoes to give a reddish color. Half-cook split peas separately. Half-cook small pieces of chicken separately. Put burnt onions, tomatoes, split peas and chicken in a pot with the rice and add salt to taste. Pour water into the pot to a level of 1¼ inches above the rice surface. Add geerah and a touch of mango achar and stir well. Boil for three-quarters of an hour.*

The London press, not nature's gourmands, enjoyed and recommended it.

The Luckhoos now had five children. The youngest, Mark Edward, born in England while his father was the accredited representative of two other countries, could lay legal claim to three nationalities. Mark has another out-of-the-way distinction. It is customary, indeed necessary, to register a boy at birth for entry to the better-known English public schools. After Mark's birth, Lionel wrote to Harrow, where his other son Michael was already entered. By mistake, a secretary addressed the letter to Harvard instead of Harrow. It brought back a reply from Harvard University that there was no precedent for dealing with the request, because no one had ever before applied for entry at such an early age, but, if Mark could meet the normal entrance requirements when the time came, he would be accepted.

Their friends in the Diplomatic Corps saw Lionel and Sheila as the happiest of couples. But their relationship was no longer as close as it had been, And, when the question of Lionel being sent to Venezuela as Ambassador arose, Sheila refused to go with him. She wanted to remain in England. Lionel knew that if he went alone it would break up their marriage, and he wanted to preserve the family unit. There were other considerations that had to be weighed. His physical health had deteriorated; a chronic stomach complaint had developed which gave him constant bouts of pain. He not only declined the appointment to Venezuela, but decided that the time had come for him to leave the diplomatic service.

Both Burnham and Barrow pressed him strongly to remain. When he proved adamant, they decided that no other person could fill the double appointment, and that, for the future, each country would have separate representation. At the end of 1969, Lionel relinquished office as High Commissioner and Ambassador for Guyana. He agreed to carry on for Barbados until he could be replaced, which was not until June, 1970.

As a personal speculation, I would hazard that, although Lionel had served without stint, and even found zest in the diplomatic role, his heart never strayed far from the courtroom. It was there, even when not a participant, that he found his greatest delight—watching Sir Patrick Hastings, whom Lionel and many others regarded as the most deadly cross-examiner of his day, handle a hostile witness; or Sir Norman Birkett (later Lord Birkett) of the wonderful voice make comments to the jury in such dulcet tones that, although irregular, they would escape the ire of the judge. Among judges, he particularly admired Lord Reed for depth of thought, incisiveness, and clarity of his decisions.

In the New Year Honours' list for 1969, Lionel was elevated from the rank of Knight Bachelor to Knight Commander of St. Michael and St. George. It meant fulfillment of the ambition he had expressed at the age of four, of becoming an "Excellency" and a KCMG. Recalling his father's words on that occasion, he sent home a cable: "The impossible has happened!" Yet he took greater pride in the first knighthood, which had been awarded for *legal* services.

Diplomacy and the law both employ the art of persuasion, but, in diplomacy, the exercise of that talent is often a waste of time. Judges and juries have no vested interest in the outcome of a case. It is won or lost on its merits, or by skillful advocacy. Contrariwise, there is no deeper vested interest than national interest. Diplomacy might be compared with trying to win a just verdict from a jury comprising the family of the victim, the parents of the accused, a hangman, two chaplains, three psychiatrists, and an insurance assessor, directed by a judge holding a gun in place of a gavel. After conceding every argument, they would still be bent on seeing the prisoner set free, hanged, committed to an asylum, or the victim declared a suicide, according to their own prevailing sentiments. Diplomatic victories are not won on the facts or justice of the case, but by an appeal to self-interest, enlightened or otherwise. If on any occasion partisan minds have been swayed, the advocate may not have the satisfaction of knowing it until long afterwards, if ever. In a court of law, he wins or he loses; and, after a tenacious struggle, Lionel Luckhoo enjoys the taste of open victory.

Both victories and defeats were precious few when Lionel, diplomacy behind him, began the practice of law in London. While in the Diplomatic Corps, he had been invited to undertake legal cases at various times, including the sensational McKay case. (Two Trinidadians were accused of kidnaping and murdering Mrs. Muriel McKay, wife of the editor of *News of the World*. Lionel Luckhoo's candid opinion is that their eventual defenders handled the case somewhat like novices!) Now that he was free, there was not sufficient work. Under the English system, barristers (the senior branch) are entirely dependent for their briefs upon the good graces of solicitors (the junior branch). A client cannot approach a barrister directly; indeed, he is lucky if he sees the man who is to defend him before the case reaches court. One justification for separating the two branches is that barristers usually specialize in one, perhaps two, subdivisions of the law (Sir Stafford Cripps was accounted exceptionally brilliant by being an expert in six), so guidance is needed to pick out the right man. In anticipation of the high fees he may receive later, a barrister can expect, and is expected, to starve during his early years.

Relationships with solicitors are formed in a variety of ways, but slowly. Lionel was a Queen's Counsel; his legal talents had gained him a knighthood; his name and reputation were established in law and diplomacy. These distinctions helped, but did not bring in the bread-and-butter cases. He made successful appearances in court. When he defended a case at the Old Bailey, pleading his client guilty to a lesser charge, the judge went out of his way to comment, "Rarely have I heard the facts of a case so succinctly put, or such an eloquent plea in mitigation"; whereupon, two solicitors who happened to be in court came to ask Lionel where he could be found. But they did not send him briefs immediately, and the time was coming when he could not afford to wait.

Lionel had heavy commitments, and a sizeable family to support. Pleas for him to take on cases in Guyana were coming almost daily. If he returned, his financial future would be assured. He was also needed at Luckhoo and Luckhoo. With Lionel in the diplomatic service, and E.V. in the judicature as Chancellor, Lloyd had been carrying a heavy burden as the only senior member of the firm, and his preference was for civil rather than criminal law.

Sheila still refused to leave England. By now, their estrangement went deeper than a difference of opinion over domicile. Although Sheila was English, she had lived as long a time in the West Indies as Lionel had in London. In the early days of their marriage, either would have been happy to live wherever it pleased the other. The idealized lovers we dote on—Romeo and Juliet, Abelard and Heloise, Dante and Beatrice—never had to face up to the daily routine of marriage. However trite, it is true to say that marriage, like life, is never stagnant, and once people stop growing together, they grow apart.

Lionel insisted that Sheila and the children should return with him to the Caribbean. Her reply was to the effect that the children were not to leave England, and that she would take steps for a divorce. A divorce was the last thing that Lionel wanted. After reaching Guyana, he wrote daily, seeking to have Sheila rejoin him. The letters received no response, and, eventually, were returned to him in a package. Finally, he himself obtained a divorce in Guyana, their place of domicile.

What Lionel feared most was the loss of his children. No compromise could be reached on the issue. To obtain custody meant a legal battle. The oldest, Sharman, was 12; Michael, 10; Marina, 6; Mark, still a baby. Courts everywhere are reluctant to take young children away from the care of the mother. It would be immeasurably difficult to persuade an English court to decide against an English mother in favor of a father of foreign nationality, and allow him to take the children outside the court's jurisdiction.

Before the case came up, Lionel went through all the formal motions of engaging senior counsel, junior counsel, even employing two sets of solicitors. Then, when the date for the hearing arrived, he found that he could not go through with it by such a method. If he wanted his children, he must plead for them himself. He thanked the array of legal representatives for their services, and told them he had decided to conduct his own case.

The judge was alarmed when he stood up. "Are you sure, Sir Lionel, that you wish to appear for yourself?"

"Yes, m'lud, I wish to do so."

On the tip of every lawyer's tongue is the adage "A man who conducts his own case has a fool for a client." The tempting retort, naturally, is "Better a fool for a client than a fool for a lawyer." During one of our talks, I asked Lionel Luckhoo whether he would appear in his own defense if he were charged with murder. "If innocent, yes. If guilty, no," he replied. I suggested that, if guilty, he might stand most in need of his own special talents. Would he have as much confidence in anyone else? "Perhaps E.V.," he said. I stayed skeptical. Lionel regards his brother Sir Edward Luckhoo as being the better lawyer . . . but in a murder trial! I pressed the issue. "Wouldn't you really prefer to do it yourself?" Lionel gave it fair consideration, then said, "Really, I suppose I would."

The case took two weeks. Lionel had Sheila's only brother, Michael, and his wife Shirley to give evidence on his behalf. But in his final plea he stood alone, in what he considers to be the greatest court battle of his life. But, in this instance, he did not feel he was alone. He remembered the saying "With God, one is a majority." He had the consciousness that he was being upheld throughout the worst ordeal he had ever faced. He fought desperately, and, in the end, the case was decided in his favor.

Ironically, the first new client to seek Lionel's help to defend him on a murder charge, when he returned to Guyana, was a man who confessed to having killed his wife and two small children by deliberately setting fire to the home. It was, and remains,* the only murder case Lionel Luckhoo ever turned down flat.

2

Lionel Luckhoo has been a faithful father to his children. To make a home for them was no easy proposition. Lloyd and Doreen readily came to Lionel's assistance, and, for over a year, he and the children shared their home. Then Lionel bought a house, and set himself up as a bachelor father. He learned how to keep house, but was never too proud to call for help. If he ran out of milk, he would still drive to Lloyd's house and borrow a pint from Doreen.

Nowadays, Marina helps him with the shopping list, but it is her father who collects it. (A small awkwardness is that one or two shops refuse to accept payment if Lionel himself calls, because a member of their family owes freedom to his defense; so to them he sends his driver.)

In the household, I came to know there were three children closely attached to their father. One Father's Day, they pooled their pocket money and bought a small silver cup, with the inscription, "To the Best Father in the World." To

* *At the time this was written. But see Chapter 28.*

this, Sharman, Marina, and Mark added their own note, which read, "Daddy, you are the best father and mother anyone could ever have." (Michael, at this stage, was going to school in London.)

Lionel's workdays are punctuated by quick dashes home to transport the children to or from some activity. Late in the evening, he will interrupt work on a brief to collect Sharman or Marina from a party or a picture show.

One afternoon, with no time to spare between two important meetings, Lionel rushed home to take Mark to a meeting of his scout troop. Both field and pavilion were deserted—apparently, the event had been postponed without any notice being given. Father and son took the inconvenience, for the one, and the disappointment, for the other, with calm philosophy.

Sharman was spending the evening with a group of teenage friends. After dropping her at the house, Lionel wondered aloud if the young people might like some ice cream, drove three miles to the center of town, queued for twenty minutes, and took back several quarts as a surprise treat.

At any time, the Luckhoo home is a refuge for up to a dozen stray animals the children have rescued—kittens, puppies, a duck, and a rabbit or two. Sharman, especially, is fervent in the cause of animals, and has become an uncompromising vegetarian—which throws the meal schedules into disarray. When they indignantly accuse their father of not showing as much concern for the strays as they do, he gently points out that, when the children are away, or forgetful, it is he who feeds the animals.

Already, the Luckhoo family has sixteen members in the legal profession. Does Lionel want to see any of his children join them?

"Heaven help me, no!" he cries. "I think a lawyer works much too hard, and if he doesn't work too hard then he is no lawyer. In law, you learn nothing before you qualify. It's after a lawyer qualifies that he has to keep abreast and always be a student. What the law requires is dedication. I have to live, sleep, and dream law. If I had to live my life again, I'd probably do the same thing—but then, I'm a fool."

He resumes in a quieter vain. "The main point lies in the

French quotation, *Il n'y a pas de sal metier, il y a de sal gens.* (There is no such thing as a dishonorable profession, but there are dishonorable people.) If a boy wants to go and sweep the road, fine! But he must aim at being the best road-sweeper. If a girl is going to do hairdressing, then she must aim at being the best hairdresser.

"At Christmas time in London, I used to give a party for my Guyanese and Barbadian nationals. With true West Indian spirit, they often brought me little gifts. One year, a Bajan came and handed me—well, hardly handed; he nearly bowled me over with—an enormous parcel. I am hopeless, just cannot bear to wait for Christmas Day to open gifts, so I opened it at once. It was a giant roll of bread. 'My goodness!' I said. 'Where has this come from?' My Bajan friend stuck out his chest with pride. 'I am a baker, Sir Lionel,' he said. 'I have a one-room baker shop . . . but one day I will be the best baker in London.'

"It is not what a person is professionally, but what he *really* is, that matters. Mr. Sealey wanted to be the best baker. He proclaimed that he was a baker with as much gusto as if he were announcing that he was the president of U.S. Steel. This is the only kind of approach that satisfies me. I want to see my children succeed in whatever is the vocation of their choice."

And that, of course, does not necessarily rule out the law.

3

Family devotion created a tragedy that took Lionel Luckhoo into court for his first important criminal defense after his return to Guyana. It could be called The Case of the Loyal Son.

Two young men, Ralph Hansraj, twenty-one, and Basil Persaud, twenty, were the closest of friends. Both were fishermen, and lived with their families at the village of Fyrish on the Corentyne Coast of Guyana. Early one morning, Ralph noticed that Basil's fishing boat had sunk under water at the Albion Koker, where it was moored.

A *koker* is a small reservoir, or lock. A heavy door, operated by a wheel, controls the water. On either side of the koker, the dam is built up to a height of about twelve feet. This particular morning, the door had been raised, and the sudden rush of water had swamped the boat.

Ralph went and told Basil what had happened. If the boat could not be rescued in time, the strong current would take it out to sea, and it would be lost. It was natural that Basil should ask Ralph's help in recovering the boat, which he was very willing to give. Neither could foretell that this simple act of friendship would lead to the death of one, and that the other would stand charged with his murder.

Ralph went to fetch two of his workmen. Together with members of Basil's family, they started on the salvage operation.

They had not been working long when Ralph's father, Archibald Hansraj, appeared on the scene. He, too, was on friendly terms with Basil and the Persaud family, but now he was angry. He had expected his son to be out in their own fishing boat, making an early catch. Instead, he was wasting hours at the koker on somebody else's boat.

Father and son started to quarrel. Archibald picked up a bamboo stick and waved it at Ralph as if he were going to strike him. It was then that Basil made his mistake. He took up a stick to defend his friend from his irate father. He aimed a blow at the old man.

Immediately, Ralph switched his allegiance. "You cannot hit my father!" he cried, and, seizing a stick, made a wild swipe at his friend. Basil fell off the dam into the koker and disappeared.

It was a case of simple tragedy, plain as the movements of three pawns on a chessboard. The son goes to help his friend. The father is annoyed with him for neglecting his own work. He makes a move to chastize his son. To stop him, the friend lashes out at the father. The son resents anyone daring to lay a hand on his father, even in his defense. He attacks his friend, who stumbles into the water and is drowned. Anger, frayed nerves, a sudden act, and unpremeditated reactions. Clearly, it was not murder. Nonetheless, murder was the charge when Ralph Hansraj was brought to trial.

Senior Counsel Bhairo Persaud pleaded self-defense on his behalf, claiming that Ralph was acting in defense of his father, with the alternative defense that he had accidentally struck Basil Persaud before he fell into the koker. All the witnesses testified to Ralph having rushed to the help of his father when Basil gave the old man a blow.

State Prosecutor Ragnauth did not press the charge of murder, but demanded a conviction for manslaughter. Life was not cheap, he argued in his final address. The father was in no real danger. The deceased merely struck the father to prevent him from attacking the accused. These circumstances did not warrant the use of a force sufficient to topple the deceased from the brink of the koker into the water below.

Summing up, the judge, Mr. Justice Collins, said that the defense was one of self-defense, the accused contending that it was accident which caused the death of his friend. He directed the jury that, if they did not accept self-defense, then the proper verdict was one of manslaughter.

After being out for more than three hours, the jury returned with the verdict: not guilty of murder, but guilty of manslaughter. Ralph Hansraj was sentenced to four years' imprisonment.

Lionel Luckhoo was back in Guyana in time to be asked to conduct the appeal. The fishermen of Fyrish were united in their belief that Ralph Hansraj had been unjustly convicted. Members of Basil Persaud's own family were among the group which came to retain Lionel's services. One of them remarked, "Sir Lionel, Ralph didn't look for trouble, trouble look for he."

In a statement made from the dock at his trial, Ralph Hansraj had described how, when Basil Persaud struck his father, he went between them and picked up a stick.

"I swung the stick to frighten Basil," said Ralph. "I got a slide on the mud dam and became unbalanced. That is how the stick hit Basil and he fell into the river."

There was confirmatory evidence of there having been a rainfall that morning, which had made the mud dam slippery.

The main ground of appeal advanced by Lionel Luckhoo rested on the failure of the trial judge to put this defense adequately or fully to the jury.

"Implicit in that statement of the accused," he argued, "was that it was no voluntary act of his that caused the death of Basil. If A swings a stick to keep off B, who is attacking, this is not an unlawful act. If A slips on a mud dam, overbalances, and the deceased B is hit accidentally, this is a defense which, if accepted, could exculpate A entirely. For the act was independent of his will, it was not a conscious act, it was not controlled by his mind. And it was not a dangerous act.

"The accused was entitled to have this defense placed before the jury, and not merely the statement of the general principles of self-defense and accident. A defense may have several facets. Counsel may advert to some only, but it is the duty of the trial judge to refer to *all* of them. Unless he did so, he was not placing the defense for the consideration of the jury. A statement of the law, without applying the facts of the case to the law, was useless."

The defense had not been adequately put to the jury, Lionel contended, nor was the jury assisted in the application of the facts to the law. On these grounds, the appeal should not be allowed.

The Court of Appeal, presided over by Chief Justice Bollers, agreed that the defense of accident had not been put to the jury fully, and set aside the conviction.

When Ralph Hansraj walked out of court a free man, the relatives of the *victim* were jubilant—perhaps the most remarkable sight ever to greet a restored prisoner!

During the many months he had spent in jail, Ralph Hansraj had lost twenty pounds in weight. Before they parted on the steps of the court, Lionel Luckhoo asked him, "If your neighbor's boat got into trouble again, would you help him?"

Hansraj did not hesitate. "Of course I would. This could not happen twice. Once in a lifetime is enough."

Chapter 18
The Case of the Blindfolded Witness

Who saw him die?
"I," said the Fly,
"With my little eye,
"I saw him die."
—*Tommy Thumb's Pretty Song Book*

At this late date, the Fly cannot be subjected to cross-examination. A pity! For, conceivably, his testimony might be as shaky as the evidence of so many other eyewitnesses has proved to be. Let us hope he was more reliable than most.

They say that seeing is believing. We like to believe, not only what we ourselves have seen, but what we are assured by others they have seen. Such acceptance is too readily given. After the controversial book, *The Third Eye*, was published, two British national newspapers interviewed its author, the pseudonymous Lobsang Rampa. Their descriptions, run together, pictured him as being tall, short, slim, bald, dark-haired, clean-shaven, with a beard.

Human observation is fallible. Sir Walter Raleigh learned this, when, while a prisoner in the Tower of London, he decided to begin the second volume of his history of the world. He gave it up next day, when he found that he could not accurately describe a fight he had seen in the courtyard beneath his window.

No two witnesses of the same incident see it alike. Nowadays, an almost routine little playlet is performed at advanced police training classes. Two, maybe three, people rush into the room; a few threatening words are exchanged; one of them is shot or knifed. The class is then invited to write accounts of what each has witnessed. It is taken for granted that there will be wild discrepancies in their recollections of what the actors looked like, what they were wearing, what was said and who said it, even which was the murderer and which the victim, and whether a gun or knife was used. And the people taking part in these classes are trained observers of a contrived event, not laymen thrust into the midst of a real-life drama for the first time in their lives.

The great bank robbery that excited Georgetown in 1970 had the elements of a screen thriller. In fact, the plotting of a similar crime had been featured in a sellout film shown at local cinemas not long before, which may have given someone an idea. Five bank employees, who lived through the panic, later appeared in court as witnesses. The bank guard was murdered, so his recollection could never be tested.

Kitty, an attractively named and normally quiet suburb of Georgetown, has, for no known reason, had more than its share of sensational crimes. One murder case began with a body being conveniently left in a parked car almost opposite the police station.* The Kitty branch of the Royal Bank of Canada was robbed by three armed men on October 6. A month later, the police arrested and charged Kirkpaul Sookdeo, Dharampaul Sookai, and Yadunauth with the crime.

The robbery had taken place between 1:00 and 2:00 P.M., when the bank was officially closed for lunch. How did the robbers gain admittance? The murdered guard Percival Pollard must have opened the door to them. And, for him to do this, he must have known the person who sought entry.

The prosecution alleged that this was Kirkpaul Sookdeo. Some time before, either by chance or intention, Sookdeo had become acquainted with Winston Ramessar, who was employed by the Royal Bank as messenger. They met at a wedding, became friendly, and Sookdeo would often call at the bank to borrow Ramessar's motorcycle. These visits usually took place during the lunchtime closure. Pollard came to know Sookdeo, and would let him in. All of this was attested

* *See Chapter 28, "The Case of the Vicarious Victor."*

to by Winston Ramessar when he took the witness stand. On the day of the robbery, Ramessar was not at the bank.

Another suspicious circumstance was that, since the date of the robbery, Kirkpaul Sookdeo had been spending money freely. He no longer had to borrow a motorcycle; he had bought one of his own. No longer was he badly dressed, as he had been; now he wore fancy clothes. A girlfriend, Lynette Mangal, gave evidence that he had given her money to keep for him.

Yadunauth and Sookai had made confessions after their arrest. Sookai introduced the only element of humor that entered into the case, while explaining how he had buried $5,000, his share of the proceeds. "You would never believe it," he waxed indignant to the police, "but someone went and stole $1,000 from it."

When Kirkpaul Sookdeo was arrested, he said nothing. To convict him, the police would have to depend solely on the identification of eyewitnesses.

Wilfred Carr was the branch manager. Before he went to lunch that day, all the money was locked up in the safe, as was customary. It amounted to $24,000 in cash, plus some foreign currency, travelers' checks, and securities.

Carr returned about 1:25 P.M. He heard the sound of a radio from inside the bank as he approached the door. This annoyed him, as the employees had no right to play it so loudly. The door was opened to him by a stranger holding a knife. "Get inside!" he ordered. Carr identified Yadunauth as the man at the door.

Inside the bank, he saw the guard Pollard lying on the floor, face downwards, his head covered with a bag. Two other bank employees, Krischenchand Persaud and Andrew Persaud (not related), were tied up and being guarded by two East Indian men armed with batons. Carr was unable to identify either.

One of the robbers demanded that he open the safe. Carr said, "I'm afraid I don't know how."

The man said, "Quit stalling and open it."

Wilfred Carr asked Andrew Persaud to give him the combination. Persaud called out a series of numbers. Carr purposely dialed them wrongly, so that the safe would not open.

At that, the robber became impatient, and threatened, "If you don't give us the right combination we'll do you in!"

Persaud repeated the numbers. He was then made to assist Carr in opening, first the outer, and then the inner, safes.

When Krischenchand Persaud and Andrew Persaud gave evidence, they admitted they could not identify any of the three accused.

Neither could Clara Cumberbatch, who said she had arrived at the bank, knocked at the door, and was let in by a man holding a long knife. He had pointed the knife at her and said, "We come to rob this bank, and if you don't cooperate we will kill you." She had almost collapsed. Her hands had been tied behind her back and elastoplast stuck across her mouth.

The case against Kirkpaul Sookdeo had not been advanced a step further by the evidence of these witnesses, though all four had been given ample time to memorize the features of the men who made them prisoners. The star witness for the prosecution, on whose word Sookdeo's fate was to depend, was a bank employee who, during most of the time she spent in the robbers' presence, had been blindfolded.

Gail da Silva had not left the bank that day. She ate her lunch on the premises. "It was about 1:20 P.M.," she testified. "I had just finished my lunch when Kirkpaul Sookdeo entered my room. I did not know him before. He had an open knife in his hand. He said, 'Go to the manager's room.' I was afraid, so I obeyed him. We went to the manager's room. There I saw Sookai with Pollard the bank guard. Pollard was shouting murder, and Kirkpaul Sookdeo went and overpowered him. Pollard was small of stature, about five feet, two inches. Sookdeo was almost six feet. When Sookdeo had overpowered him, he tied Pollard's feet and hands behind his back, and passed the cord around his neck so that when he kicked, the cord became tighter. In his struggle to get free, Pollard strangled himself.

"Sookdeo still had the knife. He turned to me and said, 'Lie down.' He tied my hands and feet, and then he put elastoplast over my mouth and eyes. I did not see anything after that."

State Prosecutor Kennard (now a judge of the High Court)

asked her, "Mrs. da Silva, are you sure you recognize Kirkpaul Sookdeo?"

"Yes," she answered. "I also recognize Sookai."

While the sensational trial, that had crowds flocking to the Supreme Court every day, was taking place, Lionel Luckhoo was still in London. The defense was led by J.O.F. Haynes (now Chancellor of the Judiciary). In cross-examining Gail da Silva, he concentrated on her identification of Sookdeo.

"Mrs. da Silva, after you saw this man as you allege on October 6, when next did you see him?"

"I saw him at an identification parade on November 5."

"You gave evidence in the magistrate's court?"

"Yes."

"Did you then say that, when you went to the identification parade, you identified no one?"

"Yes, I did say that."

"Sookdeo was in the parade?"

"Yes."

"Yet you did not pick him out then."

"That is correct."

"Could you explain why you did not pick him out?"

"Well, after the parade I spent about ten minutes thinking about it, and it came back to me that this was the man I saw at the bank."

"It came to you in a flash, Mrs. da Silva?"

"Yes."

"Mrs. da Silva, you knew you were going to identify a person whom you had seen that day, and who was responsible for the death of Pollard, and who robbed the bank?"

"Yes."

"So you were identifying the occasion with the person in the identification parade?"

"Yes."

"Then how come you did not identify the person at once, if you knew him?"

"Well, I was afraid, and I was not sure."

"That's two things you have said. You were afraid, and you were not sure?"

"I was afraid, and I was not then sure."

"What did you do after ten minutes?"

"After ten minutes I went and spoke to Inspector Lall."

"After you spoke to Inspector Lall, were you sure that it was Kirkpaul Sookdeo, the Number One accused, whom you saw that day at the bank?"

"Yes, I was sure."

"What did Inspector Lall do to make you feel so sure?"

"He did nothing."

"Yet after you spoke to him you were sure?"

"Yes."

"And before you spoke to him you were not sure?"

"That is correct."

"Mrs. da Silva, I put it to you that you were influenced by the Inspector towards the recognition of this man?"

"No, that is not true."

Haynes was tireless in his cross-examination. Gail da Silva was on the witness stand for two full days. To the end, she maintained that she could identify both Sookdeo and Sookai.

Judge Akbar Khan summed up strongly against the accused. He more than once told the jury that they could accept Gail da Silva's evidence, and that her evidence had established the identification of Kirkpaul Sookdeo. Although Sookai and Yadunauth went back on their confessions, there were too many police witnesses against them for the denials to carry much weight. The jury returned verdicts of murder against all three prisoners.

It was inevitable that Kirkpaul Sookdeo would appeal; almost as inevitable that Lionel Luckhoo, newly arrived from London, should be briefed to appear for him. For three days, Lionel addressed an appeal court, comprising Sir Kenneth Stoby, Sir Harold Bollers, and the Hon. Victor Crane, on the question of identification.

There were five surviving witnesses to the crime, he said. Three had failed to identify any one of the accused. The manager, Wilfred Carr, had identified Yadunauth as the man who let him into the bank. Gail da Silva had identified Sookai. Then, after failing to identify Kirkpaul Sookdeo at the parade held for that purpose, she had afterwards become convinced that she recognized him.

Yet Gail da Silva had had less opportunity than any other of the witnesses to observe the robbers carefully. Within a short time of their unexpected intrusion, she had been blindfolded. The others were free to take a good look at their captors, but not one of them could support Gail da Silva in her identification.

"This court is not concerned with whether the accused is guilty or not," Lionel told the judges. "This court is concerned with whether there is sufficient evidence to warrant the verdict of guilty. That verdict was based on Gail da Silva's evidence. She failed to identify the accused when she saw him, but later went back and claimed it was he. Her identification is not strong enough to swing a cat, much less hang a man.

"I feel that many innocent persons have been wrongly convicted because of one-witness identifications of persons whom they never knew before. One day, we will have this kind of identification placed in the category of requiring corroboration, or the jury being warned that it would be dangerous to convict on such evidence without corroboration.

"No garnishing by the judge of Gail da Silva's evidence can rehabilitate the poverty of her identification. I am confident that the highest court in our land will not permit this conviction to stand."

His confidence was justified. The appeal succeeded, and Kirkpaul Sookdeo was set free.

2

Witnesses may weave a circumstantial web of evidence against an accused from which, it seems, there can be no escape. In Lionel's Luckhoo's last case of 1977, his two-hundred-sixth murder defense, the client was entangled in such a web. He shattered it by daring to ask just one win-or-lose question.

Lloyd Bunbury and Barbara Gordon were lovers. They did not live together, but slept with each other when they could, often at the home of Lloyd's sister Claudette. Her house, like so many in Guyana, was built high on stilts as a protection against floods, which are an endemic problem.

On January 22, 1977, a young girl, Roxanne Williams, was playing under Claudette's house, when she saw drops of liquid dripping through the floor above her. Roxanne caught a drop on her finger, and saw it was blood. She ran from under the house, towards the front steps. Coming down the stairway was Lloyd Bunbury. He passed her quickly, without speaking.

Roxanne hurried up the steps and through the front door, into the house. She found Barbara Gordon lying on the floor, in a state of collapse. Blood was pouring from a deep, punctured wound in her upper thigh. Roxanne went for help. Barbara was taken to the hospital, but died of shock and hemorrhage soon after arrival.

The first person the police looked for to interview, not surprisingly, was Lloyd Bunbury. Before they could find him, his relatives had already called on Lionel Luckhoo and asked to retain his services. He advised that Bunbury should give himself up to the police, but should make no statement. He did this, and was at once charged with the murder of Barbara Gordon.

When the case came to court, there was a general assumption that, when Roxanne Williams saw Bunbury, he was leaving the scene of a crime he had just committed. Lionel cross-examined, and the girl agreed that she could not see the front steps from where she was playing, nor had she seen Bunbury enter the yard. The first time she saw him was when he was coming down the stairway. She had found the front door closed, but not locked.

"Was there anyone else in the house?"

"I don't know."

"Did you go into the bedrooms or the kitchen?"

"No."

"So there could have been other people you did not see?"

"Yes."

To sound the alarm, Roxanne had run out of the house and across the street, leaving the door open. Anyone who was inside the house could have left after her. Such a possibility was not much help to the defense. Roxanne's cries had aroused the neighborhood, and anyone leaving the house after she did was not likely to have escaped detection.

Claudette Bunbury gave evidence that, on hearing Roxanne calling for help, she ran back to her house. She found Barbara Gordon lying bleeding on the floor. She had tried to get her to speak, but she was unconscious. Claudette had seen no sign of any weapon.

"From what you saw, the blood and Barbara's state of collapse, did it strike you that this had happened some time before?"

"Yes, that is how it struck me."

A lay opinion on such questions did not have much value.

There was testimony that the course of love, true or otherwise, between Lloyd Bunbury and Barbara Gordon had not been running altogether smoothly. The evening before she died, Michael Allen was out walking with Barbara, when they met Lloyd Bunbury. He was with a girl and, Michael Allen said in evidence, they were walking very closely together. Bunbury became angry when he saw Allen with Barbara, and threatened him.

Lionel Luckhoo asked, "Did the accused speak to Barbara?"

"No, he spoke only to me," Michael replied.

"Did he say why he was threatening you?"

"No."

"He made no reference to Barbara Gordon?"

"No."

"Did you see a policeman walking quite nearby?"

"Yes, I saw P.C. Rolston."

"Did you report to P.C. Rolston that this man was threatening you?"

"No, I never reported to him."

"If you felt that the threat were a serious one, would you not have reported it?"

"I might have reported it."

"You regarded what the accused said as just a form of vulgar expression?"

"Yes."

"Did Barbara Gordon say anything?"

"No."

"You knew that Barbara and the accused were not living together permanently?"

"Yes."

"And he had other girlfriends?"

"Yes."

"And she had other boyfriends?"

"Yes."

"And, indeed, you saw him walking out with one of his other girls?"

"Yes."

Then came the last witness for the prosecution. Yvette Hinds was a neighbor of Claudette Bunbury. She told how Lloyd Bunbury had come to her and said, "Go and see what happened to Barbara." She went over to Claudette's house, and saw Barbara lying there as if she were dead.

Ordinarily, there would be no point in questioning such a witness at length. The most the defense could expect from her would be a description of Lloyd Bunbury's demeanor after the event.

"When the accused asked you to go and see what had happened to Barbara, he spoke as one who was deeply concerned?"

The witness agreed. Normal sound practice would have been to leave it at that, but Lionel did not do so. This was one of the times when some sixth sense, that has stood him in useful stead in cross-examination, gave him the feeling that something might be gained by probing further.

"Where were you when Lloyd Bunbury came and spoke to you?"

"I was sitting at my window, looking out."

"Does your window face Claudette Bunbury's house?"

"Yes. It is directly across the street."

"You were at your front window?"

"Yes."

From his own visit to the scene, Lionel knew what the answers must be to his next two questions.

"You could see the front stairway leading to Claudette's house from that window?"

"Yes."

"There are no trees in between?"

"Did you see the accused come directly from Claudette's home to where you were sitting by your window?"

"Yes, he came directly over, crossing the roadway to my home."

Lionel had the impulse to press on, over more dangerous ground. He looked at Yvette Hinds with a steady gaze.

"Had you seen the accused go into Claudette's yard?"

"Yes, I saw him walk into Claudette's yard."

"And did he walk up the stairway?"

"Yes, I saw him walk up the stairway."

The next was the vital question. The wrong answer could convict his client.

"But he did not enter the house?"

The witness paused a second that seemed to stretch to an hour, while the court waited in silence.

"That is true. He did not enter the house."

The hundred-to-one chance had paid off!

"Is there a glass window to the house by the top of the stairway?" Lionel knew there was.

"Yes."

"And did Lloyd Bunbury lean over to look through the glass window?"

Yvette Hinds thought for another long second. "That is correct. He did look through the window."

"And thereupon hurried down the stairs and came over to you?"

"Yes."

"How long had you been sitting at your window before you saw the accused?"

"Well, at least half an hour."

"If he had entered the house through the front door during that period, you would have seen him?"

"Yes, had he entered I would have seen him."

"If he had come from the house by the front door to go down the stairs, you also would have seen him?"

"That is so."

"So I would be right in saying that you saw Lloyd Bunbury enter the yard, he walked up the stairway, peeped through the window, then walked down the stairway, came directly to you, and said, 'Go and see what happened to Barbara'?"

"Yes."

"From your front window, you would not be able to see the back stairway of Claudette's home?"

"No, I could not see the back stairway."

"But there is a back door which could give entrance or exit to anyone?"

"That is so."

"And a person could have gone through the back of the yard, gone up the back stairway, attacked Barbara Gordon, and could have left by the same back stairway, and not been seen by you?"

"Yes, I agree with that."

As a result of his cross-examination of Yvette Hinds, defense counsel was able to argue that no case had been made against Lloyd Bunbury that warranted his being committed for trial before a higher court.

Without Hinds' evidence, Lionel said, it might be suggested that, when Roxanne Williams saw the accused coming from the house, he had just committed the assault on Barbara that led to her death. But what Roxanne saw was the final movement of the sequence, as described by Yvette Hinds. Her evidence was that Lloyd Bunbury had not entered the house. Looking through the window and seeing the girl lying on the floor, he had rushed to alert the nearest neighbor, Hinds. This conduct was consistent with that of a person suddenly and unexpectedly coming across a body on the floor.

Circumstantial evidence, Lionel Luckhoo urged, should point unequivocally to the guilt of the accused, and be inconsistent with any other reasonable explanation. In this instance, the evidence failed to establish a *prima facie* case.

The magistrate, Mr. O.A.M. Small, agreed with the submission, and Lloyd Bunbury was discharged. It was a popular verdict. A crowd of neighbors, present in court, cheered it loudly.

Chapter 19
The Case of the Political Cow

Hey diddle diddle,
The cat and the fiddle,
The cow jumped over the moon;
The little dog laughed . . .
—Mother Goose's Melody

In our story, the cow jumped only ten feet. But so much "moonshine"—$25,000 worth—was written about the alleged phenomenon that any little dogs who happened to be around could hardly be blamed for laughing. It was enough to make a cat laugh as well, if that sensible animal were not busy on the fiddle.

The pejorative piece below appeared in the *Mirror* of Guyana, under a banner headline:

PM'S COW ELECTROCUTED

A hefty 300 lb. zebu cow was electrocuted when she stepped on the live electric wire surrounding the spacious farm of the Prime Minister aback of the Botanical Gardens on Sunday evening.

*The animal has been identified as belonging to the PM. On instructions it was sent to the zoo where the lions and tigers were to have it for their evening meal. So far there are conflicting reports as to what exactly happened to the carcass, though it is widely rumoured that the meat was carted by a few persons connected with Congress Place.**

* *Headquarters of the People's National Congress, Prime Minister Forbes Burnham's political party.*

> *The live electric wire, it is reported, has been installed with the purpose of warding off prowlers and thieves from entering the PM's private farm. Now that crops of eschalot and tomatoes are near their harvesting period it is understood that the current has been put on in full blast.*
>
> *The unfortunate cow, only one in a large herd of cattle reared on the farm, came near the fence to graze but was thrown some ten feet in the air when it came in contact with the wire.*

A story sizzling with innuendo! Whether innocent or malicious is for the courts to decide, but all kinds of implications might be read, and the Prime Minister—or, at any rate, his legal advisers—read plenty. They did not regard the *Mirror* as a newspaper with an attitude towards the Prime Minister of disinterest except for his news value. The *Mirror* supported Forbes Burnham's main opposition, the People's Progressive Party, led by Dr. Cheddi Jagan. Indeed, the editor was his wife, Mrs. Janet Jagan, herself a political activist.

The Prime Minister's lawyers understood the story to say, among other things, that the Prime Minister was responsible for installing live electric wires, constituting a trap set in a place to which the public had access, namely, the Botanical Gardens—an act calculated to endanger the lives of innocent subjects of the State, as it provided for sufficient electric power to throw aloft a three-hundred-pound cow and kill it; that, by the said act, which constituted a criminal offense, as well as being shameful and inhuman, the plaintiff was prepared to jeopardize the lives of man and beast, to the selfish purpose of merely protecting his kitchen garden; that it showed his unfitness to be Prime Minister, or to hold any office involving responsibility and concern for the welfare of the people of Guyana, and his unfitness to be a Senior Counsel and Barrister-at-Law, through which offices he should have been acquainted with the law and should have realized the impropriety of his infamous and disreputable conduct.

Their statement of claim ended with a flourish: "In the result the plaintiff was brought into public odium, contempt and ridicule, and was otherwise damnified." Damages of $25,000 and costs were sought.

A defense was entered, admitting publication of the article, but claiming that it was published without malice or gross negligence. A full apology had been printed and $1,500 paid into court by way of amends. Allegations of injury to reputation were denied.

This was how matters stood when the opposing forces lined up in court before Judge Dhan Jhappan. Lionel Luckhoo and J.T. Clarke represented Prime Minister Forbes Burnham; Dr. Fenton Ramsahoye, a former Attorney General during Dr. Jagan's term as Premier, appeared for the defendants Janet Jagan and the New Guyana Co. Ltd.

The main witness was the subeditor, who had authorized publication of the story. He stated that part of his duty was to check for libel. "When I check for libel, I look for anything that is in a bad light for any person's character." If he had any doubt, he referred the copy to the editor, and "in things like libel, the editor consults the lawyers." This particular item was not shown to the editor "because I felt, to my mind, that the Prime Minister was not in any way connected with the matter. I thought that the cow was his cow and the farm belonged to him. I thought the electrifying of the fence was done by a workman, and that the Prime Minister was not personally involved, as he was too much of a busy person."

The subeditor rejoiced in the name of Mohamed Ali. Subjected to what the judge later described as a brilliant cross-examination by Lionel Luckhoo, he displayed none of the skills in attack or defense associated with his famous namesake. On the contrary, Mr. Ali's admissions revealed a quite startling naivete.

The cow? "I did not check to verify if it was the Prime Minister's cow which was electrocuted. I have not since checked."

The "spacious farm" of the Prime Minister? "I did not check this, nor have I checked since."

He believed what was published. "Until this moment, I believed what the reporter wrote was true as regards the whole article, but at no time at all did I think that the Prime Minister was involved."

He believed that some workman had done the electrification without the Prime Minister's knowledge. He thought another farm worker had put the current on at full blast. "I cannot explain why I thought so."

He realized it was a serious matter, involving the lives of men. He thought the workers would have been in danger. "I did not think that people reading the newspaper would have thought that the Prime Minister was involved."

But "it did strike me that the Prime Minister must have known about the cow. Knowing this, then, the Prime Minister must have known that his farm fence was electrified."

Mr. Ali was sorry, and he was not sorry, or, perhaps, the other way around. "At this stage, I am not sorry for the publication, because it never struck me that the Prime Minister was in any way connected with the electrocution of the cow, but my lawyers told me that the matter might be libelous. I am prepared to be guided by them. I now say I am sorry for the publication."

And then, under cross-examination, came the fatal admission: "I now say that the publication is fictional."

A partial explanation of his somewhat singular outlook could be found, perhaps, in Mr. Ali's statements: "I do not think anyone who cares for his tomatoes more than for human lives should be put out of office as Prime Minister. I would associate with a man who cares more for tomatoes than for the lives of people." If fruits and vegetables had a vote, surely Mr. Ali himself would be a candidate for Prime Minister!

In his address for the defense, Dr. Ramsahoye contended, "At its highest, this libel has to be that the Prime Minister went further than was proper in dealing with persons stealing his property. It is not accurate to put it that the Prime Minister was callous as to the safety of man and beast. The highest that that can be put is that he was callous in dealing with thieves. To bolster his reputation, Mr. Luckhoo must suppress some little part, or add what is not true. The Court has to see what the words, in their ordinary sense, must have meant. The article says the Prime Minister has his farm, people go there to steal, and the fence has been electrified.

"Whilst, for the purposes of this matter, it is assumed that the Prime Minister was in some way personally concerned with the electrification, it is clear that some reasonable people would not necessarily have drawn that inference upon reading the article.

"The allegation that the fence was electrified does not make it a public nuisance, and a criminal offense at Common Law would be committed, not by the presence of the electrified wire, but by the electrified wire doing something to someone.

"The next point to consider in relation to the gravity of the publication is how ordinary people will react, as they think of a man in Guyana who takes an extreme measure against thieves, who never sow, but who, after the farmer has sown, appear ready to reap. The Court, sitting as a jury, puts itself in the category of ordinary people. In the climate of opinion in this country, the ordinary man would have no sympathy with a thief."

Dr. Ramsahoye submitted that whatever errors were made were not made maliciously, in the sense of a calculated attempt to impugn the character of the Prime Minister. Carelessness, by itself, was not malice. Unreasonable belief was not malice. Gross negligence was negligence to a degree that bordered on recklessness. A man was reckless when he did not care what he was doing. A man was never reckless if he applied himself to what he was doing and made a mistake.

For the plaintiff, Lionel Luckhoo refuted the idea that it was a question of a man seeking to protect his land from thieves. It was a complete fabrication against the Prime Minister. To have attacked him publicly would not have been as effectual as to attack him in this calculated, fictional way. The allegation was that the Prime Minister thought so little of the people of his State as living creatures, or of animals such as his own cow, that he was responsible for turning on so much power that the electricity killed a cow grazing nearby.

"Where the venom seeps hard on libel cases, no amount of apology can properly compensate," claimed Lionel Luckhoo. The defendant's case had aggravated the damage. The witness called had negated the very respect which the defense sought to establish.

"Ali has shown that he was guilty of the gravest negligence possible for any editor. His failure to inquire shows malice. Contrition does not come from the mouth of Counsel; contrition must be shown by the words and actions of those who should be contrite. The demeanor of the witness shows no contrition. Up to today, he has made no inquiry as to whether the publication is true or not.

"If the defendants made no inquiries from the time of publication on February 8 up to June 5, then they must have known at the time of publication that what they were publishing was wholly without foundation, false, and fictitious. They must have known that an inquiry was incapable of revealing any extenuating circumstances or explanation. The apology contains a word that is highly relevant, pregnant with meaning, and gives rise to a number of consequential deductions: '*Now* the *Mirror* is fully satisfied. . . .' This means that the witness had, in fact, made inquiries and full investigations. The denial of Mr. Ali in respect of any inquiry can only mean that the inquiry discloses something which the defendants wish to hide from the Court. If the apology was inserted merely for the purpose of reducing damages, then that is a falsehood."

When Judge Jhappan gave his decision, he endorsed all the innuendos set out by the plaintiff, awarding $25,000 damages and costs. The case then went to the Appeal Court.

The Chief Justice, Sir Harold Bollers, was scathing in his dismissal of the appeal. Mr. Ali's excuse that he did not refer the news item to the editor, because he felt that the Prime Minister was not connected in any way with the matter, was "as lame as it was audacious." His explanation that he believed the electrification of the wire had been done, and the current put on at full blast, by a farm worker, was incredible, "and would not have fooled a ten-year-old child." His statement, that he did not think that people reading the newspaper would have thought that the Prime Minister was involved, could not bear scrutiny.

". . . in my opinion, all this evidence by him that I have set out was strong evidence of the actual malice that existed in his mind and that of the appellants (who must bear the responsibility), at the time of the publication, rather than any proof of the absence of malice. It appears to me that the evidence of this witness did the appellants' case more harm than good.

". . . in the apology which appears in the amended defense, the appellants had stated that 'the *Mirror* is now fully satisfied that the said statements were wholly unfounded, and desires to express its regret to the Prime Minister.' Yet at the trial, the subeditor, in his evidence, stated that no inquiries up to the present date had ever been made, and he believed the publication to be true. It seems to me to be pellucidly clear that the apology was saying that inquiries had been made, and as a result the appellants were satisfied that the statements in the offending publication were without foundation; yet here was the subeditor stating on oath that no inquiries had been made and he believed the publication to be true. . . . It could not be seriously contended that there were reasonable grounds for believing the publication to be true, when no inquiries whatever as to its veracity had been made by anyone."

The Chief Justice noted that the appellants had not produced as a witness the reporter who, it was alleged, gave the information to the subeditor, nor had they disclosed to the court even his name.

"On a survey of the evidence of the subeditor, which consisted of a series of contradictions, inconsistencies, and incredible statements, the inevitable conclusion must be that the appellants knew that the news item was false at the time of publication, or at least that they had no genuine belief in its truth when they made it, which would be conclusive evidence of malice.

"Was the apology full? In order to be full, the apology need not be an abject one, but it does at least require a complete withdrawal of the imputation, and an expression of regret for having made it. The apology does express regret, and apologizes for any embarrassment suffered by the respondent and any inconvenience which may have been caused to him; but it does not demonstrate a complete withdrawal of the imputation which the offending publication sought to disseminate, as it omits its last paragraph, which is perhaps the most damaging statement of all, and that is that the unfortunate cow, which was only one in a large herd, came near the fence to graze but was thrown some ten feet in the air when it came in contact with the wire. Implicit in that statement is the further suggestion that other cows in the herd might suffer a similar fate if any of them happened to come in contact with the wire.

"The offending publication appeared on the front page of the newspaper, for which a banner head was reserved. In bold type, it read, 'PM'S COW ELECTROCUTED'; but, in contrast, the apology appeared on the back page under the heading 'Apology.' It is at once noticeable that, while the abbreviation 'PM' on the front page might at once attract the attention of the reasonable reader, it cannot be said with equal conviction that the word 'Apology' at the back page would attract the notice of such a reader, as he might see the caption but not bother to ascertain to whom the apology is being made. . . . For these reasons, then, the apology could not be said to be a full apology.

"Furthermore, the respondent, by effective cross-examination through his counsel of the subeditor, and the introduction of other issues of the same newspaper, was able to show the existence of strong and positive evidence of actual malice and gross negligence. I hold that the learned judge was right when he found that the appellants had failed to prove that the libel was inserted without malice and without gross negligence, and that the apology was not a full and frank apology."

The other judges, Chancellor E.V. Luckhoo and Justice V.E. Crane, gave separate judgments. The court was unanimous in dismissing the appeal with costs, and refused to reduce the award for damages.

Although the court admissions make it difficult not to deduce otherwise, the *Mirror* did not give birth to a work of unalloyed fiction. The unfortunate cow was real; it was found dead, showing no signs of violence, not far from the Botanical Gardens. The lions and tigers were real; and they did have the cow for their supper. The Prime Minister was, and is, real; and he did have wiring around his fences, with strong lights, to discourage thieves. But *the wires were not electrified.*

The root of the trouble was that it was a running issue which of Burnham or Jagan, both being Socialists, had the more genuine concern for the people. Jagan's standpoint, naturally, was that no one cared more than he did, and he cared much more than did Burnham. So, when a newspaper allied to Jagan's cause imputed conduct to Burnham that indicated an indifference to the safety of people and animals—well, that was $25,000 worth of libel.

We do not know on what basis Judge Jhappan assessed damages, the highest award ever made up to that time in a libel suit. But the circulation of the *Mirror* was 6,500, so —allowing four readers to a copy, which is not unreasonable—it worked out at just about a dollar a head.

A new record was set in libel damages when Lionel Luckhoo appeared once more for Prime Minister Forbes Burnham—again, in a suit brought against a newspaper. This time, it was the Guyana *Graphic* that had published the alleged libel, in a column written by Archibald Codrington.

Codrington had stated that the Prime Minister, who, not long before, had made an appeal for austerity, was receiving $1,000 a month as a housing allowance. Forbes Burnham asked him to make a correction. Codrington agreed. Later, when the correction did not appear, the Prime Minister asked why, and was told by Codrington that he was relying on the *Official Gazette*, which showed that the Prime Minister had been receiving the $1,000 a month. He then published a letter which questioned, "Did the *Official Gazette* err?"

The *Gazette* entry referred to an Act that had been amended.

The *Graphic* did not contest the subsequent legal action, but Codrington did, with a plea of fair comment. In cross-examination, Lionel Luckhoo was able to get him to adopt the stand that he had not apologized because he still believed that the Prime Minister was drawing $1,000 a month, in addition to living rent-free in a government house. Forbes Burnham, who had often watched Lionel in court, remarked that he had never heard him to better effect.

The effectiveness rated an award of $40,000 damages with costs. Judge Massiah said that the answers to Counsel, and Codrington's refusal to correct the publication, made him conclude that it was actuated by malice. The plaintiff had sought peace. Twice he had sought for a correction, and twice his olive branch was refused. The defendant wanted war, and had continued in his callous course of disregard. Codrington relied on the defense of fair comment, said the judge; but there were no comments—only statements of alleged facts which were damaging and defamatory.

2

Cows in Guyana, if not high flyers when left alone, do seem to be capable of inspiring politicians, journalists, even petty larcenists, to flights of fancy. A man charged with stealing a cow came to Lionel Luckhoo, protesting his innocence. Lionel asked him what had happened.

"Well," said the accused, "I went to the backdam, I cut my grass, looked after my plants. I have a long rope I always take with me. I was going home, dragging the rope along, it is quite a long rope, and—you would not believe it, sir—I found the cow tied to the end of the rope when I got home."

Chapter 20
The Case of the Disappearing Double

Double, double, toil and trouble!
—Macbeth

You can double your trouble by having a double. And the toil it gets you might be hard labor.

All of us at some time or other have hailed a stranger because of the close resemblance he bore to a friend, or have been greeted by someone who mistakenly thought he knew us. Such mistakes are common. The Duke of Wellington was once approached in the street by a man who addressed him as Mr. Smith. "Sir," said the outraged Duke, "if you believe that, you'll believe anything." But the rest of us cannot take such pride in our singularity as befitted the victor of Waterloo.

When the great American wit (and con man) Wilson Mizner founded the Millionaires' Club in New York, one of its "fixtures" was a three-hundred-pound man who was a near-double of former President William Howard Taft. Mizner had installed him there, with a newspaper and a highball, as sucker bait. The deception ended when "Taft," one night, stuck a knife into a waiter for bringing him watered whiskey.

The most oft-quoted case of double trouble to occur in this century is that of Adolph Beck, twice convicted at the Old Bailey for frauds on women. Beck served a total of seven years' penal servitude before his innocence was proved. He then received *two* King's Pardons (meaning "we were wrong, but we forgive you"), and £5,000 compensation.

The case of Clifford Shepherd in the United States involved double doubles. Both he and his landlady were arrested in lieu of a couple who had been passing forged checks in the neighborhood. Ten local merchants appeared as witnesses against them, and they were each sentenced to nine months. On the day of their release, they were arrested again on similar charges, another group of merchants testified, and they were again sentenced. Shortly after Shepherd came out of prison, it happened again—but this time his alibis were believed. He had been in prison on the dates the merchants thought they had seen him in their shops.

A sympathetic member of the third grand jury hired the Burns Detective Agency to look into Shepherd's case. His double was identified as Edward Sullivan, known as the Phantom Forger. Later, Sullivan and his wife were arrested and convicted of other forgeries. When appealed to, Sullivan confessed to the crimes for which Shepherd had already served sentences. But Shepherd, his life ruined by the jailbird tag tied on him, had to fight eleven more years before he got a full pardon.

When Nurse Reece appeared before the Recorder of Cardiff, Mr. B.F.Williams, there were no fewer than twenty witnesses lined up against her. Each testified that she had fraudulently obtained money from them by claiming she was collecting for hospital funds. She escaped conviction because warders and wardresses from Gloucester Prison were able to swear that, at the time of the frauds, she was in that prison awaiting trial on similar charges. At Gloucester, there had been another twenty or more witnesses willing to swear to her identity. And she had escaped conviction there because, at the time of those offenses, she was in Staffordshire Gaol, awaiting trial on yet another series of charges.

There are plenty of other instances where justice has miscarried, and life and liberty have been placed in jeopardy, merely because guilt and innocence wore the same features. Years ago—in 1950, to be exact—Lionel Luckhoo was defending a Chinese man, named John Ying, who was charged with receiving stolen paint. Ying strongly protested his innocence, but there was nothing to weaken the evidence against him . . . until Lionel noticed that the accused and his brother Thomas, though they were not twins, bore a close resemblance to each other. It enabled him to pull off one of the cleverest tricks he has ever managed in court.

He waited until the main witness had testified to selling the accused a tremendous quantity of paint for a ridiculously small sum, then asked that the witness should stand out of court while he made an application to the judge.

"Your honor," he addressed the Bench, "I would like to make an unusual application. Here is the brother of the accused. Will you permit him to go into the dock in place of his brother, so we may see whether the witness can identify him as not being the person to whom he handed the paint?"

Mr. Justice Hughes said, "I'm afraid I cannot do that."

"Then would you allow the accused to come out of the dock, and let his brother be called, so they can stand up, side by side?"

To this the judge consented.

The brothers looked alike. They were dressed alike. The one visible difference between the two of them was that the one who stepped down from the dock did not wear glasses, while his brother did. Lionel told him to take off the glasses, then stood them together near the dock, where the jury could see them.

The witness was recalled. Lionel said, "Now, which of these men bought the paint?"

The witness must have thought he was seeing double. He said, uncertainly, "You've got two of them there now."

"Of course I have. But to which of the two did you sell the paint?"

The witness hesitated, made a wild guess, and guessed wrong. The case was won.

John Ying and his counsel were fortunate that a double was at hand who could be brought forward. When Lloyd Harris was arrested on charges of murder and rape, the double who should have taken his place in the dock had disappeared.

2

You won't find the name on any signposts, but every town has its Lovers' Lane, where young couples seek seclusion and

—the lucky ones—find tender romance (or did, in Grandmother's day). Nowadays, in most places, the hopeful lovers are likely to be outnumbered by muggers and rapists.

Georgetown, even today, lags behind many capitals of the western hemisphere in progression towards violence. So when Kenrick Ashe, a twenty-two-year-old soldier and gymnast, walked down Woolford Avenue with his girlfriend Merle, they had no reason to fear that they were being followed.

Woolford Avenue is Georgetown's Lovers' Lane. It is lonely at night. The strolling young couple came to an open area, Sproston's Sports Ground. There they lay down on the grass. A minute later, the romantic setting they had chosen became a scene of nightmare and brutality.

Only Merle lived to tell the story. Men who must have trailed them down the lane came up from behind and attacked them. Kenrick Ashe was overpowered. Merle was held, and a scarf tied around her eyes. She was four times raped by three assailants. After what seemed an endless time, the men left. Merle tore the scarf from her eyes, and saw Kenrick Ashe lying nearby. He was bound, and he was dead.

Merle ran to the headquarters of the Guyana Defense Force, of which Ashe was a member. Hundreds of police and military joined in the manhunt for the murderers and rapists. Kenrick Ashe, too, had been sexually assaulted before being strangled to death. The criminals were not found.

A month later, Merle was walking down the street when a man on a bicycle went past her, then looked back. Merle kept on walking. Still looking back at her, the man turned into a yard. Merle sought a policeman. She took him to the yard where the cyclist had dismounted, pointed to him, and said, "He is one of the men who raped me."

The man was Lloyd Harris. He was arrested, and charged with the murder of Kenrick Ashe.

Lloyd Harris was a stranger to town life. Physically, he was impressive. He stood six feet, two inches, and was powerfully built. But he was a country boy, the typical bumpkin, who had wandered into Georgetown from the west coast of Berbice, and had no permanent place of abode. He worked with a man named Naipaul, and usually slept in Naipaul's lorry.

Like any good lawyer, Lionel Luckhoo never concerns himself with the guilt or innocence of a client. After a case is over, he may form his own view. While it is continuing, he simply assumes that his client is innocent, and, in his own words, "fights to prove it!" In the case of Lloyd Harris, however, he could not escape the feeling, almost from the start, that Harris was a victim of mistaken identification.

There was one other witness, apart from Merle, who placed Harris near the scene of the crime soon after it was committed. Leslie Babb was the caretaker of a clubhouse, and at five o'clock that morning, he had found a naked man sleeping on the premises. He did not call the police. At the trial, he identified the man as Lloyd Harris.

When Lionel cross-examined, Babb admitted that he had never seen the man before that night. The clubhouse was no more than 600 yards from the scene of the murder. Babb heard the hue and cry. He saw the police conducting a search. Yet he never reported the presence of the strange, naked man on his own premises. When Babb could offer no explanation for his silence, Lionel suggested he was trying to shield someone.

Merle told her story before a crowded court. She claimed that Lloyd Harris twice had intercourse with her, each time over a period of about half an hour. Her eyes were covered with a scarf, and she only heard his voice for most of the time. But, during the second rape, the scarf slipped from her eyes. She then saw his face by the aid of a bright light on a nearby lamppost, before the accused retied the scarf.

Her identification was firm. Lionel Luckhoo cross-examined her relentlessly. Her story was tragic, but, if the result was to convict a man whose guilt was in doubt, it would only compound the tragedy. Merle admitted, in answer to questions, that she did not know, had never seen, Lloyd Harris before that night.

"What description did you give to the police?"

"I told them he was big and dark and had piercing eyes."

"Had he any other peculiarities?"

"No."

"You have seen hundreds of men to whom the description you gave would apply?"

"Yes."

"You say the scarf slipped from your eyes, and the interval between then and when the accused retied it was the only time you saw him?"

"Yes."

Lionel produced a stopwatch, and asked her to evaluate the time. "How long was the scarf off your eyes? Starting . . . now!"

There was complete silence, as the court waited on Merle to speak. "Time!" she said.

The stopwatch clicked. "Thirteen seconds."

Lionel turned again to the witness. "You were blindfolded for a long time before the scarf fell off. Surely, it took some time for your eyes to accommodate to the light and surroundings?"

"Yes, I suppose so."

"How long did it take before you could see his face clearly?"

Again the stopwatch went into operation. Merle signaled the interval. It was eight seconds.

"Eight from thirteen leaves five seconds. So you are saying that, having seen a man's face for five seconds, you can recognize that face a month later?"

"Yes."

"You were able to identify your assailant by the light from the lamppost in Woolford Avenue?"

"Yes."

"Without that light, you would not have been able to identify him?"

"No."

"You have identified the area of attack as being by the junction of Sproston's Sports Ground and the Boy Scouts' Ground?"

"Yes."

"The nearest lamppost in Woolford Avenue is about two rods, that is, thirty-three feet, from there. That is the lamppost of which you speak?"

"Yes."

Lionel Luckhoo paused, then, slowly and deliberately, said, "But, witness, that is the only lamppost in Woolford Avenue which carries no light. It has never carried a light. There is no provision for a light to be placed there."*

The court was in an uproar. The judge called for order. Merle was the only calm and unruffled person in court. When order was restored, she said, "There was a light there that night. I saw the accused, and he is the man."

An official land surveyor was called by the defense. He produced a plan of the area, and gave evidence that there was a lamppost near where the assault took place, but neither before the incident, nor since, had it ever carried a light. The nearest street light on Woolford Avenue was 228 feet away.

There was strong public sentiment against Lloyd Harris throughout the trial. Lionel Luckhoo's final address to the jury was delivered in a hostile court. At one point, he spoke at length on how people often resemble each other, and honest mistakes of identification can be made.

While Lionel was speaking, he looked around the crowded courtroom. One man appeared to be listening very attentively, his head bowed down. Lionel stared. The man moved slightly. If Lloyd Harris had a double, this could well be he.

Lionel turned to look at the jury, swung around, and pointed a finger. "Does that man remind you of anyone?"

The man lifted his head. He was the "spittin' image" of Lloyd Harris.

If it had been a Perry Mason story, that would have been the end of the case. The stranger would have been held, interrogated, and, if he had not confessed on the spot, his connection with the case would have been quickly proven. As it was, he shuffled quickly out of court without being stopped. No one knew who he was. He just disappeared.

Afterwards, Lionel Luckhoo tried to trace him, but failed.

The trial had lasted twelve days by the time the judge had completed his summing up. A mixed jury of seven men and five women then retired for two hours, and came back with a verdict of guilty. When sentence of death was passed, Lloyd

* *Incredibly, almost, and for no known reason, this one lamppost had never been fitted with an extension arm to carry a light.* Ergo, *it could not be lit.*

Harris said nothing aloud. He just kept repeating quietly, as if to himself, "I want to go back home to the country."

One of the women jurors came up to Lionel Luckhoo before he left court. "I'm sorry," she said, "but if a man did that to me and I saw his face for one second, I could never forget him." Perhaps this was the opinion that had swayed other members of the jury in reaching their verdict.

Despite a natural sympathy with the victim, and a willingness to believe that a raped woman carries the face of her attacker, once seen, printed indelibly on her mind, the jury might not have been so ready to accept Merle's identification had they heard the fresh evidence that Lionel Luckhoo applied to have admitted before the Appeal Court.

There were many grounds of appeal. Lionel contended that the judge had erred on many aspects of the trial. His more important submissions were based on the new evidence laid before the court, consisting of Chancellor J.O.F. Haynes and Justices Persaud and Crane.

This evidence was the statements given by Merle to the police, now made available by the Director of Public Prosecutions. At the time of the trial, Lionel had been told by the State Prosecutor that the evidence given was the same as appeared in the statements. This was not so.

In her first statement, Merle had said, "At no time did I get to see the faces of the men who had sex with me."

In her second statement, she had said, "I saw the face of the man who was having sex with me. He looked like a negro."

In her third statement, she said, "When the man was having sex with me, my head-tie slipped from my eyes. I got a clear glimpse of the man for about fifteen seconds. He was wearing a handkerchief from about his nose down."

Even allowing for the emotional distress of the victim, the discrepancies in her statements were gross. In her statements, she referred to two men having raped her; whereas, in court, she said three. More important, she had said she could not recognize the face of either of the men. In the second statement, she claimed to have seen the face of one man, but was uncertain of his race, and said she could recognize him only by his voice. In the third statement, she declared she had glimpsed the man for fifteen seconds. Her estimate at the trial, when this recollection was tested, proved to be only five seconds. And—the most vital point of all—she had never mentioned, while making her identification of the accused at the trial, that the lower part of his face had been concealed by a handkerchief.

In giving judgment, the Court of Appeal criticized the failure of State Counsel to inform Counsel for the Defense on the existence and contents of Merle's statements to the police. He had a duty to do so, which should not be regarded as a favor to the accused. The court considered the problem of identification; Merle's opportunity to observe the features of her attacker, taking into account the quality of the light, and the defense proposition that the judge had not given full directions on the matter. In giving its decision, the court cited a passage from one of former Chancellor E.V. Luckhoo's judgments: "The jury was left to roam at large over the rugged terrain of critical evidence without the guidance and enlightenment which would aid its estimation or appreciation."

The appeal was allowed. On his release, Lloyd Harris the simple country boy rushed to find transport to take him back home. His farewell words to Lionel were, "Sir, this kind of thing don't happen in the country." For him, the city lights had lost their glamor. He has never returned to Georgetown.

3

Although, in most societies, it is no longer considered to be a fate worse than death (without having experienced both, it is difficult to judge), violent rape is a foul crime. Terror and revulsion at the outrage can leave deep mental scars, even should the physical damage be only slight.

But in rape, as in most crimes, there are many degrees of culpability. Rape by strangers, as in the crime of which Lloyd Harris stood accused, is usually a simple question of identification. Rape between friends, so to speak, is about the most difficult crime on the statute book to fairly assess. An innocent, flirtatious, or stupid woman may place herself in a situation where she gets more than she had bargained for; a man, thinking he has been coyly led on, may use more coercion than he had intended. When, in order to protect herself, or from motives of malice or revenge, the woman cries "rape," the wisest of judges may have difficulty in deciding whether the accused deserves a drastic sentence or the sympathy of the court. One of the ways in which women are superior to men is that they are more convincing liars. Even Solomon, judging between two women, could not say which one was telling the truth.

Joseph and Janet had been sweethearts for six months. They had a quarrel one night, and Joseph found himself in unexpected and serious trouble.

Special Reserve Constable Albert was patroling down Sussex Street, in the village of Alexander, when he heard the resounding cries of a female in distress. He did his duty, as a good policeman should, and rushed to the rescue.

When he arrived at the scene, Albert found Janet weeping bitterly. "Constable," she said, "this man snatch me ring and me twenty-five cents from me."

"Ah!" Constable Albert seized hold of the appalled Joseph. "A choke-and-rob thief, eh! You come with me." He took Joseph to the Ruinveldt Police Station. A tearful Janet trailed behind.

After Constable Albert had made his report, the Station Sergeant turned to Joseph. "What you got to say about it? You rob this girl?"

Joseph told his story, how he had met Janet six months before. "Since then, we have been friendly, so friendly that I met her often and we have sexual intercourse. Tonight I had an appointment with she, and we went to our usual place at Alexander Village. I had an affair with her, and it is because a quarrel break out that she make the allegations against me. I can tell you, sergeant, what underwear she is wearing, and . . ."

His speech was interrupted at this point by Janet. She held her head in her hands and dramatically stated (in effect), "Woe is me, officer. I have been raped."

So Joseph was charged with rape and, in due time, arraigned in the High Court.

At the trial, Constable Albert gave evidence of hearing the cries for help, of being told by Janet of the alleged robbery, and of Joseph making a statement to the sergeant that there was no robbery, but that he had been having an affair with the girl; whereupon, Janet blurted out she had been raped.

" Constable," Lionel Luckhoo asked him, "when Janet made that statement before the sergeant, was it the first time she was complaining that she had been raped?"

"Yes, sir."

"Did Joseph deny it at once?"

"Yes, he did."

"Did Joseph go on to say to the sergeant that the girl was wearing a pink petticoat that had frilled lace?"

"Yes, he did say that."

"And that her panties also had frills. but their color was blue?"

"Yes, he said that."

"Did the sergeant check that she was wearing a pink slip or petticoat, and blue panties?"

" Well, the policewoman checked."

"And she found that Joseph's statements were correct?"

"Yes."

"And the garments were not torn?"

"No, they weren't torn."

When Janet gave evidence, she stuck firmly to her story that she had not known Joseph before that night.

"You were not choked and robbed, were you?"

"No."

"Then why did you say you were?"

"Well, I was ashamed and wanted the police to hold him first, then when I had settled down I would tell them the whole story."

"Did he have intercourse against your will?"

"Yes."

"Did you attempt to struggle?"

"Yes."

"You are a big person, Janet?"

"Well, not so big."

"Did you get any scratches?"

"No."

"Were your clothes torn?"

"No."

"Did he take off your clothes?"

"No."

"Do you know how he was able to describe your undergarments in such detail?"

"I don't know. He must have guessed."

Two doctors gave evidence. Predictably, they canceled each other out. The prosecution witness said he had examined Janet and found "slight generalized tenderness" of the vagina, and expressed the opinion that such tenderness is never caused by intercourse where there is consent. The doctor called by the defense disagreed with that opinion.

However difficult to decide, the case was a simple issue of consent or no-consent. Joseph admitted having had intercourse. Janet denied it was with her consent. Lionel Luckhoo, addressing the jury, pointed out that Janet had made no complaint of rape to Constable Albert, the sergeant, or anyone else, until Joseph, in answering the charge of robbery, sought to prove their intimate relationship by describing her petticoat and panties.

The judge was not impressed by this argument. He told the jury that they could take into account the fact that, at a very early stage, Janet had complained that she was raped. The jury took an hour to return a verdict of guilty. The judge nodded his head. It was the verdict he had expected, and he inflicted a sentence of five years' imprisonment on Joseph.

Fortunately for Joseph, the Federal Appeal Court disagreed with judge and jury. Lionel Luckhoo laid great stress on the trial judge having invited the jury to regard Janet's statement to the sergeant as a complaint made shortly after the deed, that would show the consistency of her conduct in negating consent.

Justices Rennie, Archer, and Wylie held that Janet did not make a complaint of rape. Her complaint was that she was robbed, not robbed of her chastity, but of twenty-five cents. What she said to the sergeant later could in no way negate consent, for it was only when Joseph said, "I can tell you, sergeant, what underwear she is wearing, and I could describe it to you because I took a fancy to it," that she then in reply blurted out that she was raped.

"The question now arises what this court should do in a case of that kind. Except in exceptional circumstances, a Court of Appeal will not upset the verdict of a jury, for the simple reason that the jury had the opportunity of hearing and seeing the witnesses when giving their testimony. We consider this is an exceptional case, and one coming within the provisions of s.16 (1) of the Federal Supreme Court (Appeals) Ord., 1958, which provides: 'The Federal Supreme Court on any such appeal against conviction shall allow the appeal if they think that the verdict of the jury should be set aside on the ground that it is unreasonable or cannot be supported having regard to the evidence.' This is a conviction that we think cannot safely be allowed to stand. The appeal is accordingly allowed, the conviction quashed, and the sentence set aside."

This was a case where three heads were better than thirteen. The Appeal Court accepted the common-sense view that the evidence suggested nothing more than a lover's quarrel. Why? Because a woman raped would be much more likely to cry "rape" than "robbery" as soon as a policeman appeared. And because a rapist would be less likely than a lover to be able to describe, in fond detail, a girl's petticoat and panties.

It was lucky for Joseph that Janet wore such dashing underwear. Still luckier that the colors and frills captured his fancy.

Chapter 21
The Case of the Maligned Lawyers

St. Peter and the Devil were arguing one day about who was going to fix the broken fence between Heaven and Hell. Finally an exasperated St. Peter declared, "You mend that fence or I'm going to sue you!"

The confident Devil replied, "Go ahead and sue. Where you gonna find a lawyer?"

—The Rev. Eugene Dunn, in Reader's Digest

Plato had a low opinion of lawyers, judging them to be small and unrighteous of soul. Aristotle said that Solon's laws were written in obscure language so as to create more lawsuits. Thomas More excluded lawyers from his Utopia. Carl Sandburg wrote, in vitriol:

Why does a hearse horse snicker
Hauling a lawyer away?

Evidently, millions of *Reader's Digest* readers are thought to believe that it is easier for a camel to pass through the eye of a needle than it is for a lawyer to enter the Kingdom of Heaven—why else would the Reverend Eugene Dunn's story be accounted funny?

All this is not just hearsay prejudice. Public opinion polls in the United States indicate that citizens who have had need to hire a lawyer have stronger feelings against them than others who have steered clear of the profession.

The reverse of the coin shows that most Americans give greater trust and respect to jurists of the Supreme Court than to any president or to either arm of Congress. And, although the first president, George Washington, shared the popular prejudice to the extent of instructing that the arbiters of any dispute over his will should lend no ear to lawyers, two-thirds of the men elected by voters to succeed him have come from the legal profession.

The British attitude is as curiously contradictory. The law has more representatives in the House of Commons than any other profession. But, during the present century, the Prime Ministers who have been lawyers might be counted on the fingers of a crippled hand.

Maybe we need to develop a comparison made earlier on. The man who takes his spiritual or physical sickness to a priest or a doctor can, by changing his outlook or his intake, play a part in effecting his cure. He does not have the feeling of concrete and malign forces being arrayed against him, save he be paranoid. If he does not completely recover, his condition usually improves, unless the disease is terminal—and, in that unhappy event, he is no longer around to complain of being short-changed by his advisers.

The man who goes to a lawyer feels both helpless and hopeless. His case will be decided on past events that his present conduct, or future intentions, can in no way change. Dimly, he realizes that, as Victor Hugo put it, "The law is a machine that cannot move without crushing someone." In a civil suit, either he or the other party must lose. If he wins, he may still be dissatisfied with the award. If an agreed settlement is reached, he may feel that his lawyer could have done better. The winners often see themselves as losers, in terms of the time, trouble, and lost tranquility their victory has cost them.

In the criminal courts, there are few winners. Either by reason of a guilty plea or an adverse verdict, the vast majority of cases that go to trial end in conviction. Again, the winners are also losers, having tasted prison while on remand, or, if allowed bail, having suffered loss of job, friends, and reputation.

The law has become so complex that no one person knows it fully. When a case hinges on a technicality, the layman might never understand how the decision came about. Small wonder if his fear and distaste for legal processes is transferred by osmosis to his lawyer, an officer of the court to whom he has bared his blemished soul in one of the few relationships, other than that of husband and wife, which carry absolute privilege.

Lawyers themselves, like all professionals, can be good, bad, or indifferent. Caught up in a system that guarantees a preponderance of aggrieved clients, appreciation is likely to come only from those whose gain far outweighs their losses. One compensation of being a specialist in murder is that the client whose neck has been saved will be genuinely grateful. Another reward, though this applies in any branch of law, is the esteem of legal brethren, who are best qualified to appraise the effort and skill that go to winning a verdict.

Perhaps the best tribute a lawyer can earn is to have a learned friend seek him out as a client. When the great American defender Clarence Darrow faced a charge of suborning witnesses, he chose Earl Rogers to defend him. Rogers, the successful defender in nearly 100 murder trials, whom Darrow himself had declared to be "the greatest jury lawyer of his time," won the case. But such opportunities come rarely. Either lawyers, as a class, are more law-abiding than most, or their sins seldom find them out. Certainly they come near the bottom of any trade or professional poll of murderers. (Doctors of medicine would so easily top any such poll that it sometimes seems questionable for what skills the letters "M.D." have been awarded.)

2

Sooner or later, the trial lawyer meets most of his legal brethren. Daily, they are his adversaries in court. After nearly forty years as a defender, Lionel Luckhoo has had exceptional opportunity to weigh the merits of prosecuting counsel. Sometimes he has been critical of their conduct, when they have unfairly attacked a client.

"Do not be misled by the demands of the prosecutor," he has warned the jury. "The prosecutor is merely seeking to express his feelings in language strong. Your determination must be on evidence strong."

Or, in a closing address: "If the prosecutor were the jury, there would be no need for retirement; the prisoner would stand condemned. Indeed, if the prosecutor were the jury, there would be no need for evidence to be presented, because he has determined the guilt of the accused upon reading his files."

And, in another instance: "The prosecution is based on shouting and histrionics. That is not the role of the prosecutor. The prosecutor should present his facts impartially and coldly, for he is a minister of justice."

Lionel prosecuted a number of cases for the Crown before independence, and his presentation was described by the then Attorney General E.O. Pretheroe as "strong, but fair." He believes that is what the prosecution should aim at.

"Conduct of a high order is expected of all in our courts of justice," he says. "Our judges set a standard comparable with the best in the world. Some of our younger prosecutors should remember that they do not win or lose a case, they present a case. They must do so fully, without inhibitions, but they must not persecute. The late Sir Stanley Gomez used to say that, when prosecutors became persecutors and ceased to exercise their role as quasi-administrators of justice, then the very basis of our criminal prosecutions would be shaken, and the entire country must suffer. For me, Stanley Gomez represented the ideal prosecutor."

When Lionel Luckhoo was prosecuting in an arson case (*R.* v. *Bramwell*), he saw that, in their original statements, the two eyewitnesses had failed to recognize the accused. He advised accordingly, and a *nolle prosequi* was entered. Incidentally, his only prosecution in a murder trial (*R.* v. *Seepersaud*) ended with a conviction and a hanging.

Looking back, Lionel recalls examples of fairness, similar to his own conduct in the arson case, that have earned his respect:

"Not long ago, Mr. Justice Bishop commended State Prosecutor Stanley Moore for informing the jury, in his opening address, that a witness who would testify to the identity of the accused had said, in her first statement, that she did not recognize him. When I took the Lloyd Harris case to appeal, I remember the Director of Public Prosecutions, Mr. George

Jackman, bringing it to my attention that the girl who was raped had made previous statements which were clearly in conflict with her evidence on oath. This is what I would have expected from George Jackman. In congratulating him, later, on behalf of the Court, the Chancellor observed that it was the duty of State Prosecutors to bring such matters to the attention of defense counsel.

"The winds of change have left untouched the sacred concept of a prosecutor's duty, which has become enshrined in the firmament of our legal system. Again, I recall the present Director of Public Prosecutions, Mannie Ramao, bringing a statement to the attention of defense counsel which was in conflict with the evidence a witness was giving on a material aspect of the case. Yet Mannie Ramao was a firm prosecutor, a searching cross-examiner.

"More recently, I witnessed a case in which a young prosecutor, in his zeal and enthusiasm, failed to observe these high principles. You cannot sweep such conduct under a carpet. The law is an honorable profession. The role of the prosecutor is high and honorable. Today, we have a number of Caribbean-trained lawyers, and I do not criticize the standard of their efficiency, or the depth of their legal learning. But I feel that, prior to their graduation, they should receive from the hands, or, rather, hear from the mouths, of such leaders of the law as the Chancellor, the Chief Justice, and other legally eminent persons, lectures on ethical standards; such concepts as are not in the textbooks, yet have been fully appreciated for hundreds of years in the profession.

"This is not urged with a view to converting would-be tenacious prosecutors into milk-and-water representatives of the State. But some basic tenets do appear to have been neglected, in recent times, by a few of our younger prosecutors. I feel that, if the high standards which we respected in the old days are underscored, then the traditional quality of the judiciary will be maintained."

Chapter 22
The Case of the Woeful Weddings

And thou art wedded to calamity.
—Romeo and Juliet

Love laughs at locksmiths, they tell us. And at murder, too, sometimes, it would seem. As many as twenty—that is to say, almost 10 percent of the total of murders that Lionel Luckhoo has been involved with—have taken place before, during, or after a wedding ceremony. Most often, it is after the wedding, when the guests have become convivial in celebrating two people having been joined together, that an unlucky someone is put asunder.

Members of the Singh family came together from all parts of Guyana for the big occasion of Julie's wedding. Leonard Singh was specially fond of his sister, and theirs was a happy reunion.

Drink was plentiful at the wedding. It was the bridegroom Arjune who drank more than was good for him and became quarrelsome. When he began to beat Julie and she cried out, Leonard rushed to her aid. He hit Arjune on the head with a stick. Arjune died, and Leonard Singh was charged with murder.

Perhaps the most important thing a cross-examiner needs to know is when to sit down. The classic warning is in the story of the lawyer who was defending a man alleged to have bitten off the ear of the complainant. He succeeded in getting the main witness to admit that he had not actually seen the accused bite the victim's ear. That was where he should have stopped. Instead, he indignantly demanded to know how the man had the nerve to come and testify against his client.

"Because," said the witness, "I saw him spit it out."

The sequence of events leading to the death of Arjune is seen most clearly in Lionel Luckhoo's cross-examination of Rajkumarie, mother of Leonard and Julie, who was one of the principal witnesses for the prosecution. Rakjumarie proved an unusually fair and objective witness, stretching no point in favor of her son.

"When your daughter Julie cried out that she was being beaten, did Leonard run to her assistance?"

"Yes."

"Then there was a scuffle between Leonard and Arjune?"

"Yes."

"Arjune was stronger than Leonard?"

"Yes."

"And Arjune was getting the better of Leonard?"

"Yes."

"Did Leonard run away from Arjune?"

"Yes, after hitting him on his head with a stick, Leonard ran."

"Did Arjune pursue him?"

"Yes."

"In running down the back stairway, Leonard was in front and Arjune was behind?"

"Yes."

"Arjune had picked up the stick with which Leonard had hit him?"

"That is so."

"Did Arjune stumble and fall from the step as he was chasing Leonard?"

"Well, not exactly."

Lionel backtracked. "Arjune was upright when he was chasing him?"

"Yes."

"Did he roll down the steps?"

"Yes."

"At the bottom of the stairway there is a concrete base?"

"Yes."

"Did he hit his head on the concrete?"

"I couldn't tell."

"But you saw him lying at the bottom of the stairway with his head against the concrete?"

"Yes."

"And it was from that position that he was lifted and given first aid?"

"Yes."

The medical evidence was that Arjune had died from an injury to his skull. There were signs of only one injury. From this, Lionel argued that the State would have to connect the death with the original blow, which was admittedly dealt by the accused, before they could establish a case for the jury. If Arjune had died immediately after the blow from the accused, then it might well be murder. But, after the blow, the deceased had continued the scuffle with Leonard and had chased him. It was only after he fell down the stairway and hit his head on the concrete that he died.

The court upheld the submission, and Leonard Singh was discharged.

After his client was freed, Lionel asked the relatives who had witnessed the incident whether Arjune had tripped or whether he appeared to have swayed and fallen from a delayed effect of the blow to his head. They all said that, at the top of the staircase, Arjune had seemed to pause before plunging forward. It was the question the prosecution should have asked, to establish the link demanded by the defense.

If Lionel had not stopped short of asking the question in court, he might have got his client hanged.

2

The Chief Justice of Guyana, Sir Harold Bollers, has said to me of Lionel Luckhoo, "In murder cases, he never asks a question the answer to which he does not reasonably foresee will be the answer he desires." Lloyd Luckhoo had told me how Lionel could be "rough and tough" in demolishing the testimony of a witness, when the occasion made it necessary. Both these facets were shown when I went with Lionel to New Amsterdam for the preliminary inquiry into a wedding-night murder.

Two brothers, Deokarran "Ricky" Dhanraj and Harrichand "Jerry" Dhanraj, were accused of killing Lorick Ramkissoon in the street outside the house where the wedding party was in progress.

The evidence for the prosecution was that Lorick and six of his friends had met together, early that evening, at a rum shop. "I can't remember who ordered the rum," Deodat Jainauth testified, "but bottles were coming and we were drinking. Everyone was merry, and we decided to go to the wedding house at Mackanlall." Anyone can go uninvited to an Indian wedding and be made welcome.

Rejendranauth Narine, known as Vernon, told a similar story, except that he denied he had been drinking rum. He said he drank beer from 6:00 to 10:00 P.M. Then the boys all went to the wedding party.

The prosecution case was that the group had left the wedding house and were going down the street, when Ricky suddenly appeared and attacked Lorick with a cutlass, fatally wounding him. But the father of the two defendants, Etwaroo Dhanraj, alleged that two incidents, in which the deceased and his friends had been the aggressors, had occurred earlier in the evening.

Dhanraj said he was at the wedding house when he received a warning that a gang of boys was coming to kill Ricky. He looked for his son, but could not find him. He walked over to a neighboring yard, and there was surrounded by a group of armed men, led by Roopchand "Bob" Narine and Lorick Ramkissoon. Narine had two knives; Ramkissoon, a cutlass. They put their blades to his belly, and he had to beg for his life. Back at the wedding house, he saw the same men beat up Seeraj Bipta, called Mukesh. They threatened Mukesh not to tell about the beating. Both Dhanraj and Mukesh gave statements to the police.

Cross-examined by Lionel Luckhoo after giving evidence, Vernon denied the attacks on Dhanraj and Mukesh. He said he did not know Mukesh.

"Did the police ask you whether you beat up Mukesh?"

"Yes."

"Did you ask the police, 'Who is Mukesh?' Or say, 'I don't know Mukesh'?"

"No." Vernon's hands were shifting about on the rail of the witness box as he spoke.

"You seem agitated." Lionel's tone was almost solicitous. "Your hands are moving up and down. Is it because you are not speaking the truth?"

Vernon made no answer. Lionel shifted direction. He was to come back to the matter of Mukesh later on.

"When you left the wedding house and were walking down the road, can you tell us who was in front and who behind?"

"Lorick was in front. I was to his left. No one was to his right."

"You were walking side by side. How were the others walking? All in a line?"

"No, by twos."

Here was a discrepancy. Deodat Jainauth had testified that he, Lorick, and Bob were in front; the others were four abreast, behind.

Vernon was asked to describe the attack. He first saw Ricky, he said, when he was about fourteen feet away, running towards them. "He struck Lorick first, and then he struck me. He struck Lorick once. I did not see the cutlass until he chopped Lorick."

"The night was bright?"

"Yes."

"There was no moon?"

"No moon, but the place was bright."

"If there was no moon, where was the light coming from?"

"Light was coming from the house opposite the school, Cocoa Boy's house."

"If this house had had no lights, you would not have been able to see, because there was no moon."

"No, I would not have been able to see."

"Would you like to change that answer? I'm not taking any advantage of you." Vernon stood silent. Lionel resumed. "Where in Cocoa Boy's house were the lights?"

"There was light on the landing."

"This landing was in the open, not enclosed?"

"Yes."

"How many lights were on the landing?"

"One."

"And how far was the house from where you were standing?"

"About sixteen feet."

"Were there any lights in the house?"

"Yes."

"How many?"

"I can't say how many."

"But it is true the house had burning lights?"

"Yes."

Vernon had testified that, after receiving a blow from the cutlass, he ran home. He had heard no one call out, and could not say what happened to the others, except that he saw Lorick get a chop in the neck. He reached home by 11:15 P.M.

"How far is the police station from your home?"

"Three or four miles."

"Now, if I take a cutlass and chop your neck, it is a serious matter. Here you have a man running amuck with a cutlass. Why did you not go to the police station?"

"Because I had no conveyance."

"If you had had a conveyance, you would have gone?"

"Yes."

"Do any of your neighbors have bicycles?"

"Some of them do."

"But you didn't think of borrowing a bicycle?"

"No."

"If you had thought of it, you would have gone and tried to borrow one?"

"Yes."

"This man Lorick could be bleeding to death. This man was your friend. You had been drinking together. But you didn't think to borrow a bicycle. Am I not right in saying that you were all so drunk you did not know what had happened?"

"No, it's not true that I was so drunk."

Vernon had said he was with his friends, drinking beer, from 6:00 to 10:00 P.M. Lionel now shot at him, "You went out at 2:00 P.M.—to Doon's beer parlor. Is that wrong?"

"I can't remember."

"Because you were too drunk. You don't remember what time it was, or how long you spent at Doon's parlor?"

"No, I don't remember."

"You spent four hours at the rum shop, later?"

"Yes."

Lionel switched back to an earlier line of questioning. "Did you ever see a man named Mukesh?"

"No."

"You can give no reason why the accused should attack you?"

"No."

"I won't keep you long. I see your feet are beginning to tire." The witness was shuffling uncomfortably. "I'll give you one last chance. Were you at the police station when Mukesh was making a statement?"

"No."

"Corporal Ralph did not point him out to you?"

"No."

"Mukesh didn't go to the hospital to be examined by the doctor at the same time as you?"

"No."

"Your story is a true story—everything is as true as the statement you make that you did not know Mukesh?"

If the witness answered yes to this, he overturned his entire testimony. Lionel could produce irrefutable proof that he knew Mukesh very well. Vernon answered, "Yes."

"And if Cocoa Boy's house had had no lights, you would not have been able to see?"

"No."

"There was light on the landing?"

"Yes."

"And lights in the house?"

"Yes."

"But you cannot say how many?"

"No."

Vernon, tangled in a tissue of lies, was in a pitiable state. The cross-examination had achieved, with deadly effect, the discrediting of the witness.

Lionel had visited Cocoa Boy's house and the beer parlor, and had interviewed independent witnesses.

Evidence could be called that Vernon had been drinking for eight hours before going to the wedding party—double the time he admitted.

Evidence could be called that there was no electric fitting

on the landing of Cocoa Boy's house, so there could have been no light; inside the house, there was only one bulb, and the windows were opaque, so no light could have shone through.

Evidence could be called that Mukesh was pointed out to Vernon at the police station, the two of them were taken to the hospital together, and as boys they had gone to school together.

He and his friends contradicted each other in their evidence. Vernon said they left the rum shop to go to the wedding house at 10:00 P.M. Others among them had it as early as 9:00 P.M., and as late as midnight.

Vernon said that, when attacked by Ricky, they were walking in double file, himself and Lorick in front. Jainauth had said Lorick, Bob, and he were in front; Vernon, behind, with the others.

Under Lionel's interrogation of the witnesses, the variations multiplied. Sometimes it was not clear whether it was six or seven of them who had been walking down the road together. There was moonlight—there was no moonlight. Only Lorick was chopped—Vernon and Bob were chopped. Jerry spoke, and was seen before Ricky attacked them—no one spoke, and Ricky was alone. All except Bob and Lorick ran away—no one ran away.

Lionel Luckoo submitted that Jerry's mere presence at the scene was not sufficient to make a *prima facie* case against him for murder. He committed no overt act to show his implication in aiding and abetting, or acting in concert. Lionel cited cases in support of his contention. The magistrate Mr. Hugh Hanoman agreed, and Jerry was discharged.

The magistrate commented that the cross-examination of the witnesses had been so effective that it was difficult for him to say whose version could be relied upon, in respect of Ricky. This must be a matter for a trial jury to decide.*

3

Marriage is a civil contract. At the time of his marriage ceremony, Tom Francis Olivetti** was on his deathbed, so

* *The State later entered a* nolle prosequi *against Ricky.*

***Names of parties in this case have been altered.*

its legality did not concern him for long, if at all. It did, however, become a matter of pressing concern to his assumptive heirs, and to the courts of Barbados.

Tom Olivetti was a leading member of the Democratic Party in the northeastern United States, and a millionaire. For a man of substance, his will was of the simplest kind. Everything had been left, without reservation, to his wife Thelma, the mother of his eight children. Then, in 1970, Thelma died.

Tom was 67 when he became a widower. Two years prior to this, he had met a lady named Jennie LeBaron, and, after the death of his wife, this friendship blossomed. In October, 1972, Tom bought Jennie a ring worth nearly $10,000, which may have been intended as an engagement ring. A few weeks later, on November 20, they sailed together from New York for a Caribbean cruise aboard the Sagafjord, sharing a cabin as Mr. and Mrs. Olivetti.

During the cruise, Tom Olivetti became ill. By the time the ship reached Barbados on December 6, his condition was critical. An ambulance took him to Queen Elizabeth Hospital, where immediately he was placed in the intensive care unit. A Roman Catholic priest, Father Lawrence Temple, was sent for, to administer the last rites.

Tom Olivetti entered Queen Elizabeth Hospital at 2:45 P.M. At some time between 7:30 and 9:30 that evening—the exact time was to assume great importance, later—Father Temple performed a marriage ceremony, at the bedside, between Tom and Jennie LeBaron. Olivetti died at midnight.

When the Olivetti sons and daughters in the United States learned about the deathbed marriage, they challenged its validity, claiming that their father could not have appreciated the nature and quality of his act and the ceremony; he never gave his consent or agreed to the marriage. They contended that LeBaron had fraudulently arranged the marriage to benefit herself, and deprived the relatives of their legal rights under U.S. laws.

Lionel Luckhoo was briefed for the plaintiffs to challenge the deathbed marriage. A remarkable case—for hundreds of years, there had been no similar cases to annul a deathbed marriage.

Dr. Winston Austin, a specialist in the intensive care unit of the hospital, gave evidence for the plaintiffs:

"I had seen Tom Olivetti that evening, and again later the same evening. At the second visit, there was no improvement, and he was able to respond very little to stimuli."

Dr. Austin said he stayed with Olivetti for almost an hour, between 7:00 and 8:00. When he saw him again at 9:30, he was clearly dying. It was then he heard about the wedding ceremony. No one had asked him at any time whether the patient was in a fit state to be married. In his opinion, he would not have understood that he was getting married. Cross-examined by J.S.B. Deare, the doctor said that Olivetti's loss of consciousness was due to severe diabetes mellitus and liver failure. If the diabetes was the major contributing factor, his level of consciousness could have risen as a result of treatment, but, from the doctor's observation and the record, this had not happened.

Dr. Willis Butlin, a surgeon, testified that, when he saw Olivetti at about 7:30, his subjective impression was that he was slightly better; that he could understand, but was drowsy; he did not respond in a coherent manner when spoken to. He saw him again at two minutes to 9:00. At that time, Olivetti was in a coma, virtually gasping for breath, and appeared so ill as to be on the point of death. He could neither speak nor understand what was taking place. Certainly, he could not have understood a marriage ceremony.

A slight, but important, difference of opinion had emerged in the evidence of the doctors. Dr. Butlin was willing to allow that the slight improvement he observed in Olivetti's condition around 7:30 (he was never sure of the exact time of that visit) might have been sufficient for him to be capable of understanding and taking part in a marriage ceremony. In fact, during that visit, he was asked to be a witness, and had agreed. But both doctors were agreed that, going on nine o'clock, Olivetti was incapable of understanding or responding to what was taking place.

The last witness from the hospital was Sister Martha Mendel, the nurse in charge of the intensive care unit. She said that at 8:30 the patient's condition was critical, and she could get no response when she spoke to him. At nine o'clock,

Olivetti was no better, and would not have been able to recognize people or his surroundings. It was at or before 9:00 that Father Temple spoke to her about a wedding, and asked her to be a witness.

"The ceremony was between 9:10 and 9:15 P.M. The patient was still in the unconscious state," Sister Mendel testified. "He did not in the course of the ceremony nod or shake his head. The priest read the marriage ceremony. The patient did not repeat anything that the priest said to him. The patient never did or said anything to show that he knew what was happening. When the priest asked the patient if he would have this woman to be his wife, there was no reply.

"Then the priest said, 'Can you hear me?' Again, there was no reply. The priest asked again, 'Can you hear me?' in a louder voice, and closer to the patient. A muttering sound or groan was heard from the patient. There were no other sounds from the patient during the ceremony, which lasted, roughly, ten minutes, if so long. I did not see the priest take the hand of the patient and join it with the hand of the respondent. All the priest wanted the patient to say was 'I do'—but there was no response."

Had the patient signed or made his mark in the register?

"I did not see a pen being put in the hand of the patient. After the ceremony, I went back to my desk to prepare my records. After three to five minutes, the priest brought over a bound ledger, and pointed to the line on which he wanted my signature. I signed there as a witness. I do not remember seeing any X on the volume when I signed."

Under cross-examination, Sister Mendel maintained that she had first heard talk of a wedding, and was asked to be a witness, at about five minutes to 9:00. It was possible that Dr. Butlin came in at around 7:30, but she had no record of it. Father Temple came in about eight o'clock, and she thought Dr. Butlin had come in after him. She did not agree that the priest came in as early as 7:30, or that the wedding took place at twenty to 8:00. She was sure that it took place about 9:10, because the night shift had come on.

The respondent Jennie LeBaron gave evidence that Tom Olivetti had proposed and had given her an engagement ring in October. He had wanted to be married on board ship, but she had asked him to wait until they got home. Then he got ill, and became progressively worse.

Her description of the wedding ceremony differed from that given by Sister Mendel. When she entered the intensive care unit with her daughter and Father Temple, she said, Olivetti's head was turned away. She called his name, and he turned around and looked at her. She said, "Tom, we'll be married like you wanted to." Olivetti nodded his head, and said, "Yes." Then Father Temple fetched the nurse, and they stood around the bed.

Father Temple asked Olivetti if he wanted to get married, and he said, "Yes." He asked Olivetti if he understood what he was doing. Olivetti said, "Yes," and nodded. When the priest started the vows, Olivetti had answered very softly, and Jennie had said, "Tom, I can't hear you." At the end, Father Temple said, "Will you take this woman to be your lawful wife?" Olivetti said, "I will." Then Father Temple took his hand and placed it on the book, and Olivetti made a cross. It was around 7:30 or twenty to 8:00 when the ceremony took place.

Cross-examined by Lionel Luckhoo, the witness said that the cruise was intended to be a honeymoon. Olivetti had not wanted the publicity of a marriage in the United States. There was a Catholic priest on the boat who could have married them, but the first three days she was very seasick. After that, they talked about marriage, but, as they had booked as Mr. and Mrs. and everybody now knew them, she was embarrassed to get married on board.

In the hospital, Olivetti had never spoken a whole sentence, just the words "Yes," "No," and "I will." Dr. Butlin had told her, before the ceremony, that Olivetti's condition was stable, and he appeared to be quite alert. His eyes were wide open, and he was not drowsy. He was sick, but he knew what he was doing. She then thought he would get better. If Dr. Austin had been there between 7:00 and 8:00, she would have seen him. There was no personal animosity between her and Dr. Austin, but he was mistaken. Nurse Mendel, too, was wrong about the time. The marriage was not at ten past 9:00, but between 7:30 and 8:00 P.M.

The respondent's daughter Patricia LeBaron gave evidence that supported her mother's testimony. But these witnesses were interested parties. The court was unlikely to accept their version of events and to reject that of two independent witnesses: a doctor who said he had been with the patient between 7:00 and 8:00, and no marriage took place during that period, and a nurse who stated that the marriage took place after nine o'clock, by which time (the two doctors were agreed) the patient was not competent to participate.

One witness had yet to be heard. Much depended on what he might say, for lawyers and laymen alike are predisposed to believe that a priest does not lie. Father Lawrence Temple took the stand.

He stated clearly that the marriage of Tom Francis Olivetti and Jennie LeBaron took place at 7:40 P.M.

That swung the weight of evidence the other way—unless the priest could be discredited by cross-examination.

"Father," Lionel Luckhoo began, "this was an unusual request—being asked to marry a man who was dying. The particulars of that marriage would be firmly fixed in your mind. When did you receive the call?"

"At about 6:00 P.M."

"You could not have made a mistake about this, could you, Father?"

"No."

"And it was about an hour and three-quarters after the call from the ship that you married these two persons?"

The witness agreed.

"That would make the time about a quarter to 8:00?"

Again, agreement.

"So, if you received the call at seven o'clock, the marriage would then have been at about a quarter to 9:00?"

"Yes, that is so. But I received the call at six o'clock, and the marriage was at about twenty or quarter to 8:00."

"Would you agree that your memory might have been fresher two years ago than it is now?"

"Well . . . maybe."

"Look at this statement which you made two years ago. It says, "I received the call from the ship at about seven o'clock.' Did you make that statement?"

"Yes."

"Is the statement correct?"

"No, it was six o'clock."

"Was six o'clock always firmly in your mind?"

"Yes."

"Then how did you come to write seven o'clock?"

"I made a mistake. It was six o'clock."

"Have you made a mistake in the interval between the call and the marriage?"

"No. About one and three-quarter hours would be the time."

"Now, Father Temple, I ask you to look at a further detail in your statement made two years ago. Did you say then that the wedding was at about a quarter to 9:00?"

"Yes, but that is not so."

"Has your memory improved in the last two years?"

"No!"

"Then what makes you so sure it was a quarter to 8:00, and not a quarter to 9:00?"

"Well, I recollect that while I was performing the ceremony I had a visual look at the clock on the wall, and it said twenty to 8:00."

"Father, did you say *visual* or *vision*?'

"Visual."

"And that is why the time of the marriage burned itself into your memory?"

"Yes."

"And from that moment you remembered that it was twenty minutes to 8:00 when you married the sick man and this woman?"

"Yes."

"Did you have that recollection when you made the statement two years ago?"

"Yes."

"Then why did you not say 7:40 in your statement?"

"I made a mistake."

"What you put in your statement, two years ago, was 8:45?"

"Yes."

"But that is wrong?"

"Yes."

"Did you deliberately put the wrong time in your statement?"

"No, it was a mistake."

"But when you were writing 8:45 in the statement, in your memory the time was 7:40?"

Hesitantly, wretchedly, the witness admitted, "Well, yes."

"Father Temple, are you not lying to this court, and seeking to justify that you married a man who did not understand what was taking place?"

"No, I am not lying. I am a priest."

"Are you aware at this moment that, because of the evidence of the doctors, the question of time is vitally important?"

"I believe so, but I am speaking the truth."

"And, although you remembered the precise times, you wrote the wrong times in your statement?"

The priest seemed paralyzed, looking limp and ragged, with sweat pouring down his face. He could only repeat the same weak reply: "Well, I made a mistake."

Lionel Luckhoo's cross-examination of Father Temple destroyed what chance the respondent had of winning her case.

In giving his decision, Judge Williams said, "Father Temple can be said, in one respect, to have an interest to serve, in that he was the priest who officiated at the ceremony and would not be likely to admit any impropriety. This did not mean that his evidence must be discarded; a balanced assessment of it must still be made. But his contradictions on time placed a great strain on his credibility. . . . I was completely unimpressed by his explanation of the visual recollection of the clock showing twenty to 8:00. Maybe it was his misfortune that his belated visual recollection of the clock happened to match so well the time being put forward by the respondent and her daughter as the time at which the ceremony took place. But it is a matter which I cannot ignore."

Sister Mendel, said the judge, had given her evidence well, and he accepted that the ceremony took place at about nine o'clock. He also accepted the opinions of the doctors, and found that, at the time of the purported marriage, Olivetti "was not in a fit condition to be asked to consent to marriage, and was incapable of understanding the significance of what was being done at his bedside, or of a meaningful participation in the ceremony. In my view, though Father Temple went through the normal ritual of the marriage ceremony, he was following the form rather than the substance—an empty and meaningless formula, since one of the participants was present, essentially, in body only."

The marriage, Judge Williams declared, was null and void. It was a historic decision, for never before in the English-speaking Caribbean had a deathbed marriage been annulled.

Chapter 23
The Case of the Artful Advocate

The object of oratory alone is not truth, but persuasion.

—Macaulay

After Aeschines had spoken, the Athenians would say, admiringly, "What a fine speech!" When Demosthenes spoke, they said, "Let us march against Philip!"

Oratory is not an art to be assessed in the abstract. It purposes to produce an effect. The printed report cannot adequately show how the effect has been created. Too much is missing that can never be recaptured. Ambience of time, place, and circumstance; tone and timbre of voice; inflection given to word or phrase; gesture or avoidance of gesture—all are matters of fleeting moment. Every great speech is shaped to a particular audience on a particular occasion.

In a courtroom, the jury, theoretically, at least, has no predilections in favor of either side. But juries are human. When a crime arouses emotions of fear, anger, or revulsion, they feel that someone should be punished. They may then take a look at the prisoner in the dock and think to themselves, "If he is not guilty, why is he here?"

Mr. Justice Boland has said that Lionel Luckhoo has the ability to mesmerize a jury. "I have watched the process time and again," he says. Lloyd Luckhoo explains it, less esoterically, as a genius for bringing out a line of defense which will not only impress the jury with its sincerity, validity, and the logic of his presentation, but which is attractive to them as being reasonable in accord with their understanding of human nature, while it may transcend (without ignoring) legal principles in its appeal to justice. "He is never despondent if a case looks bad or the outlook bleak," Lloyd says. "He will probe into it in depth, and is always able to extract a point of view which might not be apparent to, or could not be put over by, someone else." On the lighter side, Chief Justice Bollers recalls an occasion when, as Crown Counsel, he was prosecuting a man charged with stealing a bull. "Lionel was defending. He convinced the jury that the accused was on his way to the police station to return the animal when he was arrested."

The power of persuasion is Lionel Luckhoo's most potent gift. The pillars of persuasion are *preparation*, which involves learning more about the case than anyone else, down to the smallest incidentals; *presentation*, which calls for a clear mind, and the ability to employ simple language to arrange an argument in orderly sequence; and *personality*, which is the distinctive, but indefinable, essence of the man himself. Add to these knowing what questions to ask and how to ask them, and good advocacy might be described as watching your P's and Q's.

Lionel was once briefed at the last moment just to address the jury. Three men had been charged with wounding-with-intent. Two had lawyers. The third was not represented. He had insisted that he wanted only Lionel Luckhoo, but he could not raise the fee. After all the evidence had been heard, his relatives went to see Lionel in chambers.

"Sir Lionel," they said, "one of the lawyers was good enough to give us his notes of all that has taken place at the trial. They are very full notes, and we have had a clerk type them out. We want you to read them and then, if you are willing, we would ask you to give your service for only one day. Will you go tomorrow morning and address the jury?"

Lionel read through the typescript. The notes were well taken. The request was unusual, but he was impressed by the trouble the people had gone to in their eagerness for his services. He spent the night familiarizing himself with the case. Next morning, he addressed the jury for three hours without having seen or heard any of the witnesses. When he sat down, the judge, Mr. Justice Hughes, said in open court, "This is the most remarkable address I have heard in my life.

Counsel has not been present for any of the four days of the hearing, yet in analyzing the evidence which has been led he has not missed a single thing. It is incredible!—a fact which has nothing to do with you, members of the jury. You are still to consider the case in the manner and form which I shall put it to you. But I would like to compliment counsel on his feat."

The verdict went in favor of Lionel's one-day client. All three men on trial were acquitted.

Preparation for a case more commonly begins the moment a client enters Lionel Luckhoo's chambers. Mention is made in Chapter 1 of a case at which I watched Lionel at work from the start, giving advice to the man on what he should do if he were arrested, and, almost immediately afterwards, going to view the scene of the incident. The man was arrested that same day, and the next step was to visit him in prison. There Lionel questioned him at length, on his background, his own and his wife's antecedents, his business experience, what he knew about the man who had died. Then more questions about the incident, what time it happened, how brightly lit was the place, how many people were there, what were the exact movements of both the client and the deceased. This is by no means a complete analysis, just a skeleton on which body will be built later.

It is important at the first prison interview to let the client know that his counsel has spoken to the Superintendent of Prisons, and requested that the client be allowed to communicate with him whenever he wishes; that he is willing to receive messages at any time. It makes the prisoner feel that he is not cut off.

"Opening a personal relationship between the client, the prison authority, and yourself is useful," Lionel explained to me, later, "because he now begins to feel a little confidence, based upon the fact that I'm taking an interest in his case. The more I see of him, the more questions I will ask, and the more I will become completely immersed in his case. This enables me to understand him, to learn what makes him tick, and this I've found to be very useful.

"I haven't got a clue what the defense is going to be in this case as yet. I shall have to wait until the evidence comes out. I will do what I call the skirmishing in the preliminary inquiry, try and find out as much as possible of what the witnesses know, how they give it, the possibilities of what they might or might not have seen; did they see the man before, at, or after the shooting. Any little points of vantage which they give me I shall explore. For example, if they say that after the shooting he appeared surprised, then I would ask such questions as 'Did he appear surprised, like a person who did not expect that there would be an explosion, the sound of a gun, and didn't expect to see this man go down? You would say that he was as surprised as you were, he appeared to give you that impression?' In matters of this kind, you have to be quick to improvise, to make use of any little niche or opening. If it fails, no bother—because this is only the preliminary inquiry. You know what to avoid and what to capitalize on when the trial comes off. "

Personal investigation at the scene of the crime is a part of the preparation. Lionel learned its importance from his uncle J.A. Luckhoo, who told him that, not only should he go to the *locus*, but he should go, particularly in cases where identification was involved, at the time of day or night that the incident had occurred.

"In other words," Lionel says, "if it took place at midnight, he would really advocate that I should go there around midnight. Nowadays, with all deference to J.A., if I went up there at midnight I would probably find someone else with a cutlass there." (We had been discussing a late-night cutlass killing.)

Once, Lionel visited the scene of a crime, and then, at the trial, insisted that the jury should be taken there, to prove a point about what a witness could have seen from where he said he was standing. Lionel knew the man could not have seen as far as he claimed, because there were trees in the way. The application for the jury to visit was allowed—but when they were there, the trees had been chopped down and the view was clear. The experience taught Lionel a lesson. Now he goes to the scene a second time, just before the trial, to make sure there have been no changes, and, if it is necessary for the jury to go, they will see what he saw originally.

The intensity of his preparation, in and out of court, before and during the trial, up to the point where he makes his final address to the jury, is the first reason Lionel Luckhoo gives, to explain his singular success.

"I must know the case completely, more thoroughly than any other person taking part in the trial," he says. "The evidence of every single witness I remember without looking at a note. The pauses they make before answering I mentally record, their demeanor in answering a particular question stays in my memory. I know my own case backwards, and I know where the prosecution case has deviated from mine, or mine from that of the prosecution. Often, when I am addressing the jury, I don't look at notes at all, but am able to accurately quote what a witness said. When judges are summing up, and they give a slightly different slant to what a witness is alleged to have said, I can correct them without consulting my notes. I will rise and point out that the witness said something a little different, and when the judge checks his notes I don't recall ever having been wrong.

"You may say that this means I have a fantastic memory, but I don't. I have an excellent memory for what has taken place while I am in court. But after the case is over, I can just scrub it clean out of my mind. If I look at a case record afterwards, it means nothing to me until I have read a few sentences. Then it comes back to me what happened."

Less easy to explain than the practical preparation is the attunement with the mind of the jury that Lionel Luckhoo seems to achieve. "I put myself in the position of a juror listening to the case," he says. "I consider what would appeal to my juror mind, how I would see it, looking through a juror's eyes. The points I feel must be knocked down, I hammer at vigorously. The points in my favor which need to be stressed, I stress. But all the time I am not addressing the jury *qua* jury; I am addressing the jury as if I myself were a member."*

* *Marshall Hall was described as "The Thirteenth Juryman" by Robert Churchill, the ballistics expert who appeared as a Crown witness in so many cases. In his biography,* The Other Mr. Churchill *(Harrap), Macdonald Hastings quotes him as saying, "All his effort was concentrated on winning the sympathy of the jury. He seemed to put himself inside the box with them."*

He can be artful in the exercise of his art. One of Lionel's early cases was a charge of unlawful wounding. During the afternoon session, a juror who had eaten—and, perhaps, drunk—a good lunch, slipped off his shoes, eased himself in his seat, and took a quiet snooze. Judge Fretz, when he noticed, banged with his gavel and said accusingly, "Juror Number Four, you are sleeping." Juror Number Four quickly roused himself. "Your honor," he said, "my eyes are closed, but I listen better this way. I am not sleeping."

Lionel's client put forward the defense that he carried a knife to threaten but not to use. The injured man had tried to take the knife away from him, and that was how he got cut. In his closing speech, Lionel said, "Gentlemen, not because your eyes are closed are you sleeping. Not because you have a cigarette in your mouth are you inhaling the smoke. Not because the accused brought a knife with him was he the assailant." He gained an acquittal.

Even in the selection of jurors, Lionel's intuitive feeling at times comes into play. Once he was appearing with his brother Sir Edward Luckhoo, and felt, for no reason he could define, that a particular juror should be challenged. "He seems all right to me," E.V. decided. "Let it ride." The case ended with a hung jury, eleven of them being in favor of acquittal. The one who held out was the man Lionel had wanted to reject. Before the retrial, E.V. said, "You decide who you want or don't want on the jury. I think maybe you have a seventh or eighth sense operating."

In a murder case, the verdict of the jury must be unanimous. Not often does just one juror hold out against the rest, but it does happen. Lionel almost lost a verdict in the Punt Trench Murder Case. Eleven jurors wanted to convict, but after six hours one juror was still unwilling to agree, and a retrial was ordered. That night, Lionel had telephone calls from three members of the jury, each of them saying, "I want you to know that I was the only one to hold out for your client."

While a case is being tried, Lionel Luckhoo likes to hear the opinions of anybody and everybody on the day's proceedings—members of his own chambers, his staff, his chauffeur, his gardener, people in the street, anyone at all who is taking an interest in the case. What they are thinking might be what the jury is thinking. If their comments bring out weaknesses in the defense case, they can be allowed for, if not corrected, before he presents his final argument to the jury. Of course, Lionel does not always take the advice that is offered, and once he had cause to regret not doing so. In the Disappearing Double Case, he was warned not to have a woman on the jury. He thought he knew better—and ended up with five women in the box, who almost certainly prevailed upon the male members of the jury to bring in a doubtful verdict against Lloyd Harris. Lionel won a reversal in the Appeal Court, but his rejection of that particular advice is nonetheless astounding; it is an almost automatic ploy for defense counsel to shoo off women jurors in a case involving rape.

The final factor in winning a verdict is the indomitable fighting spirit that Lionel Luckhoo never fails to maintain. "I have implicit faith in the case I am presenting," he says. "I don't consider the question of my client being guilty at all. I have accepted his story, I believe his story, and I advance it with all the power of which I am capable."

"What if the client has told you he is guilty?" I asked him.

"This has happened on very few occasions. Then I do not put him on the witness stand, but I attack the case for the prosecution relentlessly."

This, naturally, led us to the question which so many laymen feel ought to put a lawyer on the defensive, though the logic of the legal system makes a defense unnecessary. Nevertheless, I asked Lionel, "How can you defend a man you know or feel to be guilty?"

"I am not God. I have taken an oath that I am to use my skill and my abilities in the interest of my client. A client may well be guilty, but, under the rules we observe and follow, it is necessary that the jury return a verdict of guilty on the evidence. That is the oath which every juror takes—to determine guilt or innocence on the evidence which is adduced. It is my duty, even if I know a person is guilty, to see that the Crown establishes his guilt; or, to put it another way, to establish the fact that the Crown has failed to make out a sufficient case for conviction.

"Let me ask myself another question: if my personal feelings were allowed to come into it, what happens with the person whom I feel to be innocent? Can I go before the jury and say, 'Let me swear to you that I believe this man is innocent'?* I cannot. These matters have to be viewed objectively. It is the task of the jury to decide his innocence or guilt. My job is to see that he is not convicted unless the Crown establishes his guilt. Did not Blackstone say it was better that ninety-nine guilty persons should escape penalty than that one innocent person should be convicted?

"I start off with the premise that everyone who comes to me is innocent. I do not question that at all. I am interested in what is his story. I will investigate that story and ask him questions which may elicit from him further facts that might be helpful, not always too helpful.

"What about letting clients go on to the witness stand? I never direct them. I take the view that, except in a case where it is necessary, they should not go on to the witness stand, and so advise them. Why? Because even an innocent person—and I have seen it happen so often—has such problems as nervousness and tension, and can be made to look guilty by skillful cross-examination.

"I never ask a man if he is guilty. But if he comes to me and says, "Look, Counsel, I am guilty," I will still take his case. I would not tell him to go into the witness box and tell a lie. That, to my mind, would not be honest. But I would move heaven and hell to ensure that the prosecution must establish his guilt according to law."

"When a man has admitted his guilt to you, do you still always advise him to plead not guilty?"

* *At the trial of William Palmer, the notorious poisoner, Serjeant Shee said to the jury, "I begin Palmer's defense and say in all sincerity that I have an entire conviction of his innocence." This was an "unprecedented" (Lord Cockburn) and "outrageous" (Lord Birkett) departure from the rule which forbids the advocate to express his own view. The author has heard a prosecutor urge the jury to "believe me when I ask you to do these [police witnesses] the honor of believing that what they said was true"—which is sailing close to windward.*

"In cases of murder, which is what we are talking about, principally, I have often—no, not often, but on occasion—had someone come along and say, 'I have killed X. What do I do?' I say, 'Well, it is for the State to establish your guilt.' Once, a man came to me and said he had killed X. I said, 'All right, stay put until you are charged.' He came back the following week and said, 'Counsel, I want to tell you I have killed Y.' I then became suspicious that he was making it up. I spoke to the police, asking them whether X had been killed at such a time and place, and then asked the same about Y. They told me nothing of the kind had happened. The man was firmly convinced that he had killed two people, when in fact he had killed neither.

"But this is not really the point you are asking. If there has been a murder and a person confesses, my advice to him still would be that he should plead not guilty, and let the State prove the case against him. I remember, once, a man got up in court and said, 'I am guilty of murder.' The judge said to him, 'I would advise you to enter a plea of not guilty, and let us see whether the evidence establishes that you are guilty of murder or not.' I think this is the correct approach."

"Lionel, you and the judge would approve of the Irishman who, when asked whether he pleaded guilty or not guilty, said he did not know, as he had not yet heard the evidence against him! After a really bad murder, such as the man who confessed to burning his wife and children (the case you refused), how would you feel on getting the man off, though you knew he was guilty?"

"I think when a jury returns a verdict of not guilty, then, so far as I am concerned, the man is not guilty. I have a peculiar philosophical outlook. I feel that many people who have committed crimes have paid a penalty of sorrow and retribution, and that that serves as a means of providing compensation for their crimes. The fact that a jury returns a verdict of not guilty means that it has not found them guilty on the evidence; but I am also conscious that the divine hand of Providence may well have had some play in the final determination of the matter."

"What percentage of the people you have defended for murder do you think were not guilty?"

"I would say barely 5 percent. Anyway, not more than ten or fifteen persons out of 200 did I feel strongly to be innocent. At the time of taking the case, the question does not arise at all. It is only in retrospect, when the case is over, that I permit my mind to consider the matter of innocence or guilt. And only with that bare 5 percent would I be willing to put my head on the block and say these persons were not guilty. But it is not my function to judge. I would be avoiding the true purpose of my vocation, negating the oath which I have taken, if I did not defend each and every one with all my skill and ability.

"And, again, I am not God. Although I personally feel someone is guilty, he may not be. So often, it happens that what you believed turns out not to be so. Indeed, a man may feel guilty of murder without being guilty in the eyes of the law.* Let me tell you, briefly, about just one case. A man was charged with murdering his friend. When I went to see him, he said, 'Sir, I am guilty of it. I don't know what to do.' Then I went into the facts, and found that he had killed his friend accidentally. He was angry. He brandished a bamboo stick in front of him to keep his friend off. The friend walked into it, overbalanced, and fell into the river, where he was drowned. His action had caused the death, but I said, 'You are not guilty of murder.' A jury agreed with me."

I suggested to Lionel, "An analysis of hundreds of trials in the United States has led to the conclusion that in only a small minority of cases does the ability of either prosecuting or defense counsel play a significant part in the result. In other words, the main factor is the strength of the evidence,

* *A man may be wholly innocent and not know it. Francisco Trapia, a New York longshoreman, was arrested by police officers who had seen him throw a sack, which proved to contain the arms and legs of a woman, off a Brooklyn pier. At Trapia's apartment, they found the head and torso. He and the woman had been drinking. Trapia woke from sleep to find her dead, and thought he had killed her during the night. Dr. Charles Norris, the Chief Medical Examiner, found she had been asphyxiated by a faulty stove flue. He appeared for the defense, and saved Trapia from an otherwise certain conviction.*

and cases are mostly won or lost irrespective of the relative merit of the advocates. What difference do you think a strong or weak prosecutor, a strong or weak defender, can make to a verdict?"

"I would say that even a strong prosecutor may likely lose a case against a strong defense counsel. By strong defense counsel, I mean a defense counsel who exploits every conceivable legitimate avenue. A case of murder comes up, and sometimes you think it will take two days; but when you begin to explore and exploit every avenue, it might take two weeks. And this is where a strong defense counsel—that is, an experienced counsel—does have a decided advantage over a weak prosecutor. Our system of law is so designed—based upon the English jurisprudential system, wherein the law leans over backwards to say that the case must be proven beyond reasonable doubt. Some judges put it differently: that the jury must be satisfied as to the guilt of a person.

"Take a matter like identification. We have had a recent case from England (Harvey Turnbull), in which the Law Lords laid down a series of principles wherein the judge must address the jury about being sure of the identification, and if the judge does not do it, then these cases are won on appeal. I won a fair number of cases on appeal because of the failure of the judge to observe the principles of directing the jury fully and properly. But, to give a short answer to your question, I think a stronger prosecutor has a better chance in a murder trial of getting a conviction than a weaker one—a case will have to be very strong, evidentially, before it makes no difference. But an experienced counsel for the defense is of much more advantage to his client than a young, inexperienced counsel. Indeed, I recollect that, when I was recommended for my Q.C. in 1954, the Governor asked me to give him my views on this very point. I told him that no counsel should be assigned to defend a man on a charge of murder who had not had a minimum of five years' active practice in the criminal courts. This I believe, although I had my first murder brief within six months of qualifying."

We spoke of British and American methods of advocacy. "American counsel are quite different from the English," Lionel commented, "but sometimes they are very effective.

They have a habit, which I like, of going right up to the witness. I do it myself, but perhaps not in so brash a manner. If I go up to a witness, I never shout at him. Oh, I have shouted at witnesses, but I shout from where I'm standing, at the bar table. If I go up to witnesses, it is invariably to cajole them, to play upon their heartstrings, to see if I can make them give the answer I want."

Lionel Luckhoo has seen the workings of American courts while acting as adviser to U.S. attorneys. I asked him if he preferred their less formal system to that of the British.

"I like the British system. Maybe because I was trained at the Middle Temple, London, and knocked around the London courts for so long. The American system is inclined to get a bit bawdy, sometimes." He laughs. "The wearing of wigs, gowns, stiff collars, bibs, to my mind, gives a degree of dignity, presence; lifts the tone, generally. Of course, in the tropics, certain changes of formal wear are necessary. But I have a high regard for the British system of justice and how it is practiced, on the whole. It reaches a terrifically high watermark."

"How about the different methods of jury selection? Under the English system, although challenge, both peremptory and for cause, is allowed in felony cases, the rights are seldom exercised. In the States, it often takes days, even weeks, to select a jury."

"In Guyana, we may object to three jurors without assigning cause. I don't like the American system of, so to speak, trying to distill the jury until, eventually, you get what you believe you want. I think there is something called the luck of the draw, and that you must take your chances. I rarely object to a person. When I do, it is usually because I say to my clients, 'If you don't like any person for any reason, let me know and I'll object.' I have on occasions personally objected because I have felt led to do so. Sometimes the accused ask me to challenge someone, but far more often they take the attitude, 'Let's ride our luck.' But, while I'm telling you this, I must add that I will never again enter into a rape case with a woman on the jury. I feel very strongly that I got a raw deal in the Disappearing Double Case because of the women on the jury. I can't swear it, I wasn't in the jury room, but, as I told you, one woman came up to me, later, and said, 'If I saw the man who was raping me for only one second, I would never forget his face.' Mind you, I may be wrong, but, to me, that attitude doesn't give my client a chance—and I think he deserves a fair chance and not a prejudiced point of view."

Guyana follows the American pattern, which allows the client to have direct access to the trial lawyer who will represent him in court. Under the English two-tiered system, the client must approach a barrister through a solicitor, and may never set eyes on his counsel until he is in court; some barristers will purposely avoid a meeting. I asked Lionel Luckhoo which method he preferred.

"To have the papers prepared and all the donkey work done by a solicitor and dished up for you is time saving. From that point of view, I prefer the British system. From the point of view of getting results, I think our way is more effective. I go through all the bits and pieces because the client comes to me. When you see your client, take initial statements, and have them typed out, the full details of the case get embedded in your mind much deeper than if you are just reading the papers objectively."

"Some of your verdicts—say, 10 to 20 percent, would you agree?—appear to have largely resulted from the preliminary spadework: observations at the scene of the crime, interviews with witnesses, questioning of the client. Without this preparation having been done personally, would you conclude that a number of these cases could have been lost; and, as a corollary, that it is less likely that your record could have been achieved in England?"

"It is difficult to say. Preparation of a case is necessary in any land to procure the best results. A more important consideration might well be the jury, for, although human nature is the same the world over, knowing the type of juror, where he comes from, what would appeal to him, is of the utmost importance. The cattle farmer, for instance, in a country area will take a dim view of any witness who has a conviction for stealing cattle. He would be reluctant to accept that a cattle thief could ever speak the truth as a witness to another type of crime. I would say knowledge of human nature, in general, and, in particular, the individual types that form a given jury, has been the most helpful factor in putting aspects of the case in such a way that they appeal to them."

Lionel Luckhoo takes both civil and criminal cases, but it is his work in the criminal courts that gets preference. "I feel that criminal law is the most important aspect of jurisprudence," he says, "because it encompasses the safety of the subject, the regulation of society, and the fundamental freedoms. Basically, law is a question of individual rights; civil law relates to damages, criminal law relates to liberties."

Legal training lays heavy emphasis on civil law. The student learns about criminal law after he is qualified; mainly, at the expense of his early clients. I asked Lionel if he agreed that the balance ought to be redressed, and, if so, how.

"The present-day approach of pupilage and young graduates compulsorily going into Chambers has rather taken care of this. In the old days—my day—after two years of study I was, so to speak, let loose on an unsuspecting public. Today, our law course in Guyana is some five years, and the young lawyer is much more 'experienced' when he goes into practice. Whether he turns out to be a better lawyer is a moot point."

Chapter 24

The Case of the Quizzical Judge

For Justice, though she's painted blind,
Is to the weaker side inclined.

—*Samuel Butler*

Judgment had been delivered by Lionel Luckhoo. A man came up to him. "Where's your dog?" he wanted to know.

"I don't have a dog," the puzzled judge answered.

"You should have. You're blankety blind."

It was not contempt of court. What Lionel had been judging was a beauty contest. And female beauty, far from being a matter for objective assessment, is notoriously in the eye of the beholder. (For the imperfect vision of our ancestors most of us can be duly grateful!)

As a judge of beauty, Lionel has had his share of criticism, even threats. Once a disgruntled onlooker muttered in his ear, "After this, you better stick to law, or someone gonna bust your head!" Another time, as chairman of the panel, he totaled the points and declared the wrong winner. When he corrected himself, and was trying to explain to an unbelieving audience that it was a genuine mistake, due to his being hopeless at arithmetic, a wag saved the day by calling out, "You mean you no good at figures!"

Lionel Luckhoo has few complaints to make against the blindness of judges in his own sphere. If on occasion the lower courts have differed from him, the higher he has taken his appeals, the more agreement he has found. Some of the judgments he has heard have puzzled him, nevertheless; some, he has resented, as being irrational or unfair.

During his first year at the Bar, he appeared before Magistrate C.R. Brown, a noted West Indian cricketer, in defense of a man charged with receiving stolen razor blades. It was a case that could go either way, and, after Lionel had addressed, the magistrate reserved his decision. Several weeks later, Lionel received notice that judgment was to be given. "Ah, Mr. Luckhoo," said Magistrate Brown, "I remember your address so well. Is there anything else you would like to say?"

Lionel thought this sounded a bit ominous. Why would the magistrate ask him for further remarks if he was going to decide in his favor? He replied, "No, your worship. I have had a full say, and you appeared to understand the points I was making."

So the magistrate ran through his notes: how witness A for the prosecution had said this, and he was impressed by it, and witness B for the prosecution had said that, and he accepted it, and so on. After giving all the possible reasons for convicting the accused, he ended by saying, "For the reasons which I have given, in the course of my judgment, and because I remember so vividly the address of counsel for the defense, I must dismiss this case. " Lionel still wonders how he won it!

On occasions when he has had cause to be irate with judges, Lionel has usually avoided the heated clash in favor of the icy comment. After an annoyingly bad summing up in a murder trial, the judge turned to him and said, "Sir Lionel, would you like to add anything, or make any comment on what I have said?" Lionel responded, "My lord, I am fully aware of the law of contempt. I do not wish to find myself in the embarrassing position that might arise if I were to make any comment." And he sat down.

A similar invitation to comment was offered by a judge who had summed up strongly against his client. "My lord," said Lionel, "your directions of law the jury are bound to follow, and it would be impertinent of me to suggest that your lordship has incorrectly construed the law to them. Your lordship's views on the questions of fact I do not agree with at all, but this is a matter which neither you nor I can determine. It is a matter for the jury."

A lapse into rudeness by way of a private comment led to one of Lionel Luckhoo's most embarrassing moments in court. He was halfway through a case of murder and, as always, had arrived a few minutes early to relax before the battle, when a colleague came to him and said, "How is the judge taking it?" "Oh," said Lionel, "the old fool never indicates one way or the other until he is summing up, and then you know on which side he falls." Then from behind him he heard the gentle voice of Mr. Justice Manning, an English High Court judge, who had come in quietly and unobserved: "Yes, Mr. Luckhoo, the old fool believes in the principle of not making up his mind until he has heard all the evidence."

The worst blowup Lionel had with the Bench happened within two years of his going into practice, and not as a defender, but in the role of prosecutor. But it was a private prosecution, in which his client was very much the underdog.

David Reginald Hay-Neave was a prize pukka sahib, a relic of the outdated breed—even in 1942—who regarded themselves as born to rule the "lesser breeds without the law." An English public-school product, he had served with the 10th Lancers in India—where his favorite sport was pig-sticking! —before taking a commission in the Colonial Police. It was a pig that brought trouble upon him in British Guiana, though the real trouble may have been caused by pigmentation.

The pig was missing, and Hay-Neave decided that a young black Guianese, George Hope, had stolen it. He accused him, and Hope denied it. When Hay-Neave said he was going to arrest him, Hope started to run. In a Keystone Cops kind of episode, Hay-Neave then chased young George from house to house through the village. The comedy stopped when Hope ran into his own home. Hay-Neave followed, cornered him in his room, and shot him through the backside. The bullet entered the scrotum, by lucky chance missing the testes.

George Hope retained Lionel Luckhoo. He needed him, for never before in British Guiana had an information been sworn for the arrest of a superintendent of police. When the court refused to have Hay-Neave arrested for attempted murder, Lionel proceeded by way of an amended charge of malicious wounding. After evidence had been led to show his previous hostility to George Hope, Lionel cross-examined the defendant.

"Mr. Hay-Neave, why did you shoot a man from behind when he was facing the wall?"

"Well, I expected he would do something to me."

"Something! What something? Hurl a bomb?"

"Well, I didn't know if he had a gun or knife. "

"Did you tell him you would shoot?"

"No."

"Why didn't you tell him to put up his hands?"

"I was out of breath from running, and if he had attacked me I could hardly have defended myself."

"But you could have asked him to hold his hands above his head?"

"Yes, I could. But it all happened so quickly."

"You are a prize shot. Did you aim to shoot him through his backside?"

"I didn't aim. I just fired."

"But it is a fact that you shot him through his backside?"

"Yes."

"Why were you arresting him?"

"To inquire into his story about the pig."

"Did you have a warrant?"

"No."

"When you left the station, did you intend to arrest him?"

"No."

"You made up your mind because he was not cooperative?"

"Yes, that is so."

Lionel accused the witness of having a superior attitude to blacks and coloreds, whom he pejoratively called "natives."

"I have served elsewhere and handled all kinds of people," Hay-Neave replied. "It is only here I get trouble."

"You mean it is only in British Guiana that the natives stand up against your patronizing, insufferable conduct. Supposing you had killed this man, what would have been your defense?"

His counsel, H.C. Humphreys, K.C., objected to the question, but Hay-Neave petulantly answered, "Clearly, self-defense."

"Who were you defending?"

"Myself and the administration."

"From what?"

"From an attack I feared might come."

"The attack had not yet come . . . had not begun?"

"No."

"Then is not this an excuse?"

"No. The law must be respected."

"You respect nothing. Neither law nor people. Only your own pigmentation."

When, after this, the magistrate Kenneth Stoby ruled that there was no *prima facie* case, and discharged Hay-Neave, Lionel rose, wild with anger. "If that is your conception of justice," he told the magistrate, "then all I learned at the Inns will have to be revised."

"Are you being rude?"

"Hardly, sir. I am being truthful."

"Young man, you are showing contempt for the court."

"No, sir. I am deeply concerned that there should be no contempt for justice. I propose to bring this matter to the attention of the Attorney General."

Lionel did write to the Attorney General, but received no satisfaction. He then wrote to the Governor and the Secretary of State for the Colonies. The Governor telephoned to tell him that Hay-Neave was being transferred within the next twenty-four hours, and he was.

2

The view from the Bench has never appealed to Lionel Luckhoo. As long ago as 1954, he was offered a judgeship by the then Governor of British Guiana, Sir Derek Jakeway. From time to time, he rejected other offers of appointment, until, in 1976, Prime Minister Forbes Burnham suggested that he should accept for a limited period, as a form of national service. So the day came when the parties assembled in Criminal Assize Court No. 2 rose to the entry of Mr. Justice Luckhoo.

It would be stretching it a bit unfairly to say that, as a judge, he was a good defender. But Lionel himself confesses, "It was difficult to get over the fact that I was no longer defense counsel, and I committed the cardinal sin of asking too many questions. I just couldn't see a question remaining unanswered because counsel was not asking it. Maybe I was also a bit lenient in my sentences, but I sought to give a square deal to every accused."

This inclination towards the weaker side—the defense, with the full armory of the State arraigned against it, is always the weaker side in a criminal trial—did not save Lionel Luckhoo from being threatened by a convicted prisoner. This sooner or later is the fate of every judge, though the threats are hardly ever fulfilled.

Oliver Hinckson, a former Intelligence Officer in the Guyanese Defence Force, was notorious for having introduced a new dimension of crime into the country. He had gathered a bunch of criminals around him, and planned their robberies like military operations. His latest scheme was to dress his accomplices in guards' uniforms, provide them with guns, and send them to the home of the manager of the bank at Linden. After forcing the manager to open the bank, they were to kill him and throw his body into the river, in a sack loaded with weights so it would not surface. The police would then find an open safe, money gone, manager missing, and could make their deductions accordingly. The plot came to light before it could be put into action, and Hinckson was caught with the uniforms, guns, sacks, and weights in his possession. He came before Judge Luckhoo on the minor charge of possession, while more serious charges concerning other crimes were being prepared. Lionel saw that he had a fair trial, but covered the case as fully as possible in his summing up. When he was found guilty and sentenced to two years, Hinckson said, menacingly, "It is because of you I am convicted, and this I will not forget."

Already, he must have planned his escape. He was taken from prison to face charges, at a preliminary inquiry, of obtaining $84,000 by false pretenses from the Guyana National Co-operative Bank. A confederate with a motorcycle was waiting in the yard below the three-story courthouse. Hinckson leaped from the dock, ran through the open door, and gained the veranda, then jumped from the rail to the pillion of the motorcycle twenty feet below, and away it roared. That was the last that was seen of Hinckson in Georgetown for two years. "Wanted" posters were put up, and a reward offered, without result. Police believed he had crossed the border into Surinam, and, from there, had reached Canada or the United States. Then in September, 1978, Hinckson walked into police headquarters and gave himself up. Most of the time since his escape he had spent in Brazil and other South American countries. He had won a Casa de las Americas Literature award from the Cuban government for a book, *The Enemy Within*—and had the $1,000 prize revoked because the entry was submitted under a false name.

At times, Mr. Justice Luckhoo was stern with offenders. *Choke-and-rob* is the Guyanese term for mugging. One assailant seizes the victim with an arm around the throat from behind, while, from the front, an accomplice robs him of money and valuables. Such crimes were becoming increasingly prevalent, and Lionel gave judgment in a particularly vicious case:

"Although students of human behavior disagree as to the purpose of punishment," he said, "it must be accepted that punishment is basically necessary for control of individual and group behavior. I accept the theory of deterrence. Wrongdoers must be punished to discourage others from committing similar crimes.

"Choke-and-rob, robbery with violence, is so prevalent in Guyana that people fear to walk the streets. Our streets must be made safe for all users. Choke-robbers are not easy of detection—they strike and flee. This case is a particularly heinous one, a shameful and outrageous crime. The statement made by prisoner Reis to the police sets out the history of the crime. He confesses that two of his confederates and fellow-conspirators criminally assaulted one of the two victims. I shall not take this into account in the infliction of penalties, as they were not charged with rape. But knives were certainly used at the throats of the victims. The victims were, literally, kidnaped. One was bundled into the trunk of a car, where he lost consciousness. Their money, jewelry, and goods were taken away and divided. There were five in the gang. Two are missing, and I ask the State to spare no pains in seeing that they are brought to trial."

After giving a written statement to the police, Reis had later denied that it was free and voluntary, and he pleaded not guilty at the trial. Lionel had ruled that the statement was admissible, so far as Reis was concerned. Of course, it could not be accepted as evidence against the other defendants.

"Let me say that the law views this as a crime of the utmost gravity," the judge declared. "The physical results of an assault can be cured. The assault on the mind may make a much more lasting impression. Such sufferings are not overtly perceived. The trauma, the shock, the effect on nerves and mind, can wound mortally.

"Society must be protected. I feel that for too long many have received lenient sentences, which are all too quickly served. Then the same individuals return to the foray to continue their careers of crime. The law prescribes, for robbery under arms, not only imprisonment for life, but a whipping or a flogging. In my view, these prisoners must receive corporal punishment—this is the infliction of pain by whipping. They must also receive mental punishment by a long custodial sentence of such a nature that all might know the manner and form in which the courts of our land are extending themselves to protect the lives, sanity, and property of individuals who are pounced upon by gangs of hoodlums bent on the use of brute force to take that which is not theirs.

"It is for this reason that I asked the prisoners to show cause why they should not be sentenced to life imprisonment." (The accused had pleaded that, although they had records, it was several years since they had been in trouble. "You mean, several years since you were caught and charged," the judge observed, dryly. "I give warning that this court will not hesitate to order life sentences for fit cases of choke-and-rob.)

"Each prisoner is sentenced to six years on each count, and, in addition, to receive eight strokes each. The sentences are to be concurrent. They showed no mercy to their victims, and they must expect none from the court."

(The usual penalty was five years for a bad case of choke-and-rob. Lionel gave six years, rather than longer sentences, because he did not wish too great a disparity between his sentences and those of other judges. To make up for the shorter sentences, he ordered the whippings, which is what hardened criminals greatly fear—most would gladly take a couple of extra years on their sentence to escape it.)

Mr. Justice Luckhoo never tried a murder case. "Perhaps it was just as well," he admits, "because I think, almost unconsciously, I would have fought for an acquittal."

Lionel Luckhoo still sits in judgment on occasion. He is chairman of a disciplinary committee that looks into any charge of breach of ethics brought against a barrister or solicitor. In this court, the accused are all qualified to plead for themselves, but, should they falter, they can surely count on the defense case not going by default while Lionel Luckhoo is one of the judges.

Chapter 25
The Case of the Dumbstruck Defendant

History is little else than a picture of human crimes and misfortunes.

—Voltaire

Since his arrest, the man accused of murder had said not a word. Fortunately for Lionel Luckhoo, it was his brother Lloyd who had been assigned to the defense: there was just no way to defend a man who would give no instructions. The prisoner kept silence up to and throughout the very short trial. When he had been convicted and sentenced to be hanged, he spoke just one word. That word was "Thanks."

When Lionel was faced with the problem of a silent client, it was not that the man was unwilling to speak, but that he was unable. A bullet, fired through his mouth, had deprived him of the power of speech. And, on the face of things, it seemed that no degree of eloquence on his part could have lessened the weight of the case against him.

Up to the time that he was charged with murder, Alvin Yellery had lived a Samuel-Smiles-style success story, the sort that school-leavers are, traditionally, encouraged to emulate. Starting out as an office boy, he had risen through the ranks of junior clerk, senior clerk, assistant manager, and manager, to managing director of one of the largest business firms in Guyana. Now, it appeared, *hubris* had overtaken him. In an hour of frenzy, he had murdered his wife, attempted his own life, and, failing, rushed to the nearby graveyard, where he embraced his mother's tombstone before he was arrested.

It was tragedy of a Sophoclean order. Told in the prosaic prose of the police, the main facts of the case appeared to be incontestible. Sergeant Roberts lived only a few doors away from the home of the Yellerys. "I heard one shot, then, thirty seconds later, another shot," he testified at the trial. "I looked out of the window and saw the accused running down the road. I found this strange. I went to the home of the accused, and there I found the wife of the accused, dead."

A prison guard, Leonard Cumberbatch, took up the story from there. He was walking down the road, and Yellery rushed by him. He saw him go into the Georgetown cemetery. He did not follow him. Yellery had appeared to be sobbing as he went by.

Police Constable Victor had made the arrest. Alvin Yellery was leaving the cemetery and heading back towards the house, still running, when Victor caught and held him. He did not say anything when cautioned. He was bleeding from the mouth, and had to be taken to the hospital.

Cross-examined by Lionel Luckhoo, the constable admitted that, if the accused had wished to speak, he could not, owing to the wound. When Lionel had interviewed his client, he was still unable to talk, but gave instructions and answered questions by writing on a pad.

The surgeon specialist who examined Yellery at the Georgetown Public Hospital had found an entrance hole, made by a bullet, on the inside of the mouth, but no hole of exit. When X-rays were taken, the bullet was seen to be lodged about an inch and a half below the right temple, and an inch and a half in front of the right ear, at a depth which would make any attempt to remove it dangerous.

In answer to a question from Lionel, the surgeon said the accused had been tested for alcohol. The test was negative. For four months, Yellery had not been able to speak at all. He was gradually regaining the power, but his speech was still very halting. The bullet remained where it was, in a position that made it a constant threat to his life.

The main witness to the events leading up to the shooting incident was a nephew of the accused. He said, in evidence:

"My uncle and I had been to cricket that day. We returned home together. I left him at his house and went to my own home, which is in the next building. Half an hour later, I heard a quarrel. The sound seemed to come from my uncle's house. The quarreling lasted about half an hour. The voices went on and on. Then I heard the sound of a gun, as if a revolver had gone off. I did not know what had happened.

"Ten minutes later, I went over to check at my uncle's home. I went in and found my aunt lying back on the rocker. I called out to her, and then I saw she was dead. I went to my uncle's room, and there I saw him, sitting on his bed, bleeding from his nose and mouth. In his hand he held a pistol. I became afraid, ran out and left the house, and reported to others what I had seen."

For the purposes of the defense, it was necessary to combat the implication that a quarrel between the Yellerys had resulted in murder. Lionel's first question led straight to that point.

"You know the voices of your uncle and his wife?"

"Yes."

"You would recognize those voices if you heard them?"

"Yes."

"Yet you did not recognize the voices you heard quarreling?"

"No."

"You would not say that they belonged to the accused and his wife?"

"No. I do not know to whom the voices belonged."

"The houses in the area are set very close to each other?"

"Yes."

"And it was difficult to tell where the voices came from? You could not be sure it was from your uncle's home?"

"No, I couldn't be sure."

"It might have been the voices of others living nearby that you heard?"

"That is true."

"Did your aunt and uncle get on well together?"

"Yes."

"Was he kind to her?"

"Yes, very kind."

"Would you agree that he was never unkind or cruel to her?"

"No, never. They both got on well together."

Lionel Luckhoo began his address quietly. He pointed out that Alvin Yellery was one of Guyana's outstanding citizens. By his application, ability, and dedication, he had worked his way to the top, winning the respect of all who had come into contact with him. He and his wife were devoted to each other. There could be no suggestion of ill feeling between them. Then what had happened on that fateful night?

"Only two people know what happened that night. One of them is dead. For four months or more, the other could not tell his story. Now that story will be told."

Alvin Yellery did not attempt to give evidence. It was his counsel who told the story.

"That night, they heard the sound of quarreling of neighbors—and considered themselves fortunate that their home was one of peace and love. Then, while changing his clothes, the accused took out of his pocket the revolver he had carried with him that day. He showed his wife how the safety catch operated. He told her what a wise precaution it was to have it on, in the event of an inadvertent pull on the trigger. And, while he was demonstrating, the gun went off. His wife slumped forward. He looked at her with astonishment, then anguish, when he found that she was dead—shot through the heart.

"In the agony of that moment, conscious of the fact that by his stupidity he had caused the death of the wife he loved, Alvin Yellery resolved to take his own life. He put the pistol to his open mouth and fired. It was a near-certain way to cause death. He should have died the moment he pulled the trigger, but fate decreed otherwise. This was not to be his end. By what seemed a miracle, he lived.

"Throwing the gun aside, he rushed out of the house as a man demented. He ran to gain comfort and help from the mother who had succored him as a child. He ran to the place where she rested—the burial ground. There in the cemetery, he lay on her tomb and wept and wept. He wept until his eyes could bring forth no more tears. But, while his eyes could weep themselves dry, his heart continued to cry in unending remorse.

"The depths of his feeling only he could know. Would a man kill that which he loved above all else? Would a man take the life of one who had been his loyal and devoted wife? Never!" Lionel's voice rang out the word in a hushed courtroom. Many were weeping. Quietly, he then pleaded, "This man's suffering and mental torture will live with him all his life. The sharpness of the mental pain which prevailed, the anguish which enveloped him, caused him to react by attempting to take his own life. Today, with the passage of time, the hurt may be assuaged a little, but the knowledge of his responsibility for the death of his wife will abide with him forever."

The State had been able to produce no evidence of malice aforethought. The prosecution had, accordingly, reduced the charge to manslaughter arising from the gross negligence and recklessness of the accused in handling a dangerous weapon. It was to Judge George Pompey that Lionel Luckhoo addressed his plea for clemency:

"Manslaughter can extend from near-murder to what is little more than common assault. It can extend from an act which borders on murder to the mischance or misfortune of a purely careless act. The State has now agreed that this is no case of murder. On the facts as I have described them, which mesh with the facts known by the State, the accused humbly pleads for an understanding heart of the Court—this is what Solomon chose, and the choice so pleased God that, not only was it granted, but with it he received all the things that had gone unasked. The continuing punishment of the accused is already twofold: firstly, living with the memory of what he has done; and, secondly, walking by day and sleeping by night with a bullet within him that can claim his life at any moment of time.

"A brief moment, an irresponsible act, a careless act, and for the rest of his life he must bear this cross, the like of which no court can impose—the deep sadness of being responsible for the death of the person whom he cherished—his wife. Within this setting, I implore the mercy of the Court to permit him to sign a bond, that he may leave this Court, and, indeed, this country, forthwith, to try to begin life anew in some other part of the world."

It was a moving and impassioned plea for the sympathy of the court. As Lionel Luckhoo drew the picture of a mind that had been pushed to its limits and had shattered under the strain, there were few dry eyes in the courtroom. The judicial response was to release Alvin Yellery on bond—the judgment for which his counsel had prayed.

It was the first time for Lionel that such a sentence had been imposed for an offense as serious as murder reduced to manslaughter.

2

Blood, demonstrably, is thicker than water; but, like water, it can become contaminated. When Alvin Yellery was on trial, his nephew gave testimony as favorable to his uncle as the circumstances allowed. The uncle of Chanderpaul Singh tried hard to get his nephew condemned.

It was the uncle, Harry Singh, who informed the police that he had found his brother Dyal Singh lying stabbed in his bedroom. After checking on the body, the police asked him three questions: Who else lives in the house? Who had reason to kill your brother? Whom do you suspect?

Harry Singh gave the same answer to all three questions. Just one name: that of his nephew Chanderpaul Singh, the eighteen-year-old son of the victim.

Police inquiries confirmed that Dyal Singh and his son had lived alone together. Other witnesses besides the uncle were found to testify that there had been frequent quarrels between Chanderpaul and his father. Some said they had heard the youngster make threats against the older man.

But Harry Singh remained the vital witness. Only he claimed to have heard the sounds of a scuffle from his brother's house next door, on the morning of the murder, and then to have seen his nephew leave the house. Shortly after, he discovered his brother's body, face downwards on the floor, with a knife sticking in the back. Clearly, the case would be won or lost on the cross-examination of Harry Singh.

Answering Lionel Luckhoo, Singh said there was a gap of about thirty-six feet between the two houses. Although he had heard what seemed to be a fight going on, he had heard no voices. He did not go at once to see what was happening.

He did not shout to ask what was wrong. When he saw Chanderpaul leave, he did not call out to him. He waited fifteen minutes before going over to his brother's house.

Why did he not go over at once, when Chanderpaul came out of the house? Because he thought all was well. Then why did he go fifteen minutes later? In order to check that all was well.

"You could have checked by calling out to your brother?"

"Yes, I could."

"Did you try to do that?"

"No."

"Then why did you go over?"

"I wanted to be sure that all was well with my brother."

"You were anxious to go over as soon as you saw the accused come out of the house?"

"Well, why didn't you go over immediately?"

To this there was no answer. Even when the question was repeated, Harry Singh made no reply.

Lionel turned to the matter of motive. Dyal Singh had left no will. He had no insurance policies or large sums of money in the bank, from which his son might expect to benefit.

"What property did your brother own at his death?"

"Only the house he lived in."

"In whose name was the house?"

"It was in the names of my brother and myself."

What did Harry Singh do when he found his brother lying on his face, arms outstretched? He said he had not touched anything in the room. He had gone straight to the police station, half a mile away.

"Did you turn the body over?"

"No."

"Did you speak to your brother?"

"No."

"Did you know, at that stage, whether he was alive or dead?"

"No, I couldn't tell. My first thought was to run and bring the police."

"You did not try to give him first aid, see if he was breathing, anything at all?"

"No."

"The knife was stuck in your brother's back, as if someone came on him from behind and did it?"

"I couldn't say. All I can say is that the knife was in his back."

Then Lionel put it to the witness that he and his brother had not been getting on well together. He had wanted to sell the property, and Dyal had opposed the sale.

"And you are the person who stabbed your brother?"

Judge Hughes stepped in quickly, to warn the witness that he need not answer. "You need not answer," Lionel allowed, "but I am giving you an opportunity to think about the question and to answer it. Did you stab your brother?"

The seconds stretched out, to the waiting court. Finally, Harry Singh said, "I am not answering that question . . . but I did not kill my brother." A strange and curious reply.

The cross-examination must have raised doubts in the mind of the jury. If Harry Singh thought there had been a fight, why had he waited for fifteen minutes after Chanderpaul left the house before going to see what had happened? Why had he gone half a mile to fetch the police before making sure that his brother was not alive and needing medical aid?

There was nothing to support Harry Singh's story of a fight. Sergeant George, the first police officer on the scene, testified that Dyal Singh's house had shown no sign of disturbance. The medical findings were that, apart from the knife wound, the only mark of violence the body bore was a bruise on the forehead. This would be consistent with his having fallen on his face when he was stabbed.

The inference to be drawn from Harry Singh's evidence was that Dyal had been stabbed during a violent quarrel with his son, with a likely presumption of it being a face-to-face encounter. The medical witness stated that the fatal stab was a downward thrust between the shoulder blades.

"If two persons were facing each other," Lionel Luckhoo asked, "is there not a greater likelihood that one would stab the other in the chest or abdomen, rather than in the back?"

"Possibly," was the cautious answer.

"The knife was driven in with some force, was it not?"

"Yes."

"And a shorter person would find it very difficult to encircle his arm around a taller person and drive in the knife with a downward thrust, in the position it was found?"

"It might be difficult, but it could be done."

"How tall was the deceased?"

"He was five feet, ten inches."

"How tall is the accused, would you say? About five feet, five inches?"

"I would say so."

"And how tall is the witness Harry Singh?"

"He is about five feet, nine inches."

Chanderpaul Singh gave evidence on his own behalf. He said he had not left home at eight o'clock on the morning his father died, as his uncle alleged, but an hour earlier. Before Chanderpaul left the witness stand, Lionel had him perform a mock struggle with the marshal, who was several inches taller, to demonstrate how difficult it would be for him to strike such a blow as had killed his father, if they were facing each other in a fight.

During his address to the jury, Lionel pointed to Harry Singh, whereupon the star witness for the prosecution attempted to leave court. The judge stopped him.

"He may seek to flee the wrathful words uttered by a mere mortal," Lionel commented to the jury. "He cannot flee from the judgment of the Immortal, which, one day, he must face."

After Judge Hughes had summed up in favor of the accused, the jury took only fifteen minutes to bring in an acquittal.

Chapter 26
The Case of the Hypnotized Witnesses

Yea, when men speak,
that man I most detest
Who locks the verity within his breast.
—*Homer*

Women, too. For, until Women Libbers succeed in having literature rewritten in "worser English" (as Robert Frost might put it), the male will continue to embrace the female. In our present case, the silence of the mother and daughter was unnatural. Not that they kept quiet in court about what they had seen; there, on the contrary, the suspicion was that they had not seen as much as they claimed. What jarred, what clamored for explanation, was that, beforehand, they had whispered not a word to anyone of the damning evidence they could give. Not even to each other. Or, so they said!

Seudat Persaud was the owner of Taymouth Manor, an estate near Queenstown, Essequibo. On May 10, 1977, Seudat was bulldozing a section of his land. With him were his young son Ramesh and a tractor boy. Late in the afternoon, his wife Dhanwantie and her daughter Brijwantie went out to where Seudat was working.

Nearing seven o'clock, Seudat stopped work. He sent the tractor boy off with the equipment. Ramesh went with him, riding the tractor boy's bicycle. Seudat Persaud intended to walk home with his wife and daughter.

They set off east, along Capoey Dam. Brijwantie held her father's hand; Dhanwantie took hold of his shirt sleeve on the other side. They had gone no more than 100 yards, when there came the blast of a shotgun. Seudat fell to the ground.

Both women turned. The shot had come from behind them. What they saw, or did not see, became the main issue, when three tenant farmers—Doodnauth, Jairam, and Harriram, long-time friends of Seudat who, more recently, it was alleged, had threatened to beat and kill him—were put on trial for his murder.

Dhanwantie then tended to her husband. "I went to the trench, dipped water, and threw some on my husband's face. He drank two mouthfuls. Then the breath was gone. He was dead."

Mother and daughter ran to the public road. Brijwantie hurried on ahead to get help. She returned in a car with four neighbors: Narine the car owner, Clement Paul, Dennis, and Sam. They all went back to view the body of Seudat. They then drove to the Persaud home, took Seudat's car, and, with Narine still driving, went to the Anna Regina Police Station.

"Me husband got shot!" Dhanwantie informed Sergeant Tucker.

She did not say who had shot him.

Although Dhanwantie and her daughter were at the police station until four o'clock the next morning, giving statements, she mentioned the name of only one of the three men who later were charged with Seudat's murder. She had seen Harriram and two others running away, she told Sergeant Tucker, when she turned around after hearing the gunshot. At the trial of Doodnauth, Jairam, and Harriram, she claimed to have recognized all three.

The discrepancy emerged when Lionel Luckhoo, defending the three accused, applied for the original statements to the police to be put in evidence. This was made possible by virtue of rulings, in the Baksh case (Chapter 1) by the Privy Council, and in the Harris case (Chapter 20), that such applications should be granted, where statement differs from testimony.

"Me husband got shot," were the words Dhanwantie used to Clement Paul, when Brijwantie first brought the neighbors to the scene. She did not tell him the names of any persons she saw. No, she said, in reply to Lionel, she had no reason for withholding the names.

Dhanwantie had asked a man named Martinboro, whom she described as her closest friend, to make arrangements for Seudat's funeral.

"Did you tell Martinboro, 'Me husband got shot'?" Lionel asked her.

"Yes."

"Did he ask how, or words to that effect?"

"No."

"If he had asked, would you have told him?"

"No."

Dhanwantie said that, although she looked at her husband's back for signs of injury, it was too dark to see exactly where the shotgun blast had hit him.

"You were within a foot or two of him?"

"Yes."

"You couldn't see his wound, yet you purport to recognize three running men from behind, when they are forty or fifty yards away?"

"I did see them."

"Yes, you saw three men, but you cannot swear it was these three men."

"I maintain that I saw them."

"Were you stunned by the event . . . gunfire . . . your husband falls?"

"Yes."

"Did you rush to your husband's aid immediately?"

"No, I was too confused."

"Were you so confused that you couldn't really say which of the accused ran where?"

"Well . . ."

"Could you have made a mistake about the directions the men took?"

"Yes."

"Would you prefer to say that you saw three men running, but you can't say who ran where?"

"Yes, I can't say which accused ran where. But I saw them."

"And you were anxious that they should be arrested?"

"Yes."

"Was there a large crowd of people when you reached the public road?"

"Yes."

"They would be willing to help you?"

"Yes."

"Yet you never told them that these three villagers, whom everyone knew, shot your husband and ran away?"

"No."

Brijwantie Persaud was fourteen years old. Her evidence, in all important particulars, supported that given by her mother. They had walked about 100 yards along the dam, when she heard the gunblast. "Oh, God," her father said, and he fell to the ground. She turned quickly and saw the three accused men running away. One wore shorts; the others, beach pants. All three wore long-sleeved shirts. They were all forty to fifty yards away when she first saw them, running north. Then they turned to the east.

Cross-examined, Brijwantie said her mother had told her what had happened in court earlier, but she had not told her what questions were asked. She could not have identified the three men from behind, had they continued north. She saw their faces, and recognized them, when they turned east.

When shown the depositions from the preliminary inquiry, Brijwantie agreed that she had not told the magistrate that the fleeing men had changed direction and gone east. She realized that, if what she had said in the magistrate's court were true, she could not have identified the defendants, so it was important to explain that they went east. She could not explain how she came to omit it.

The omission must have seemed even more inexplicable to the jury when Brijwantie revealed how well she had kept her presence of mind at the time of the shooting. She did not run to hide. She did not run to get water. "I was more concerned to see who did shoot him. It struck me I would have to give evidence. I tried to recognize the men."

But then, having recognized them, Brijwantie remained silent. "I realized it was important, yet I did not tell my mother. I did not ask her if she knew the men running. She did not tell me, either. It was not until after I gave my statement to the police that I learned my mother had recognized the men who were running away."

To undergo cross-examination in court would be a considerable ordeal for most girls of fourteen. Brijwantie kept the cool she had so admirably preserved, apparently, from the night of the murder.

"I was not anxious to tell my mother that I had seen and recognized the men," she confided to Lionel Luckhoo. And her reason for silence? "I wanted to keep it for the court. I never told my mother what I knew. My mother told me she saw the men, when we went home [at 4:00 A.M., after giving statements]. Even then, I did not tell her anything."

How the men were dressed appeared to have created a certain amount of confusion in Brijwantie's mind. In court, she said one man was in short pants; two, in long pants. She had told the magistrate that they all were wearing short pants. In her statement to the police, it was long pants, but this she now denied having said.

Although she admitted it was getting dark, and the men were fifty yards distant, and running away, Brijwantie said she saw the gun that one of them was carrying, even to the "hole in front"—meaning, the muzzle. She regarded the gun as being important, but had not mentioned it to the police.

She had told a neighbor, Hillary Young, "My father got shot." She did not tell him she saw men running away, and that one had a gun.

She had told the car driver Narine, "My father got shot." He did not ask how her father got shot. If he had asked, she would not have told him more than she had.

People in the crowd outside her home asked what was wrong. She told them, "My father got shot." They did not ask her who shot him.

She did not mention the names of the accused to the police until six or seven hours after she arrived at the police station. She could not hear what her mother was saying, when Dhanwantie gave her statement, though she tried to listen. Afterward, she did not ask her mother what she had told the police. It was only at the preliminary inquiry that she heard what her mother had to say.

Towards the end of the exhaustive cross-examination, Lionel asked, "Do you think that you are a reasonable person?"

Brijwantie answered, "Yes."

"Now, I want you to be honest with the court. This is the story you are telling the jury. A gun sounded. . . . My father dropped dead. . . . I was not afraid. . . . I saw three men running north. . . . I could not recognize them until they turned east. Yet I never told the police nor the magistrate that they turned east. I said they ran straight north.

"I saw the men. . . . I knew them. Yet I never called their names. I never told my mother, or Narine, or the neighbors, or anyone. I merely said that my father got shot. I never asked my mother if she recognized the accused. I was anxious to tell the police my story; yet I did not tell them that one of the accused was carrying a gun, though I realized the gun was important.

"Now, witness, you have sworn to tell the truth. . . . Is it a reasonable story you are asking the jury to believe?"

Brijwantie prevaricated. "Please repeat the question."

"Is that story—and the answers you have given—a reasonable story, which you expect the jury to believe?"

Brijwantie held his gaze, as Lionel willed her to discredit her own evidence. Clearly, she had been lying. She did not flush when he asked, "Would you not agree it is an unreasonable story?" He kept nodding his head, and she began nodding her head.

There was stillness, suspense, in the crowded courtroom. Walking closer to the witness box, holding her gaze, Lionel insisted, "You will admit that yours is not a reasonable story? What you are saying is that you would not expect the jury to accept your story."

Still looking at him, she answered slowly, "I agree I could not expect them to accept my story."

"You have altered your story on material aspects. You have attacked the police who brought this prosecution. Are you not merely carrying out your mother's wishes, and seeking to accuse these persons who did not get on with your father?"

Brijwantie made no reply. Lionel had made his point; the prosecution case was now denounced by its chief witness.

The defense had expert testimony on call to prove that, if the witnesses' statements were true, the gunshot spread would have been different from what it was. The testimony was not necessary. Lionel made a submission that there was no case to go to the jury; the evidence was so unsatisfactory it would be unsafe to allow it.

Judge Kennard overruled the submission, but said that the cross-examination had so discredited the testimony that the jury might stop the case if it wished, and say it did not need to hear the defense.

After a short conference, the jury said it was satisfied. The evidence for the prosecution was so destroyed that the jury was ready to return verdicts of not guilty on each of the accused. Lionel has often cited this cross-examination as "willing" an untruthful witness to speak the truth.

2

Women leave crime to their menfolk. Less than 10 percent of the crimes of violence and fraud in Guyana are perpetrated by women. Murder? Five percent. Only twelve of Lionel Luckhoo's murder clients have been women. Why such restraint on the part of those who are so often maligned as being the deadlier sex?

"Women possess a stronger protective feeling than men," Lionel Luckhoo says. "Before a woman goes to the opposite extreme, and becomes destructive, she first has to overcome this native, natural feeling. A compelling reason is required for her to move from the passively protective to the actively belligerent. If she is with a man, she might agree with what he is doing, but rarely does she take part in the action. Her support is 'moral' rather than active.

"And women are more honest than men. Throughout my whole life, I have found this to be so. I remember, when I was president of the Turf Club, we were having a lot of petty pilfering. We started to take on women, and matters eased considerably. Of course, you might say that a man wearing a suit has a lot more pockets in which to quickly stuff away the odd dollar than a girl in a short-sleeved dress. Or, perhaps, being found out means more to her than it does to a man, so she takes fewer chances. But, whatever the reason, she is inclined to be more honest."

How about women as witnesses?

"On the witness stand, I find, a woman who is lying tends to become belligerent. This is always indicative. She will cover her mendacity, her vilification of others, by becoming loud, and even attacking. In this way, she feels she justifies what is happening. A man can often remain cool and collected while answering untruthfully, taking it as a matter of course. This is not usually a woman's reaction. Why it should be so, I don't know; perhaps a psychologist would be able to explain it. But I do find that you can get the truth much more readily out of a woman than a man.

"There is one exception—in the case of sexual offenses, a woman is inclined to be untruthful. I have had a lot of rape cases, and I know of instances in which there has been an attempt at rape, but no penetration; yet, the woman has given all the details of penetration. Why is this? Because she feels that something sacred to her has been violated, and is prepared to go the limit in her testimony, so that the full penalty will be thrown at the man."

Women are so reluctant to testify, I reminded him, that the majority of rapes are never reported.

"That is absolutely true," Lionel agreed. "But the one who reports it is the one who is willing to go the whole hog, to exaggerate, do whatever she has to do to have her honor vindicated. In other words, although nine out of ten women might not report it, the one who does is usually ready to transgress against the truth, if it helps."

"If bent on perjury, who is more likely to hold up under cross-examination—a woman or a man?"

"I would say a man. With a woman, there are usually telltale signs. She tends to lick her lips as soon as she begins to lie. The saliva dries up. Not only will she lick her lips; I have known them to call for water. And a woman, when she lies, will invariably look at you. I have found this to be a key in many cases. Once I had a counterfeit case, I remember, in which the principal witness was a woman. When she was telling where she had seen the boy put the bag of notes, she began to sweat, and asked for water. I knew at once she was not speaking the truth, so I investigated every moment of her day, and exactly where she had been. When we went to the *locus*, we found that she could not have seen what she claimed, and I knew I had been justified in pursuing a rather relentless cross-examination."

I asked Lionel to expand a little on the question of genuine and lying witnesses.

"Well, most people, going to court for the first time, must be nervous—perhaps overawed by the atmosphere, judge and jury watching, a man getting up and putting questions to him. But what happens is that, as the prosecutor goes through his story very carefully with him, and he answers yes or no, or explains what he means, then gradually the agitation wears off. He absorbs the atmosphere of the room, he becomes accustomed to the fact that he is standing and speaking, and realizes he is just telling a story of what has happened. When counsel rises to cross-examine, he may start being nervous again. But, if counsel does as I always seek to do initially—speak kindly, quietly, to him—the agitation again becomes less and less. But if he is not speaking the truth, if he is speaking only half-truth, then, when he is asked any questions which seek to go beneath the surface, he becomes more and more worried, because what his lips are saying his heart knows to be untrue.

"You were there when I asked the witness if he had seen a light on the porch. Before he answered, he pressed his hands against the rail and gave three or four short, abrasive rubs. I knew he was not going to tell the truth, but that suited my purpose. It would have been bad, from the defense point of view, if he had turned around his evidence and said he now remembered there was no light, or could not be sure. As I asked more questions, he became more agitated, he didn't know what to do with his hands, and his legs began to wobble. I could so easily have got him into a state where he was just flat out lying, but it would have served no useful purpose at the preliminary inquiry. No, that is reserved for the trial, when there will be twelve men and women who have to return a verdict. Let them see him grovel when I expose his lies."

"There must be some witnesses, the more highly strung, who remain nervous, even though they are telling the truth?" I asked.

"Yes, indeed, there are, but their nervousness will not *increase*, except when their subconscious is activated by the knowledge that they are not speaking the truth. You get them thinking that, although you may have a little bit of a reputation, you are just another person of their own kind talking to them, and it has a clearing, calming effect that eases their tension."

Chief Justice Boland regarded Lionel Luckhoo as the best practitioner of the art of gently prying out truthful answers from witnesses, that he had ever seen. Lecturing young lawyers, he cited him as an example, in that he never bullied the witness, and, therefore, the replies he received carried greater weight with the jury. In some cases—Brijwantie Persaud is an example—he succeeds in getting a hostile witness to refute the testimony just given.

"When I attempt to compel a witness to answer my way," Lionel says, "I never put the questions very loudly. I seek to make my voice caressing, and I will look the witness straight in the eyes and bow my head slowly. But, if the witness is obdurate, a high-pitched voice and a stern demeanor will often dig out the answer. By this twofold approach, I feel, truth is elicited. Perhaps the secret of it all is human understanding—being able to feel out the type of person, evaluate, and proceed accordingly."

"The first approach does suggest that, besides mesmerizing juries, as Judge Boland believed, you hypnotize witnesses, as well."

"Well, I remember one man who came out of court and said to me, 'Lawyer, you hypnotized me. I answered wrong.' He was furious. But that kind of thing happens only rarely. Talking of mesmerism, I remember my father had a clerk whose hero was Mesmer. He used to tell me that, by concentrating your thought, you could convey a message or a direction to a person. We were then schoolboys, and we used to experiment with cards, A willing B, who has made his mind a blank, to pick up what he is trying to communicate by thought. I was particularly good at transmitting, and hopeless at receiving. If I kept repeating to myself, 'ace of spades,' or whatever it might be, and the subject was asked what card I was thinking of, an uncanny number of times he would name the right card. I use this, at times, in willing a witness to say yes or no."

In a running-down case, Lionel Luckhoo had a witness who was clearly hostile to his client. He gave his evidence flawlessly—the distances involved, the number plates of the vehicles; he had everything at his fingertips. Lionel was making little headway with his cross-examination, until he had a sudden inspiration.

The witness wore very thick lenses, and Lionel could hardly see his eyes. He asked the man to take off his glasses. The witness took them off.

"Would you mind holding them while I ask a few questions?"

At this, the witness protested, and the judge was moved to inquire, "Is it really necessary?"

"You will see, your honor," Lionel said, though he really did not have a clue, himself, as to why he wished it to be done. He then asked questions, and at once the witness began to yield. He just did not seem able to remember details he had given earlier.

Lionel said, "Show me your hands, please."

The witness held up the backs of his hands for Lionel to see.

Lionel was still polite. "Turn them the other way round, please."

Slowly, with great reluctance, the witness turned his hands. Written on the palms were the data he had trotted out with such facility while giving evidence. The exposure of his patent dishonesty did much to win the case for Lionel Luckhoo's client. From the fingertips to the palms is a long stretch—and, possibly, deserves one!

The palm for sheer audacity, however, Lionel Luckhoo awards, not to a witness, but to one of his clients. The police had a strong case against Annamunthadoo, who was charged with the possession of stolen goods. It hinged, largely, on whether they had or had not found bolts of cloth in his room. Annamunthadoo contended that they were not in his room, but had been discovered in another part of the house.

Lionel succeeded in finding in the evidence discrepancies that fragmented the case. The jury brought in a verdict of not guilty, and the judge discharged the prisoner.

Whereupon, Annamunthadoo bowed and said, "Your honor, I wish to lay claim to the bolts of cloth. All along, the prosecution has been alleging that the police removed them from my room. I want them to put them back where they took them from."

Chapter 27
The Case of the Vicarious Victor

Yet do I hold it very stuff o' the conscience
To do no contriv'd murder.

—*Othello*

When I met Gowkarran Persaud, he was standing in the dock, accused of murder. It was the fourth time his case had come to trial.

The first time, after one of the longest preliminary inquiries Guyana has known, Lionel Luckhoo succeeded in getting the charge against Gowkarran dismissed. The Director of Public Prosecutions then overruled the magistrate, and ordered that Gowkarran be committed for trial.

At a full trial, the jury found him guilty. Lionel won a repeal of that verdict in the Appeal Court.

Now, Gowkarran Persaud faced a new trial. This time, Lionel Luckhoo was not available to defend him. And Gowkarran had refused to accept any other counsel. He stood alone, the first person in Guyana to conduct his own defense against a charge of murder.

He had spent the last four years in jail, for many months under sentence of death. Yet he appeared to be the most confident and alert person in the courtroom; certainly, the most buoyant character I have seen in any dock.

2

On the night of Sunday, September 9, 1973, an off-duty prison officer, named Rex Bishop, was cycling towards home. At about 11:20 P.M., he turned into Sandy Babb Street. Near the corner, across the street, at an angle from the Kitty Police Station, a white motor car was parked. The lights were on, the engine was running. No driver, no passengers; so Bishop thought. Then he noticed that the left rear door was open—and a man's foot was hanging out! He climbed off his bicycle, went close, and peered through the right rear window. A man lay between the front and back seats, his head resting against the door where Bishop stood. Looking down, Rex Bishop saw blood dripping on to the roadway at his feet.

He ran across to the police station. One of the policemen who went back with him, Constable Lyken, leaned into the car and struck a match. As it flared, they saw a brown-handled knife sticking in the neck of the now-dead man.

Minutes before Rex Bishop made his startling discovery, a telegraph operator, Brian Austin, had passed the same car at the same spot. Lights were on, the engine running, but the doors were closed. What attracted Austin's attention was that "two men in the back seat appeared to be working energetically with their hands over something between the front and back seats." Austin, feeling something was wrong, turned his motorcycle around to pass the car again. The two men "were still working away with their hands." He rode on.

What Austin saw was two men, working energetically at murder. The dead man's spectacle case was found on the dashboard. His left slipper lay under the steering wheel. He had been sitting in the driving position, apparently, when he was attacked and dragged over the back of the seat. If Austin had gone over to the police station and raised an alarm, it might have been a vastly different story. Instead, the scene was set for a sensational murder mystery, challengingly laid at the very doorstep of the police.

The victim was Victor Sheik Mahaudeen Yassin, fifty-three, wealthy owner of the Carib Hotel situated on East Coast Road, a few miles from Georgetown. Until its fatal ending, the day had been a happy one for Victor Yassin. He had driven his newly-wedded daughter to the airport and sped her off on her honeymoon. After taking his wife home, he then went on to the Carib Hotel, where he had a few drinks, his mood becoming so exuberant that he took the floor and did a little dancing by himself. When he left the hotel, three men who had been drinking in the bar were seen to get into his car with him. Within the hour, Yassin was fatally stabbed.

Obviously, the men who had been in the car with Yassin were the immediate suspects. Who were they? Yassin had not been robbed. What was the motive? The police theory was that the men were instruments of murder in a plot masterminded by twenty-four-year-old Gowkarran Persaud, believed to be the lover of Jeanette, the young and attractive wife of Victor Yassin.

Four days after the murder, the police detained Jowalla Persaud, eighteen-year-old brother of Gowkarran. The next day, they arrested Michael Boodram. They were accused of being two of the three men in the car. The Third Man was never identified to the satisfaction of the police. Gowkarran was the last to be arrested and charged with murder.

The case against Gowkarran rested heavily on the evidence of three witnesses: Police Sergeant Masood Nasir, who claimed to be a friend and drinking companion of both the victim and the accused; Mavis Young, cousin and sometime mistress of Victor Yassin; and Ramnarace Singh, a car-hire driver who told a story of fantastic journeyings on the day of the murder.

Sergeant Nasir testified that in July, 1972, Yassin had complained to him that his wife was living with Gowkarran on the east coast. Nasir spoke to Gowkarran, who said, "I don't care. I have to spend his money." When Nasir advised him to leave Mrs. Yassin alone, Gowkarran replied, "When I leave her, I will own all that Yassin owns."

Mavis Young stated that, in April, 1972, when Gowkarran attended the opening of her club, he had asked her how old Mrs. Yassin was, and were the children hers. In August, that same year, she and Victor Yassin had driven out to Beehive (where Gowkarran had rented a house, and, it was suggested, was living with Jeanette Yassin). A car driven by Gowkarran had passed them, going in the opposite direction. Jeanette was with him. On their return journey, Mavis Young saw the same car coming towards them, Gowkarran still driving. Now he had six or more young men with him, and, as the cars neared each other, they all shouted threats that they were going to "cut" Victor Yassin. Mrs. Yassin was not with them.

All these items, added together, could not be made to mean very much. It was Ramnarace Singh, described by Judge Vieira, at the first trial, as "not only the star witness, but the north star that shines brightly in the night," on whose evidence the prosecution counted for a conviction.

At about 2:00 P.M. on the day of the murder (Singh's story ran), he had been hired by Gowkarran. With him were his brother Jowalla and a Third Man. They drove from the East Coast Car Park in Georgetown to Beterverwagting, about twelve miles, where Jowalla and the Third Man went into a house. They brought back a newspaper parcel. Three miles or so further on, they stopped by a mud dam, at La Bonne Intention. Gowkarran and the Third Man left the car, and came back with Michael Boodram. Then back to the East Coast Car Park, where all alighted except Gowkarran. He told Ramnarace Singh to drive to the Carib Hotel.

Nearing the hotel, Gowkarran said to drive past slowly, then return to the car park. The other three rejoined them, and Gowkarran said, "The man is there at the Carib." He told Singh to take them to the hotel. On the way, he borrowed $5, saying he had only large notes, and he "didn't want the boys to go to the Carib and spend big money." When the others got out at the hotel, Gowkarran said to drive a way up the road and stop. By now, the time was around 8:00 P.M. Singh noticed that Gowkarran had a shotgun lying on the back seat.

After waiting about ten minutes, Gowkarran asked Singh to go back to the hotel, blow his horn, and see what the boys were doing. Gowkarran got out of the car, taking the shotgun. Singh drove off. Outside the Carib, he blew, and Jowalla came out. Singh asked him what the position was, as he wanted to go home. Jowalla said, "Hold on! If we don't get the man tonight, we can't get him again." He went back into the hotel. Singh pretended to turn the car around, but instead he drove home.

This summarizes the case against Gowkarran Persaud.

Jowalla, in a statement to the police, admitted he was one of the three men in the car with Victor Yassin that night. He named the others as Lincoln and Canie. Jowalla said he was in the front seat, next to Yassin. Passing the police station in Sandy Babb Street, Canie told Yassin to stop the car. When it stopped, Canie put a neck lock on Yassin from behind. Jowalla said, "What happen to you, boy?" Canie told him to shut his mouth; if he talked, he would get it, too. Lincoln said, "Where's the knife?" Canie said, "The knife in me socks." Lincoln took a kitchen knife and cut Yassin in the neck. Canie told Jowalla to hold Yassin's feet, to stop him kicking. Instead, Jowalla blew the horn, revved the engine, then leaped out of the car and ran off.

Michael Boodram had also made a statement, admitting that he was in the car. He said it was Jowalla who choked Yassin with his hand, while the Third Man took a knife from his pocket and bored through Yassin's neck. Boodram, when he saw blood, became scared and ran away.

Neither Jowalla nor Michael Boodram, though each accused others, attempted to implicate Gowkarran.

Two leading characters in the drama were missing, when Gowkarran came before the court for the fourth time. Jeanette Yassin was abroad, and had not been recalled by the prosecution. Michael Boodram had escaped from the prison hospital in May, 1977. After six months, he had not been recaptured.

The contrast between the two brothers in the dock was profound. During the three-week trial, Jowalla sat motionless, his handsome, soft-featured face a blank; only the flickering eyes and ceaselessly intertwining fingers betrayed his interest in the proceedings. One nail on each hand he had allowed to grow to a length of an inch and a half, while he was in prison. He spoke only once, in answer to Judge Claude Massiah, when he said, "I do not wish to add anything more to my statement."

With Gowkarran, hawklike, often smiling, always poised and ready, it was a *bravura* performance, all the way. Lawyers could never wholeheartedly approve of his conducting his own case, but his self-confidence won their respect. Lionel Luckhoo said to me, "He has had this hanging over his head for four years, enough to test the sanity of anyone; yet he has kept his composure. He believes he will do the case better, because he knows it better. He has lived it. "

Although he was unable to attend court, Lionel visited Gowkarran in the cells, at intervals during the trial, to advise him how to conduct his case. Among the points he told him to stress were that he was not seen at or near the scene of the crime; there was no evidence to implicate him in its commission; he had no motive for killing. If he was, in fact, living with the man's wife and drawing money from her, he would not want to kill the goose that laid the golden egg. What evidence was there against him? Merely, his going to the Carib Hotel and saying that the man was there. But there was no evidence that he meant the man Yassin, and, even if he did, it did not mean he was saying, "You go do harm to Yassin." The statement was innocuous. It did not point to the commission of a crime; such evidence was singularly lacking.

These were some of the arguments Lionel had put to the magistrate, who accepted them and discharged Gowkarran. After the verdict of guilty at the trial, the Appeal Court had upheld the submissions, the Chancellor saying that Lionel had a valid point that no case had been made out.

Gowkarran made submissions, cross-examined the prosecution witnesses, led his own evidence. When his mother took the stand to testify that he was at home and in bed by 9:30 on the night of the murder, he coolly asked her to speak a little louder.

The court was packed when he began his address to the jury.

3

"This is a strange and moving moment in my life. I have always endeavored to live the life of an honest man, showing due respect for the laws of our land, desiring to live in harmony with my fellowmen, and a keen care to insure that I d no man harm. After living such a life, I never thought to see the day when I would be called upon to speak in defense of my life upon such a charge as I now face. I am overawed that I must speak before a learned judge and twelve honorable citizens in a matter of such great and urgent importance that I scarcely know how to approach it. But speak I must, for who can speak for me? Upon whom can I rely to tell, with the same earnestness, depth, and sincerity, of the pain and anguish which this false and misconceived charge has caused me? To whom might I dare to delegate the defense of my life, my freedom, and, above all, my integrity? The passion which prompts my words springs from the eternal well of truth. For I am no murderer. The mark of Cain I do not bear."

It is usual for a judge to give wide latitude to a defendant who pleads his own case. Mr. Justice Massiah had allowed Gowkarran to read his address. He pulled out all stops; words poured from him in a torrent. An experienced pleader would have supplied variation of tone and pace, but not more fluency.

"In attempting to find a motive, the State has distorted, and transposed out of time, events which lent no support to their proposition that I was moved by the tidal waves of jealousy and avarice to wish, even to the point of murder, the death of Victor Yassin. Had their claim formed part of a plot in a work of fiction, we all would have been moved to commend the author. But it is a sad day when, in its frantic efforts to procure a conviction, the State must resort to tawdry melodrama. This is life; this is serious. You cannot accept an allegation on the basis of its appeal to your sense of mystery, intrigue, and drama.

"There is no more vile plague than jealousy, and, like a plague, this disease hastens all before it to swift destruction. Yet the State contends that I waited for seventeen months before conspiring to effect the destruction of the object of my jealousy, Victor Yassin. I have yet to see, or read of, a case of *patient* jealousy."

Juries are unpredictable. This one had a collectively puzzled look about it that left the judge, and counsel I talked with, in agreement that it was hard to read its reactions.

Gowkarran pointed out to the jury that, if he were having an affair with Victor Yassin's wife, then, immediately upon anything happening to Yassin, he was likely to be the first object of suspicion. It was impossible to understand the State's claim that he stood to benefit by Yassin's death. No doubt the reply would be, through his wife. But they had produced not a scintilla of evidence that she was a party to such an arrangement. She did not feature in the proceedings as an accused. On the contrary, she was a witness for the State (at the first trial), "and even from the safety and privilege of that position, she at no point hinted that I had any interest in her husband's holdings. Anyone who knew Victor Yassin would tell you that he was no fool. If there was an affair . . . he would have made quite certain that his post-mortem arrangements left his wife with nothing on which to maintain a successor. Only a fool would have hazarded an act of murder with clearly foreseeable consequences."

Gowkarran had his only serious run-in with the judge when he began to plead the case for Jowalla. Judge Massiah pulled him up sharply, and explained that he could deal with the evidence, but must not say anything affecting Jowalla's case. Gowkarran proceeded to dissect the testimony of the three witnesses against him.

"Mavis Young attempted to give to an innocent and casual inquiry—which any normal man might make about a woman who had grown-up children but still looked shapely and well-preserved—the character of a scheming and sinister introduction to a plot of deadly dimensions. Again, Mrs. Young raises the picture of a jealous lover, anxious to get rid of an inconvenient husband, by telling of a wholly imaginary incident which she alleges occurred on the East Coast Road. Why was it that Yassin took her with him on that supposed journey, rather than someone who might have been of greater use to him in the event of a conflict or subsequent test before a court of law? What could Mavis Young tell you in support of the claim that I was having an affair with Mrs. Yassin? Absolutely nothing. She never saw us together in the same house. She never found us in any compromising situation. Her contribution has been based on surmise, speculation, and spite. Remember, she is a woman who has borne her cousin, the deceased, a child; who was so enamored of him that she continued to maintain cordial, possibly intimate, relations with him, even after he married someone else. . . . Recognize that Mavis Young was in love with Victor Yassin, accept that this made her envious of Jeanette, and anxious to see her discredited, admit that she carried out a whispering campaign against this woman to her husband, sympathize with her over the loss of her lover—then damn her for the liar that she is!"

In teaching the defender's role, Lionel Luckhoo had found an apt pupil. Upon the structure he devised, Gowkarran had fleshed the bones, dressed and adorned them to his own taste and style of loquacity.

"A man is seen in the company of a woman, and, immediately, the relationship is deemed to be adulterous. A sergeant of police tells you that a husband made a report, and the report is turned over to you as though it automatically establishes the truth of the husband's suspicions. But it does not prove that Yassin was justified in making that report—and how are you to know that Yassin did make that report as alleged? Sergeant Nasir alleges that, when he told me what the deceased had said, I replied, 'I have to spend his money, and before I am done with him I have to own all he has.' He further told you that he and I were friends, and regular drinking partners, even as he and the deceased were. It is in the nature of friendships to have one friend hurl what are called 'tantalizing' remarks against the other. Nasir does not say he was satisfied I was not joking. No one can deny that both the deceased and his wife were friends of mine, or that we went places together, eating and drinking quite freely at each other's expense. That being so, what was so special about my saying I had to spend Yassin's money? Was it not true that he was also enjoying the spending of my cash? Did that mean that the one had to kill the other to get what he had? Ask yourselves if it would be reasonable for a man who had murder on his mind to disclose it, or even hint at it, to a police sergeant. Would that not be tantamount to building your own gallows?"

Gowkarran had yet to deal with the evidence of the witness whose testimony weighed most heavily against him. He began by contending that, as the proprietor of a Shell filling station, he had once had to sue Ramnarace Singh for a longstanding debt, and had been awarded damages. Evidence of the suit was tendered in court, but it remained in dispute between defense and prosecution whether Singh had been satisfactorily identified as being the other party.

"Subsequently, I had the impression there was no malice between us," Gowkarran continued. "But Ramnarace Singh had only been biding his time before wreaking a terrible and awful vengeance. Where I had sued him for money, Singh is suing me for my life. What has Singh to tell you? He did not see Yassin killed. He did not see any of us with Yassin that night. He never heard Yassin's name mentioned. It is not difficult to accept that Singh had knowledge concerning the commission of the crime, but on the basis of his own actions, claims, and description of events, his knowledge was guilty knowledge. Singh was either a conspirator, an accessory, or an active participant in that crime—perhaps, all three.

"Would you accept that a man who had three cars of his own would hire another while he embarked on a mission of murder? I suggest that a taxi would only be used if the driver were part and parcel of the plan. Again, do you think that a taxi driver would see a passenger with a gun in his car, and not even ask why it was there? Surely, the only explanation would be that he knew why it was there. According to Ramnarace Singh, I used his vehicle from about 2:30 until 8:00 P.M. Yet, he assessed his charge to me as being only $15. No taxi driver would agree to have his car on special hire for that length of time, and make all the trips he claimed, for less than three times that amount. Yet, after six days, he had made no attempt to collect even the $15 he had charged. Does that not indicate that the car was on business which concerned both the driver and the hirer? Singh also made a cash contribution of $5, according to his own testimony. Yet he would have us believe he had no knowledge as to what his passengers intended to do that night.

"Consider well his situation, and you cannot fail to understand why he chose to go to the police. He obviously knew how the deceased met his death, and at whose hands. He was, clearly, uncomfortable with that knowledge. But fate was kind to Ramnarace Singh. He was presented with an opportunity, both to remove any suspicion from himself, and to get one of his enemies out of the way for all time. After all, hadn't the police arrested me, and had he not been fortunate enough to have seen me during the afternoon and evening of the murder? He saw his opportunity, timed his moves, and chose his words carefully.

"To conclude, ask yourselves why Singh deserted his passengers on the public road, in the absence of any logical reason which he can give you. And, with that, I consign our friend Mr. Singh and his tissue of lies to your shrewd and very careful consideration."

After criticizing the police investigation, Gowkarran commented, "Superintendent Augustus and Chief Inspector Roberts were pressed by the need to solve, with all haste, a crime which had caused a furious outburst of public indignation. They fell easy victims to the net which Ramnarace Singh had spread for them, and became the tools of his vengeful enterprise.

"Bear in mind the words of John Adams, in his closing remarks to the jury, in the case of the Boston Massacre: 'Consider yourselves as knowing that the prejudices of the world about you are against you.' That jury stood firm in its conviction that only truth must ever wear a crown. Despite the threat of public dissatisfaction, they returned the verdict which they knew to be right, rather than the one they knew would have been popular.

"I leave these thoughts with you, confident that, despite whatever pressures may be brought to bear, you will let justice be done. Justice demands it, and I humbly ask it."

4

The prosecutor, State Counsel Donald Trotman, said to me, "A jury of lawyers would acquit him without hesitation. Laymen might just decide they don't like him." I knew what he meant. Gowkarran's confident, often assertive, fluency could, possibly, impress his less articulate peers the wrong way.

Earlier, Senior Counsel Gilbert Farnum, a former Attorney General who was defending Jowalla, had leaned across me to say to Trotman, "He's a damned sight more fluent than you will be. And my address will come as an anticlimax."

Certainly, it provided a contrast in styles. Farnum stood near the jury box, speaking quietly. What was the evidence against Jowalla?

"There is no evidence of murder. When he saw what was about to happen, he ran. The prosecution accepts that other people were there who are not with us. The only evidence of what happened is the evidence of the accused. His statement is uncontradicted, and is not unreasonable. Are you going to guess what happened?"

State Counsel Trotman asked the jury to accept the "solid chunks" of evidence provided by the prosecution witnesses. Decrying Gowkarran's attack on the police, he termed him one of those "men whose minds are factories of falsehood, churning out lies by the minute."

The summing up of Mr. Justice Massiah was fair and balanced. "At all times remember, you are not avenging angels," he instructed the jury. He emphasized the importance of Ramnarace Singh as a witness. Could the jury believe him? Was there other evidence which tended to strengthen or support his story? "Warn yourselves, it is dangerous to convict on his evidence alone, and each one warn the others."

The jury went out at 4:45 P.M. A painful period of waiting began for the family and friends of the accused. The most detached dared not predict the verdict. Raised voices could be heard from the jury room, as time lengthened. It took the jury two hours and twenty minutes to decide. Then it came back, the foreman twice spoke the words "not guilty"—and the courtroom became a scene of jubilation.

Darkness had fallen when Gowkarran and Jowalla Persaud were released, to savor their first breath of freedom in four years. Well-wishers surrounded them in the courtyard. Only Lionel Luckhoo was missing, and did not hear the lavish tribute paid by Gowkarran in the moment of vicarious victory.

What Judge Vieira had called "the type of case one could read in a storybook" had come to an official close. But, next day, I visited some of the places and talked with some of the people connected with the trial.

Among the people I met was the elusive Third Man. But that is no part of this story.

Chapter 28
The Case of the Mad Messiah

I talked him out of murder and suicide.
It was the biggest mistake of my life!
—Sir Lionel Luckhoo

One life only does Lionel Luckhoo regret having saved. He was not one of the 232 murder-accused Lionel has persuaded judges and juries not to hang. This man was not yet a killer. He was loved and widely respected as a man of good works. But he threatened murder and suicide, and all Lionel's persistence and power of persuasion were needed to stop him.

His name was Jim Jones.

In August, 1977, a group of young people called at the offices of Luckhoo and Luckhoo in Georgetown. The leader, Paula Adams, said that they wished to retain the personal services of Sir Lionel on behalf of Bishop Jim Jones and the Peoples Temple.

"Money is no object," Paula Adams said. "Whatever fee you ask will be paid." No mention was made of any impending litigation.

Lionel asked her if the Peoples Temple was a religious organization. She said it was. "In that case," Lionel said, "I will reserve my services on your behalf without charging a retainer."

Next day, he received a telephone call from the Solicitor General of Guyana, Joaquin Gonsalves-Sabola. An attorney named Jeffrey Allan Haas, from the United States, he said, wanted to engage the services of a senior counsel. Did Lionel have any objection if he gave Haas his address?

What kind of litigation was involved? asked Lionel. The Solicitor General said that he had not gone into details, but it concerned a body calling themselves the Peoples Temple.

Lionel said he was sorry, but he could not consider the matter, as he had already promised the Peoples Temple he would represent them in any legal action.

Two days later, the group from the Temple visited him again. Now they explained that they feared *habeas corpus* proceedings were about to be brought to take away an adopted child of Jim Jones, six-year-old John Victor Stoen. The boy's mother Grace Stoen, wife of a United States attorney, was a former member of the community. No papers had as yet been served, but they had information from America that Attorney Haas was in Guyana to launch proceedings.

Would Sir Lionel go to their residence in Georgetown and speak with Bishop Jones? He was in Jonestown, 150 miles away, in the North West District, but was linked by radio with both Georgetown and California.

"Reception was clearer than on any telephone call," Lionel says, "when I spoke to Jim Jones over his short-wave. We talked for about an hour. His voice was attractive, compelling; one could sense his presence, as though he were in the room."

"I will fight to the end of time," Jones told Lionel, "to keep the boy John Stoen, a handsome boy, a boy who looks like me." He, in fact, claimed that he was the natural father of John Stoen, and that he had sworn declarations to that effect.

The *habeas corpus* proceedings went ahead. In rapid succession, three *ex parte* applications were made and granted in chambers, by Justice Aubrey Bishop. Dated September 6, 8, and 10, the orders commanded that the body of the child John Victor Stoen be brought before the court; that he be made a ward of court; and granted leave to serve proceedings for contempt of court on Jim Jones, for which substituted service was permitted. (This allowed proceedings to be served, if personal service could not be effected, by affixing three certified copies of the court orders at three different places at the Peoples Temple Agricultural Mission at Port Kaituma.)

Every *habeas corpus* order carries the warning, "In default thereof, the said court will then, or so soon thereafter as counsel can be heard, be moved to commit you to prison for your contempt in not obeying the said writ."

The firm of Luckhoo was formally briefed. Lionel felt that the proceedings so far taken by the other party were legally wrong. No order had yet been served on Jim Jones, but, if the Luckhoos entered an appearance on his behalf, then service could be effected through them as his legal representatives. The problem was how to intervene while avoiding this hazard.

Among the bundle of papers given to Lionel was a notarized document, signed by Grace Stoen, giving custody of her child to one Joyce Touchette. A summons could be taken out by Joyce Touchette, as a person directly interested and concerned, asking to be joined as a respondent/defendant, and for the orders of the court to be set aside.

Having decided on this line of approach, Lionel Luckhoo went to the Peoples Temple residence, on September 15, for a radio talk with Jim Jones. Could Joyce Touchette be brought to Guyana? he asked. Jones said she was already at Jonestown, and was his personal secretary. She could come to Georgetown whenever it was necessary.

At first, Jones was his cool, charismatic self, when Lionel assured him that the prospects for the case were excellent. The custody papers, in her name, gave Joyce Touchette a right to be heard by the court which had ordered the arrest of John Stoen. Lionel said he felt he must succeed in getting the order rescinded, once he was able to have Joyce Touchette joined in the action.

Then Jim Jones's manner suddenly changed. Sounding suspicious and fearful, he raised a barrage of doubts. "Suppose you don't succeed in getting her joined? Suppose you don't succeed in getting the order rescinded? Suppose they come now and arrest the boy? What can I do?" His voice rose to a pitch of hysteria. "I will have to act, and all hell will be let loose!"

Again there was a change. Jones became icily calm. "If the order of the court is not removed by 5:00 P.M. today, *I will shoot the boy, kill myself, and all hell will be let loose.*"

Jones had made his demand deliberately. He meant what he said. The imbalance of mind it revealed was alarming. The time was then around noon. Lionel had been given five hours to do the impossible.

"I spoke to him of his religion," Lionel recalls. "How could a Christian adopt such an attitude?" I asked. To contemplate such acts was insane.

Jim Jones had repeated, "All hell will be let loose."

"Bishop Jones," Lionel had said, "you are a man of God. You cannot think in terms of taking a life that does not belong to you, whether it be your own life or that of the child. The Creator is the only One who should determine the severance of life."

But arguments about the sanctity of life seemed to make no impression on Jim Jones. Yet again he had repeated, "All hell will be let loose."

So Lionel asked, "What is it that will make you go to the extreme of taking your own life, and that of the boy you say you love above all others?"

Jones's reply had been enigmatic. "There are people, not only here, but abroad, who are dependent on me, and who will react to anything which happens to me."

Did the self-styled messiah even then have the intent to destroy all his people?

Finding that appeals to religion were without effect, Lionel had switched his arguments to the hard legal aspects of the matter.

"I explained that, in *habeas corpus* proceedings, the service had to be personal, or upon the jailer if someone were locked up. Jonestown itself was virtually inaccessible. If Jones had the boy there with him, he could go even further into the interior for a few days, as he often did, and be sure that nothing would happen. Joyce Touchette could be flown down to swear affidavits. I would then apply to the court immediately."

Jones had begun to show an appreciation of the legal angles which he had not given of the moral issues. "Can a judge rescind his own order?"he asked.

"Of course, he can," Lionel assured him.

"Do you have cases on the point?"

"There are many cases."

Jones had Lionel cite instances, and was impressed by a judgment given by Lord Denning that he quoted: "An order which is a nullity is automatically null and void, without more ado, though it is sometimes convenient to have the court declare it to be so. You cannot put something on nothing and expect it to stay there. It will collapse."

In the end, Lionel had instilled a confidence in the legal outcome of the case which won the day. "After much talk, I persuaded him to remove from his mind any ideas of violence. I convinced him that we would succeed in the case. He agreed to let us proceed in the manner that I advocated."

It had taken Lionel Luckhoo an hour to stop Jim Jones from committing murder and suicide.

While trying to talk Jones out of his homicidal threat, Lionel had at one stage said, "Bishop, one with God is a majority."

"I do not understand what you mean," was Jones's reply.

"I had to repeat and explain it several times before he understood the point I was making," Lionel recalls. "The seed of doubt was then, and only then, sown in my mind. Could this be a religious man? I wondered. Remember, I had not met him. I had only been speaking to him over the hi-fi set.

"I looked around their spacious building. Nowhere did I see a crucifix, a holy picture, or a Bible. When I asked the group, they said that Jones did not wish to have any of these trappings, as there were agnostics and atheists among their members. Jim Jones himself later gave me the same explanation."

Lionel felt the Peoples Temple was mocking God by calling itself a temple. For this reason, he always declined to visit Jonestown, though he was invited fifty times or more—by Jim Jones himself over the radio, by his wife Marceline, by Tim Carter, Paula Adams, and others.

The application for joinder by Joyce Touchette went forward. She claimed that both the parents, Grace and Timothy Stoen, had signed documents consenting that John Stoen be placed in her custody, and brought to Guyana, where he had been for the last three years. Although resisted by Clarence

Hughes, counsel for Grace Stoen, the application was granted.

This cleared the way for Lionel to apply for the *habeas corpus* proceedings to be declared a nullity. He contended that the three orders of court—issuing a writ of *habeas corpus*, making John Stoen a ward of court, and granting leave to commence proceedings for contempt against Jim Jones—were all irregular, and improperly made, contrary to the rules of court and the laws and constitution of Guyana.

A writ of *habeas corpus* must be served personally, Lionel argued; there was no provision in law for substituted service by nailing it to a building.

The plaintiff Grace Stoen had sworn to no affidavit in connection with the *habeas corpus* application. The only application annexed was in connection with her matrimonial proceedings in the United States, which had no standing in Guyana. Jeffrey Allan Haas had no authority in law for making his affidavit. He had not provided proof that he was an attorney, or that he was an authorized attorney for Grace Stoen, or that Grace Stoen had authorized him to receive the child John Stoen.

Lionel was asking Justice Aubrey Bishop to set aside his own orders. After a hearing that lasted weeks, the judge reserved his decision. This was in January, 1978. As time went by without a judgment being delivered, the Peoples Temple showed an increasing anxiety. Midyear, Sharon Amos replaced Paula Adams as the link between Jim Jones and Lionel Luckhoo.

"She would visit me at least three times a week," Lionel says, "to inquire about news of the judgment. They started to feed me with a mass of papers from abroad, alleging conspiracies and libels against the Peoples Temple. I told them that, if the papers were circulated in Guyana, they would have a cause for action. Meanwhile, the proper place to institute proceedings was the United States, where the papers were published and circulated."

Charles Garry, famous as the counsel for Huey Newton, Bobby Seale, Angela Davis, and the Oakland Seven, was representing the Peoples Temple in the United States. Mark Lane, noted critic of the official verdicts on the John Kennedy and Martin Luther King assassinations, undertook an investigation of Jonestown on behalf of the U.S. Citizens' Commission of Inquiry. Both lawyers came to see Lionel Luckhoo.

"Sharon Amos and Deborah Touchette said they wanted me to question Mark Lane after his visit to Jonestown," Lionel recalls, "as they needed to know what reports he would be sending back. Mark Lane told me he was satisfied that the place was *bona fide* run, and his report must necessarily be favorable."

In September, Judge Bishop called all counsel together, but not to give judgment. He stated that, because of pressures being brought to influence his decision, by people abroad and in Guyana, by telephone calls and other means, he was declining to adjudicate. He would ask the Chief Justice to appoint another judge.

The Stoen case became a major cause of Congressman Leo Ryan's investigation. Sharon Amos kept coming to Lionel with long messages from Jim Jones; usually, with an invitation to go up to Jonestown as his guest.

"The day before Congressman Ryan arrived, she came with a fervent plea that I accompany his party to Jonestown to protect Jim's interests. I said it appeared to be a political matter, and that I was strictly legal. I was willing to fight for them in court. I was unwilling to do anything extra, because the Peoples Temple was a temple of atheists. This opinion, formed earlier, had been reinforced since talking to many members of the Temple on varied occasions. I refused to go."

Sharon Amos called on Lionel again, next day, but now there was a change in her attitude.

"She brought me an order signed by the Registrar. It stated that Jim Jones was free to move anywhere in Guyana without fear of arrest. I asked to take a photocopy. She made excuses, and would not permit me. At this, I became angry. I told her I felt I was entitled to have a copy of the document, since it was a matter ancillary to the *habeas corpus* proceedings. Still, she would not allow me to photocopy it.

"When she came back to my chambers, later in the day, I was still annoyed, and sent a message that I was too busy to see her. That night, she came to my home with a copy of the document. She apologized profusely for her previous attitude.

She said she had needed to have Jim Jones's permission before handing it over, as they had received information from certain people in Georgetown that I was with the CIA. I felt she meant a foreign mission, but she did not say so outright. She went on to say that she had now cleared it with Jim Jones, who said he had made investigations abroad, and I was not CIA."

Ryan and his party had that day arrived in Georgetown, and were seeking permission to visit Jonestown. Jim Jones badly wanted Lionel to be present at any meeting with the U.S. congressman.

Why did Lionel Luckhoo refuse to go to Jonestown? The reasons he gave Sharon Amos are not wholly characteristic. Notwithstanding his own strong religious feelings, he is usually prepared to walk the extra mile for his clients, irrespective of their beliefs. On rare occasions, as instances given in earlier chapters have indicated, a kind of intuitive awareness has helped him in court. "Maybe it was my sixth sense," he now conjectures, "that did not permit me to pay Jonestown even a social visit."

The events of that week moved swiftly towards their tragic culmination. Sharon Amos, acting for Jim Jones, was cold and hostile in her dealings with Ryan. Not until Charles Garry and Mark Lane interceded did Jones agree to receive the party. They flew to Port Kaituma on the Friday.

On Saturday night at eleven o'clock, Lionel Luckhoo's telephone rang. When he answered the call, it was Deborah Touchette. "Come, Sir Lionel, come now!" she pleaded. "Sharon Amos has just killed herself and her children."

Lionel asked, "Were you involved?"

"No, no!"

"Then get in touch with the police at once," he advised.

"The police are already here with us."

At three o'clock the following afternoon (Sunday), a telephone call came from Australia. The caller was a correspondent Lionel had met when the Australian cricket team visited Guyana.

"Is it true that there has been mass suicide at Jonestown?"

"You are out of your little mind," Lionel answered. "Such things don't happen in Guyana."

"Sir Lionel, it is incredible, but true. We at the other end of the world know before you what is happening in your country."

"He was right," Lionel says, sadly. "The terrible tragedy had taken place. Jim Jones, most of the people I had known from the Temple, were dead."

After the shooting of Ryan, and four others, Jones had ordered that preparations be made for the wholesale slaughter. Joyce Touchette was one of those who poured half-gallon jugs of cyanide into the tub of strawberry Flavour-aide from which they drank. Tim Carter, deputed to take a suitcase full of money out of camp, dropped it and ran when he saw his wife and baby lying dead. Charles Garry and Mark Lane escaped by fleeing into the jungle. Paula Adams and Deborah Touchette were in Georgetown, and survived.

"What kind of a man was Jim Jones? I never met him. I spoke to him often. A clear voice, commanding in tone, yet gentle. A man who was as weak as he was strong. A mixed-up individual, suffering from schizophrenia and paranoia."

When Jones complained of his ill health, Lionel told him, "If you are sick, come to Georgetown now."

"I am afraid," Jones answered. "I must protect my life. There are conspirators anxious to get me—the FBI, the CIA, the reactionary right, are all after me. I am a hunted man. I have to take refuge at Jonestown."

"Jim Jones told me he would fight to the end of time to keep John Stoen," Lionel recollects. "Yet he was willing to destroy the boy; the innocent infant is now dead."

Lionel was approached, from America, to undertake the defense of Jones's cohorts. He declined.

Only once in his forty years as a trial lawyer had Lionel Luckhoo turned down a murder defense. On that occasion, he had just fought and won his own case for custody of his children before an English court, when a would-be client came and confessed to having killed his wife and two small children by setting fire to his home.

Again, it was the thought of the children that Lionel could not stomach. That every man is entitled to a defense is the principle he lives by. But his own emotions were too involved in this case for him to be able to plead it wholeheartedly. He told members of the Peoples Temple that he could not accept the brief for the men accused.

Jonestown still weighs heavily on his mind. A year before, the same indomitable spirit, the unrivaled talent for persuasion, that has won so many court battles when life has hung in the balance, had enabled Lionel to save Jim Jones from committing murder and suicide. He now sees his success as a damning failure.

"It was the biggest mistake of my life," he now repeats. "I wish I had failed in my persuasion. Two lives would then have been lost, but more than 900 would have been saved. I should have let Jim Jones shoot himself."

Yet, how could any human prescience have divined the holocaust that was to come?

Chapter 29

The Case of the Constant Christian

Lo, I have given thee a wise and an understanding heart.

—I Kings 3:12

Christians in Guyana are on the march! The half-mile-long procession weaves through the streets of Georgetown—four miles to go, before reaching the stadium, where a rally is being held to inaugurate the Caribbean Conference of Churches' meetings. Three bands. Dozens of church groups, each carrying its banner. By chance, though the juxtapositioning emphasizes the multidenominational, multiracial, multicultural nature of the event, Bishop Randolph of Stabroek, the Anglican Bishop of Georgetown, a black doctor of divinity from Harvard, a white theological professor from McGill, and Lionel Luckhoo, are walking before a banner which proudly proclaims the allegiance of the Akawaio and Patamonia peoples of the Alleluia Church at Amokokopai, in the Upper Mazaruni, to U'WI JIZES KRAIS.

"Our big brother Jesus Christ" is the translation, I am told by Canon William Dorman, sometime of Cambridge University, who has lived with these Amerindians for twenty years. The people marching have traveled from their homes in the shadow of Mount Roraima, where the borders of Brazil, Venezuela, and Guyana converge. A man named Abel, trained at an Anglican mission, converted the tribes. He was killed by local sorcerers. But Abel's descendants still flourish, and so does his church; one of the chief sorcerers had visions that led him to become a Christian, and to carry on the work.

The idea of the march came from Lionel Luckhoo. The Luckhoo family have been Christians for three generations, and Lionel could never be a passive believer. He is fervent, but not fanatical, in his faith. With him on the march are his two youngest children, Marina and Mark. Eight-year-old Mark proves himself to be one who, when asked to go a mile, will go two, as Jesus recommended; for, in dashing backward and forward, he must have covered twice the distance of the others in the procession.

This was Lionel's second march of the weekend. The day before, he had walked in procession with the churches of New Amsterdam, his birthplace. It was there that I heard from the Rev. Derek Goodrich, Rural Dean of Berbice, of some of the quiet charities Lionel Luckhoo performs. The beautiful interior of All Saints, the church where Lionel worshiped as a boy, was enhanced by blue carpet running the length of the aisle—a gift from Lionel Luckhoo, I was told, when I admired it. Another story I had from Derek Goodrich was how Lionel, during a service at St. Philip's, Georgetown, noticed dust descending on the congregation from on high. Next day, the vicar, the Rev. William Pheeby, received a check for roof repairs.

At New Amsterdam, it was a very slow march, which meant that the meeting to follow, at which Lionel was to speak, started sadly late. He had to tell the gathering he could speak for only nine minutes—and wound up his peroration on the second! That just allowed time to race to the car ferry for the eighty-mile trip back to Georgetown.

As it happened, the ferry boat came in late. While waiting, Lionel was recognized by a family party in the car alongside us. The mother recalled how, when she was a girl, her father had told her to go to Lionel Luckhoo if ever she found herself in legal trouble. Nearing the end of an exhausting day, on the road before five that morning, with hours of night driving still to come, Lionel readily entered into a discussion of the teenage children's future careers, and offered help in getting books difficult to obtain for their studies; even, promised introductions to eligible young lawyers for the two attractive daughters, when the mother showed worry about the dearth of suitable young men they could meet! It made me recall a remark of Doreen Luckhoo's: "Lionel will do anything for anyone, even the impossible."

He aims to live up to the motto he chose for his coat-of-arms, when he was knighted: "A wise and understanding heart." Only God can judge the wisdom in a man, but people everywhere may be touched by the warmth of understanding. Lionel could be described, literally, as a "do-gooder." This is a term one shies away from, because—the world being, as it is, irrational—it is most often used to imply derision, if not contempt. But, in the name of sanity, what is bad about doing good? Does anyone really think that to be a "do-badder" is better? It is social conscience, not ideological conviction, that, today, makes Lionel Luckhoo a strong ally of Forbes Burnham. For the shack dwellers and the homeless, Burnham's government has built 50,000 houses, more spacious and attractive in appearance than most state enterprises. On a Sunday afternoon drive around Georgetown, Lionel said, with feeling, "People sit down in their hotels and talk about social justice—*this* is social justice." Indeed, the city is so much altered that its former mayor, ignoring the directions of Marina, who knows the new estates better than her father, lost his way three times. Once, we regained the main road, seen in the distance, by surging down a narrow pathway through a backyard hung with washing, and scattering squalling chickens to the cheers of madly waving householders. Driving with Lionel Luckhoo can, if nothing else does, restore belief in the grace of God!

His own beliefs Lionel has put forward as forcibly as he would present a case in court, in a series of booklets written from the viewpoint of a Christian layman. Under such titles as *Life After Death, God Is Love, Sense of Values, The Xmas Story, I Believe,* and (in the form of an open letter) *My Dear Atheist*, he argues, pungently and with deep feeling, the case for Christianity, in a simple, direct manner much more likely to impress an ordinary reader than the narrow dogmatism, obscure creedalism, and sentimentalized meandering with which religious literature, unhappily, abounds. Lionel has also written and narrated, as a radio feature, *The Easter*

Story, a dramatization of the passion of Jesus Christ. In preparing this program, he discovered and listed ten illegalities and irregularities under Jewish law in the trial of Jesus.

Lionel Luckhoo's is a well-known voice on Guyanese radio. Usually, he talks about great court cases, not his own, bringing to life the human drama of battles fought long ago. One day as we crossed to the law courts, a stranger came up, shook him by the hand, and said, "I love to hear your voice on the radio." Obviously he spoke from the heart, and such spontaneous appreciation means a lot to Lionel.

For some years, he has been writing a column, "Lionel Luckhoo's Viewpoint," for the *Sunday Chronicle*. Occasionally, he touches on legal matters—the parlous condition of many courts, inside and outside; overcrowding in the prisons (not that many of his own clients suffer long from this); the disparities between sentences for similar offenses, encouraging the public to criticize when penalties seem unduly severe or lenient. But he covers a wide diversity of other subjects; as a random selection: cricket, religious teaching for children, beauty contests, water conservation, drugs, airline inefficiency, unlighted bicycles, wasted time, and the need for putting policemen back on the beat. His appeal for handicapped children might have been expected to succeed; more surprising was that, when he denounced a bus driver for dangerous driving, the man called at his home, apologized, and promised to take more care. Lionel was enraged, on returning from a trip abroad, to find that, in his absence, the ancient Parliament building had been painted a medley of colors—green, yellow, red, black, and white. Whoever was responsible for the unsightly spectacle (he said in his column) should be pilloried and made to drink the paint—and, with the help of the Guyana Broadcasting Service, he started a fund for repainting of the building.

His ability to turn a negative factor to a positive purpose, so often demonstrated in court, emerges in some of his articles. When an electricity failure plunged Georgetown into darkness, Lionel did not stop at criticizing the persons responsible, but read from it a useful lesson on the appreciation of sight. "To live in darkness would be a tragedy," he wrote, "yet many persons continue to live without vision"—and made it an opportunity to appeal for help for the blind.

When, in 1978, power failures became more frequent, the Prime Minister invited the critic to head a Luckhoo Commission of Inquiry into the causes of the blackouts and the general operations of the Guyana Electric Corporation. Upon concluding a six-week investigation, Lionel and two technical experts handed the Prime Minister, within forty-eight hours, a 200-page report.

The social service Lionel Luckhoo gives would be a fulltime job for a less energetic man. At present, he is a member of the Legal Practitioners' Committee, the Senior Citizens' Association, the Red Cross Society, and president of the Guyana Olympic Association. This last appointment brought real heartache when he took the Guyana team to the 1976 Olympic Games in Montreal. Because New Zealand, after maintaining sporting links with South Africa, was being allowed to compete, the Guyana team was asked home at the last minute. "It caused much hurt and pain to the competitors," Lionel says. "One or two were in tears. They had trained for years, and this was the peak moment of their lives, a chance that would never come again. They had a wonderful opportunity of winning two gold medals, possibly four, and a number of silvers. James Gilkes was the fastest man in the world. However, this is life. One doesn't always get one's own way. But I would never take a team again if there was a risk of the same thing happening."

Lionel fully agrees that South Africa should be ostracized until it changes its *apartheid* policies. But he thinks the West Indies should be sending athletes and cricketers to South Africa to coach the blacks and coloreds; then they would have an equal chance with the whites of representing their countries on merit, when conditions change and multiracial teams are to be selected.

The firm of Luckhoo and Luckhoo has flourished on forbearance, and has never fired an employee. Since Sir Edward Luckhoo left to become Chancellor of the Judiciary, and, later, High Commissioner to India, his namesake, Lloyd's son Edward, has joined the firm, showing the same zest and enthusiasm for law as his seniors. Lloyd's other son Keith and his English wife Jane, both barristers, were with the firm for some years, but are now settled in England. Although there is no formal division of labor, Lloyd's gravitational pull is towards the civil courts, and he takes few criminal cases. He spends a vast amount of time on legal homework, but finds enough leisure to do a weekly sports commentary over Radio Demerara.

While Lionel was High Commissioner, he and Sheila often used to visit old people's homes, a form of social work suggested to them by the Bishop of London. Mostly, the inmates had been sent there to pass their remaining days alone, by relatives who could not be bothered with them. One old but erect man to whom Lionel talked told him, "Of all the tragedies I have endured, the greatest is loneliness." The remark rooted in Lionel's mind, and, back in Georgetown, he and E.V. started a quiet campaign of going to the poorer districts to talk with the old and lonely. "It was a rewarding experience," Lionel says, "but, since E.V. left for India, I have to confess I have not maintained it."

E.V. has always been his guide and mentor since they went through school together. "He protected me when necessary, gave me a kick up the backside when necessary. I remember once, when I had earned a whipping, he told the headmaster that he, as a prefect, could give me a more effective form of punishment, and I would never kick over those particular traces again. The headmaster let him try. E.V. then gave me such a lecture that I begged him to let me take the flogging, instead. And I never repeated the offense." E.V. has never married, but has been a father figure to the entire Luckhoo family.

From time to time, Lionel talks of hanging up his gown. "I should say, my retirement is not far distant," he says, " because I want to do two things in life: to go and give witness to my faith, and to preach, to do some little work in winning people to the cross of Jesus. To me, this would be the greatest climax to my life, a means of thanking God for His many kindnesses to me, by seeking to give others the opportunity of the happiness and peace of mind I now enjoy because of my abiding faith."

He is patently sincere in saying this. Already, he preaches most weekends for churches of many different denominations, and in this finds his greatest relaxation. Yet, as devil's advocate, a not unfamiliar role, I had to suggest to him that God is best served by the fullest use of the talents He has provided. Not long after this conversation, Lionel secured the release of a protege of the Archbishop of the West Indies, who had been unjustly arraigned on a criminal charge. There will always be another knock on the door, another appeal to his sense of justice, another challenge to his skill and ingenuity. Preaching could never stretch his talents in the way that the law can.

On the march through Georgetown, we met Eric Williams, an old schoolmate of Lionel. They had not seen each other for years. Williams recalled a time when they were ten years old, and had gone to the backdam, looking for birds' nests—not to steal eggs, but to interchange eggs between nests, to see what would eventuate. Deep in the backdam reaches, the boys became lost. Lionel turned to Eric, and said, "You kneel down and pray. I'll look around to find a way out of the wood."

At ten years of age, Lionel Luckhoo believed in prayer; but he also knew that God best helps those who help themselves, and his instinct was to choose for himself the more active part. Today, Lionel finds joy in preaching—but it is "relaxing" (his own word), and he is a man who must *do*. I am no prophet. It is impertinent to guess; but my guess would be that the small, indomitable figure, ancient gown slung over his arm, will be seen striding across the street from his chambers to the law courts so long as health and strength, in God's mercy, allow.

Chapter 30
The Case of the Conquering Counsel

It's staggering!
—American Bar Association

The foreman was a pushy type. He had been on the jury through four successive cases at the Sessions. Each time the judge said, "Choose your foreman," he seemed to feel that, having been called, he was bound to be chosen—and took over the foreman's chair before the other jurors could so much as nod their heads.

Lionel Luckhoo had no cause for complaint. He had won all four cases. Now, the fifth case was coming up, with the same foreman. (Again, he had not been backward in coming forward!) The charges were breaking-and-entering and larceny. So strong was the evidence that Lionel had advised his client to plead guilty. "No, sir," was the firm answer he got. "I am paying you to defend me, and I would rather go down with you fighting."

"My friend," Lionel said, "go down you certainly will. I'll do my best, but I see no possibility of getting you off."

The client's defense was an alibi. Lionel would not let him go into the box to swear to it. He knew that cross-examination would tear the alibi to shreds. He had a faint hope that poverty of identification might get his man through, but that hope evaporated when the witnesses stood firm. At the close of the case, Lionel felt that his client had no chance at all.

Surprisingly, members of the jury were out for two hours. When they returned, the foreman, in a hoarse voice that betrayed the strains of battle, announced the verdict: not guilty.

"You're the luckiest man alive!" Lionel told the client.

He was crossing the street to his chambers, when the jury foreman caught up with him. "Sir Lionel," the man said, "just one thing I'd like to tell you. You have never fought harder in court than I had to fight in that jury room."

"But why? What so impressed you about the innocence of my client?"

"Oh, he was guilty, right enough," the foreman said. "But he wanted to go into the box, and I saw you advising him against it."

"How did you know what I was saying?"

"From where I sat I could lip-read. I felt you had no right to tell the man not to give his evidence on oath, when quite clearly he wanted to. I had to fight for him because I did not think you were fair. Besides," and the foreman stuck out his chest, "*I was not going to spoil my record of five straight acquittals.*"

So what is a record? One kind of record is a round, flat object with a hole in the middle; a child can break it. Some other kinds of records are as quickly broken; others outlive their creators.

Take the two sports Lionel Luckhoo most favors—cricket and horse racing. Jack Hobbs' career total of 61,237 runs in first-class cricket still stands as a record, after forty-six years. So does Gordon Richards's English record of 4,870 winners from 21,834 rides, after twenty-six years.

Where the adversary system of trial operates, every case can become a needle match; particularly, any murder charge that Lionel Luckhoo is defending, for, not surprisingly, many prosecutors are spurred by the chance of being the first to bring about his defeat. At least one judge has been known to privately predict, with human if unjudicial glee, that the case before him would end Lionel's run. So far, a jury or an appeal court has always prevented that from happening.

Yet, the longest rope has an end. And Lionel Luckhoo is ever aware that his may end in a noose.

2

What kind of people are these "murderers" whom Lionel Luckhoo defends? All kinds, saints alone excepted, almost might be the truest answer. Most of them are ordinary people who have stepped beyond their normal limits. "If they were told, on the morning of that fateful day, that they would be involved in a murder," says Lionel, "they would say, you must be out of your tiny mind. For most murders are done on the spur of the moment. Premeditation is rare." The planned murders, where an ambush is set, or poison is prepared, number not more than 5 percent of his cases.

In the largest category of cases, alcohol plays an active part. Lionel says, "Alcohol gives false courage; it releases inhibitions, causing people of not very high intelligence to give way to basic instincts of bravado, violence, and retaliation. A man whose life is circumscribed by his low position on the social ladder has limited means of enjoyment. Alcohol helps him to forget the hard work of the day, and of the morrow, frees him to express himself, lifts him above being the humble worker he is, a faceless cog in the social machine, and makes him feel he is a kingpin. He reaches a bellicose stage, and can be easily pushed into violence. His usual weapon is the tool at hand with which he is familiar—a cutlass, an axe, or a shovel, which, in his befuddled state, he employs without foreseeing the consequences."

Lionel Luckhoo feels strongly on this subject. In articles and speeches, he has advocated stringent laws to prevent more liquor being sold to anyone who shows signs of already having had enough.

Another sizeable percentage (perhaps one case in four) are crimes of passion, motivated by jealousy or rejection. A small number of killings is wholly accidental—the Hansraj case is an example. Fewer still arise through quarrels over land, as in the case of Jainarine Singh.

Having killed, how do most people react? With fear, in the vast majority of cases. When Lionel first sees them, they look up and implore God to help them—and perhaps He does. They next implore Lionel Luckhoo to help them—and he certainly does. Grown men sweat and tremble, begging him to save them from the rope. Nearly always, they protest their innocence.

A very small percentage can be deemed indifferent, and

these are, perhaps, the people who have been involved in a planned murder.

Having stood trial for their lives, how are their future lives affected? Most of them move from where they were living to a new neighborhood, and Lionel never hears of them getting into trouble again with the law. Some turn to religion; one example: Noor Mohamed became a Mohammedan priest. A few go in for a life of crime. After Lionel defended Kirkpaul Sookdeo, winning the appeal on a point of law, he told him never to come to him again if he were in trouble. Some years later, Sookdeo was arrested on a charge of kidnaping, an unusual crime in Guyana.

Enough has been said, in earlier chapters, as to why everyone accused of murder, no matter how repellent the crime, or how seemingly irrefutable the evidence against him, is entitled to a defender. The layman, though not the lawyer, may still have some slight unease that Lionel Luckhoo's skills have, in some instances, been used to free murderers who are likely to do it again. Anyone holding such qualms will be relieved to know that, of the 232 accused whom he has successfully defended, only one has been charged a second time with murder.

Oliver was seen going into a house. When the householder, Emmanuel, tackled him, Oliver struck him with a stick. Emmanuel was taken to the hospital, but discharged himself next day. He died three weeks later. Oliver was then indicted for murder. The pathologist gave the cause of death as tetanus. When the prosecution failed to connect the blow delivered by Oliver with Emmanuel's death, Lionel obtained a not-guilty verdict.

Now Oliver again faces a murder charge. He has not yet made adequate arrangements for his defense, but, should he do so, Lionel will have no qualms about defending him. "To me, every accused is innocent," he says, "and he remains so until an adverse verdict is returned—which, pray God, has not yet been forthcoming."

3

In the first chapter of this book, I referred to four widely varied cases brought by clients whom Lionel Luckhoo was interviewing, the first day I sat in his office. The *habeas corpus* case which I said might make legal history was, of course, that involving Jim Jones, and has already been dealt with in Chapter 28. It became historical in a more tragic way than I ever imagined, for it was one of the reasons that Congressman Leo Ryan went to Guyana, a visit that culminated in the Jonestown massacre.

The man accused of forgery who came to plead for help was Joseph Bansgopal. He worked as a cashier for the Guyana Rice Board, and his job was to issue sales receipts, which the customer then took to the Bond and gave to a clerk, who delivered the rice. A purchaser had bought fifty bags of rice, valued at $1,050, and there was a ticket, numbered 161221, as proof that he had paid.

When a spotcheck was made, the duplicate roll from Bansgopal's machine showed no record of that particular transaction. The contention was that the purchaser had paid Bansgopal, and he had pocketed the money.

Marks, notations, figures, and spacings on the receipt appeared to be identical with those on other tickets issued by Bansgopal's machine. But, when Lionel examined them under a magnifying glass, he noticed one slight discrepancy. On the test tickets, there was a comma placed after the thousand figure, thus: 1,050. The ticket produced by the purchaser showed no comma. Lionel was then able to argue that the ticket could not have been issued by Bansgopal's machine, as it would not have failed to reproduce the comma. The comma was so faint that it was barely perceptible to normal vision, but it was there on all the genuine tickets. The forgery must have been made by the purchaser, or some other person attempting a facsimile of Bansgopal's receipts. At this, the case for the prosecution collapsed. Bansgopal was subsequently freed, and his reputation saved, by the missing comma.

The will case had unusual and fascinating features. When Bekhan Persaud Rajnarine died, he left a coconut plantation, valued at a round million dollars, and two wills. The first will favored his son Denis; the second, his wife Stella.

Young Denis Rajnarine and his sisters retained Lionel to contest the second will made by their father. Lionel contended in court that this second will, dispossessing Denis, was no will at all. It had been drawn up in that form, and executed, merely to frighten Denis into giving up gambling on horses. If he did this, Rajnarine's accountant Latchmansingh was to destroy the document.

Lionel elicited from Latchmansingh, in cross-examination, that he was to be the sole judge of any change in Denis's behavior. He admitted that Denis had changed, and was no longer gambling. He would have torn up the will, had he not handed it to the mother, Mrs. Stella Rajnarine. After fifteen trial days, judgment is now reserved.

In another unusual case, the bar-restaurant owner accused of murder was Henderpaul Coomar. He had caught a man stealing a glass, and was making him bring it back, when his revolver went off. In the magistrate's court, Lionel demonstrated that the revolver had a very light trigger action; the slightest pressure would discharge it. Coomar was committed on a reduced charge of manslaughter.

This was not then accepted by the prosecution, and at the Assizes, Coomar was indicted for murder. Lionel renewed the fight to gain a verdict of manslaughter. He argued that there was no *mens rea*; the accused had a right to recover his own property, and, by his struggle, the deceased had caused an involuntary discharge of the gun. Manslaughter covered a very wide range, and, in this instance, the death was tantamount to an accident. At the most, Coomar might be deemed to have been somewhat careless in the use of the weapon he was employing to get the deceased to return the glass he had stolen.

Lionel won a manslaughter verdict, and the light penalty of a $10,000 fine, which Coomar was glad to pay. Had he not heeded Lionel's first advice, to make no statement to the police, he might well have been convicted of murder.

The last year, like every other year, has brought Lionel Luckhoo a varied bag of murder cases. Some have been outlined in previous chapters. Among some of the remainder is the case of Rockliffe Nedd, a policeman charged with the murder of a fellow constable.

Rockcliffe Nedd was on duty at the Parliament building in Georgetown. The midday sun was hot, and he welcomed the appearance of his friend, Constable Mason, to take over guard duty. In fact, Nedd was in such high spirits at being relieved that he started a bit of horseplay. Constable Mason was shot and died.

There was a witness to part of what had happened. Hensley Marks testified that, as she was passing the Parliament building, she saw two policemen. One was pointing a revolver at the head of the other. She walked on, and was thirty feet away when she heard the sound of a gunshot. She rushed back to where the accused was standing, holding a gun.

Cross-examined by Lionel Luckhoo, she admitted that the men were not quarreling, cursing, or fighting. "I got the clear impression they were joking, making fun with each other. If I had felt they were serious. I would have called out to them, or called for help, or raised some kind of alarm. When I went back, the accused seemed stunned. He was holding the gun, standing motionless. I spoke to him, and he started to try and help the other man."

From this cross-examination, Lionel was able to get the murder charge dropped at the preliminary inquiry. Rockcliffe Nedd was committed to stand trial for manslaughter. After a successful plea, he was placed on a bond.

This was the second time that Lionel had been called upon to defend a member of the security forces after a gun accident arising from a joke which turned sour. Edward Poole, a soldier, had a reputation as a persistent, somewhat childish, practical joker. One day, he rushed into the barrack room, pointed his rifle at a comrade, and cried, "I am from the wild west. Stand and deliver!" The safety lock was off, and the gun inadvertently fired, killing his friend. When charged with murder, the very chastened soldier said, "I will take whatever penalty is given, for I have done wrong by playing the fool and taking the life of my friend."

Lionel urged upon the court that this could not be looked upon as murder. Death was caused through negligence, and, since the accused had been in jail for many months, pending trial, that could be taken into account, and he could be bonded. Poole was acquitted of murder, and put on bond to be of good behavior for three years.

Both Rockcliffe Nedd and Edward Poole, accustomed to handling weapons, should have known better. These accidents should never have happened, but guns can be more dangerous than many experienced handlers realize. Robert Churchill, the gun expert, has records of half a dozen cases of guns firing without anyone having touched the trigger.

An *outre* sort of accident was the explanation put forward by Clive Fraser for the death of his wife. He claimed that they were making love on a chair, when the chair fell over. The lady landed awkwardly, and her neck was broken. As Lionel Luckhoo said when he took the case, thc moral must be: don't make love on a chair; if the bed is not good enough, choose the floor.

Whether chair or wife tumbled, or neither, Lionel's record nearly did. Fraser told Lionel that he had made no statement to the police, and was emphatic that his story about the chair was true. In court, the police produced a statement, made by Fraser, confessing that there was a quarrel and he lost his temper and choked his wife. Both he and Lionel were lucky to get a verdict of manslaughter.

It was Sherlock Holmes who remarked that from the grotesque to the horrible is but a step. The worst *prima facie* case with which Lionel Luckhoo was ever involved was a blood-ritual murder: the father and mother were accused of sacrificing their young son, and drinking his blood. This supposedly took place as part of the Kallimai Pooja, a festival having undertones of witchcraft.

The main prosecution witness alleged that, when the boy was missing, the mother and father came to him and confessed that, to satisfy the gods and become rich, they had killed their son and drunk his blood. Under cross-examination, it emerged that the "confession" was never made to him, but was something he had overheard. Why had he taken several weeks to report it to the police? His inability to satisfactorily answer this and like questions destroyed the value of his testimony. It was a case of suspicion falling short of proof, and the magistrate refused to commit.

Behavior both grotesque and horrible was a feature of a more recent case. Kamal Sarran Singh was a strong man who could throw a bull with his hands, and a neighborhood bully. Everyone referred to Singh as "Creature." He seemed a throwback to the Neanderthal age.

One day, Creature caught a youngster in his yard. He carried him to what was known as the gallows pole—a contraption on which he slaughtered cows—and strung him up. Then, taking a saw, he hacked at the boy's knees and his forehead.

The young men of the village met together, and agreed that, if Creature ever committed another such outrage, they would deal with him.

Over a year later, the cry went up: "Creature is taking Kennard to the gallows pole." Kennard was an old man who had suffered a stroke. Creature was being aided by his brother Buddy and two others, Isahack and Cobra.

The village youths had not forgotten the pact they had made. They ran to Kennard's rescue. There was a fierce skirmish. When it was over, Creature lay dead, hacked by cutlass, axe, and spear. Isahack and Buddy were wounded.

Seven young men were charged with murder. A delegation from the village was sent to Georgetown to retain Lionel for the defense of Suresh Balkarran, Mohanlall Ramjit, Rajpaul, Ravinda Ramnauth, Banaraj Balkarran, Ramesh Balkarran, and Jerome Ramoo.

Chief witness for the prosecution at the trial, before Mr. Justice Fung-A-Fat, was Creature's fifteen-year-old son Krishna Narine Singh. He gave a graphic account of how his father had been attacked, and chopped to bits without cause, by the seven accused, describing the combat, and how each man was armed.

His evidence was discredited when Lionel's cross-examination drew from him sixteen statements that were inconsistent with the evidence he had given at the preliminary inquiry. And then he had the boy's uncle Buddy, one of the men who had been wounded, admit that young Krishna had not even been there when the attack took place.

When Isahack told a story at variance with what the other prosecution witnesses had said, Lionel submitted that the evidence was so manifestly unreliable that it would be unsafe to allow the case to go to the jury.

The judge agreed that there were alarming discrepancies and shifts in the testimonies, but decided he could not rule that there was no case. If the jury requested it, however, he would give them the opportunity to decide whether or no they wished to hear a defense. The jury took the hint, and, after a fifteen-minute retirement, said they wanted to hear no further evidence, but to return a formal verdict of not guilty.

Lionel Luckhoo's comment was: "If the prosecution witnesses had stuck to the truth, my clients might well have gone under. But under the *res gestae* rule, the prosecution allowed them to bring in ancillary matters, how Isahack was injured, how Buddy was injured, how these boys were out to destroy Creature and his friends; thereby, seeking to blacken the case against them. When the fictional nature of some of their evidence was revealed, it cast doubt on the rest."

Lionel was able to expose the fictions because he had investigated on the spot, learned the geography of the area, taken measurements, and re-enacted what was supposed to have happened. By then, he knew more about the case than anyone in court, including those who had been present and participated in the accident.

In nearly all his murder trials, Lionel has been defending just one accused; on occasion, two. The case of Creature was unique, in that seven men were charged with the crime. If only one had been found guilty, Lionel's "brittle record" (his own term) would have been broken.

"World's Most Successful Criminal Lawyer Loses His First Case" has already been a newspaper headline. The *National Enquirer* front-paged it, in the United States, when Lloyd Harris was sentenced to be hanged ("The Case of the Disappearing Double"). Like the report of Mark Twain's death, the headline was a trifle premature, for Lionel went on to win the case in the Appeal Court. Asked, then, to comment on Lionel Luckhoo's string of victories, an American Bar Association spokesman said, "We've never heard of any individual success like this. It's staggering." And that was only the one hundred sixty-eighth case.

Now, there have been 232 successive verdicts for the defense. While working on this book, I have received news, on an average of once a month, sometimes twice a week, of another courtroom triumph. There has been some trepidation on my part that the next telegram would signal the first defeat. It has not happened. Indeed, Lionel describes the two hundred thirty-second case as "perhaps the easiest case of murder I have ever defended."

Of course, the next might be the hardest. For, hard or easy, Lionel Luckhoo still takes the cases as they come. Except in the two instances I have already mentioned, he has never refused the defense in a murder case. There is no attempt to protect the record. And, really, there is no need. The figure has climbed so far ahead of anything before accomplished that it seems certain to stand, as long as the western system of jurisprudence survives.

And the cases continue.

Chapter 31
The Case of the Perishing Attorney

by Lionel Luckhoo

An unwitting conceit, developed after many decades in the practice of law, gave me the grand illusion that I had taken part in, or had heard or read about, every conceivable type of case.

How wrong that assumption proved to be.

Suddenly, with the clarity of a lightning flash, came the stunning realization that—like billions of others on earth—I was involved, without realizing it, in a curious case which could take away the most precious possession of all: my very life.

I am talking not only of this life, but of life *after* life. And the case in reference was being made by an unrelenting, insidious, tough attorney—the most formidable I have ever encountered.

His name is Satan.

Satan, the very substance of temptation, the essence of deception, the distillation of evil, is considered by many (far too many) to be a symbol, a figurative—even, a mythological—character, a mere spiritual analogy.

If that is what most intelligent people think, then Satan has made a most convincing case for himself, and against God. To paraphrase C.S. Lewis, Satan's greatest deception is selling the idea that he doesn't even exist.

The rest of his bill of goods reads something like this: God doesn't exist (if He ever did, He is now dead); the world wasn't created by God (how could it be, if He never existed?), and just happened, when interstellar gasses and dust accumulated in space; life on earth came about through a fortunate combination of dead materials; man wasn't created, either—he just evolved from more simple living organisms. There is no heaven nor hell. When we die, we just end up six feet under. If, by some chance, there should be a heaven, all we need do to qualify for it is to be good people and do good deeds, such as being kind to our wives or husbands (one at a time, please), children, other relatives, friends, and stray dogs and cats.

Satan's bill of goods continues: The Bible is not the Word of God. It is merely interesting reading, written with beautiful simplicity and economy, containing colorful stories and some authentic history, studded with boresome statistics, family lineages, and "begats." About Jesus: how can the human mind possibly accept the story of His birth to a virgin? Why would anybody come to earth with the major mission of dying an agonizing death on the cross for the sins of mankind? How could He possibly have been brought back to life? Actually, all we need to know about Jesus is that He was a great teacher, and a highly moral and ethical man who set a fine example for us.

Some years ago—well before I realized the case that attorney Satan was building—I occasionally studied the Bible, as a lawyer would review the facts of any case. Quietly religious, I had used my reason and decided that Jesus, who lived on earth some 2,000 years ago, was God. The evidence of this was overwhelming, and the proof beyond a reasonable doubt.

As a matter of fact, I had written a little booklet on the subject, pointing out that, if I had to conjure up a God coming into this world as man, He would have had to fit in with all the requirements which Jesus, clearly, filled. Isaiah foretold, 750 years B.C., Jesus' miraculous birth—that a virgin would give birth to the Saviour of the world—even stating the circumstances and place and date of His birth.

Then there were His teachings, which enveloped the world, spreading daily for 2,000 years. Again, God, coming down as man, should have been able to perform miracles. Jesus did work miracles; often, before many witnesses: controlling the elements, stilling the winds and waves, walking on water, curing the sick, the lame, the blind, the possessed, and raising the dead.

Finally, God-who-was-man would have to conquer death, and this Jesus did, for was He not resurrected, and seen by Cephas and more than 500 individuals who could personally testify to this fact? The historian Philip Schaff vividly describes the absolute uniqueness of Jesus Christ:

> *This Jesus of Nazareth, without money and arms, conquered more millions than Alexander, Caesar, Mohammed, and Napoleon; without science and learning, He shed more light on things human and divine than all philosophers and scholars combined; without the eloquence of schools, He spoke such words of life as were never spoken before or since, and produced effects which lie beyond the reach of orator or poet; without writing a single line, He set more pens in motion, and furnished themes for more sermons, orations, discussions, learned volumes, works of art, and songs of praise, than the whole army of great men of ancient and modern times.*

Despite my keen appreciation for the man called Jesus, I was actually a "head" Christian, rather than a "heart" Christian—a Sunday Christian. I was moving along comfortably in my deep rut.

Then, on November 2, 1978, something unusual happened to me. I received an invitation to a dinner to be given November 7 by the Full Gospel Business Men's Fellowship International, at the Pegasus Hotel in Georgetown. My reaction was negative. The organization's name was long and involved. "Full Gospel," I told myself, "that's probably another church, and a Yankee one, at that. What do they want in Guyana? Don't we have enough churches already?"

I decided to decline. Then, on the seventh of November, just three hours before the dinner, I received a phone call, asking whether I would attend. Starting to say no, I ended up saying yes, for a then unfathomable reason.

At the dinner, I met Full Gospel representatives Newman Peyton and Glen Norwood, both from Houston, Texas, and West Indians Holmes Williams and Kyffin Simpson, an auto dealer, of Barbados, and a small group of Guyanese. The purpose of the get-together was to set up a chapter of this Fellowship in Georgetown. Peyton explained that the Fellowship—not a church or cult, and not seeking subscriptions or handouts—had some 1,800 chapters, and tens of thousands of members, throughout the world: businessmen and professionals, who met once a month to "lift up Jesus."

The announced purpose of the Fellowship sounded reasonable enough: if leaders of the community acknowledged Jesus, and were willing to be counted for Him, this was the best example for others to follow. Individuals in the group received Jesus as Lord and Saviour, experienced a profound change in their lives (being "born again"), and attempted to live like Jesus when He was on earth, with love as their central theme.

"Very idealistic, but not very practical," I told myself, and felt an upsurge of skepticism. One doesn't spend a lifetime in the practice of law and not become cynical. My colleagues at the Bar had often said to me, "Lionel, you seem to be able to detect within the shortest possible time if a witness is speaking the truth, or just plain lying."

Maybe I do have this ability to read beyond the words of a witness. At any rate, I brought with me to this dinner meeting an appreciable prejudice. Obviously, these characters had come all the way to Guyana to get something for themselves. Soon it would become apparent.

Carefully listening to Newman Peyton, I noted that he had an open face, and spoke calmly and evenly—no overdramatics, sanctimoniousness, or churchiness. He was firm and convincing.

"We encourage to join the Fellowship business and professionals who are not afraid to declare their stand for Jesus," he announced. "We're not looking for preachers or teachers, just individuals who can, and will, testify as to what Jesus means in their lives."

I leaned over to Kyffin Simpson, and asked, "Do you happen to know what business Peyton and Norwood are in?"

"Yes," he replied, with a smile. "Newman Peyton owns large areas of land, and has been deeply involved in the motor industry. He's quite wealthy. And Glen Norwood? He is a multimillionaire who has sold his firm, Norwood Homes, for many millions. He still owns thousands of apartment units in Houston, Texas."

Both Peyton and Norwood gave frank testimonies as to how their lives had changed when they accepted Jesus as their personal Saviour. Norwood, the epitome of a perfect gentleman, spoke quietly. His sincerity and truthfulness were piercingly patent. Without mentioning his wealth, he said, "All I have is worldly, material gains, and all of this I humbly, and yet proudly, lay at the feet of Jesus."

Something within me resonated with their message. I knew they were speaking from their hearts. They were experiencing a new dimension of life, a peace with the world, that I wished I had. Obviously, they enjoyed traveling from country to country, seeking to bring leaders of industry and nations to accept Jesus, and to experience the same joy that they had.

I learned that the Fellowship had been founded by Demos Shakarian, a Downey, California, dairyman who had had a vision that, if a sleeping giant—the layman—awoke, and if he carried out the final dictation by Jesus, to go out to the ends of the world and take the Good News with him, millions would be making a decision to go from death to eternal life.

At the conclusion, they asked all who were willing to accept Jesus as their personal Saviour—to take advantage of the fact that Jesus had died on the cross to wash away their sins—to stand up.

There was success and achievement in my life, but, nevertheless, a significant void. Within me, I was conscious of insufficiency, the necessity for completeness, which had eluded me.

I looked around at the local personalities, whom I knew intimately. "It would be a rather soft thing to stand up," I said to myself. That was not for me. Yet something happened inside. It was as if Jesus were knocking at the doorway of my heart (as in Revelation 3:20), and bidding me to open it, that He might enter. I stood up. That simple, overt act was the beginning of a complete change, a transformation of my entire life.

I was conscious then that something had happened to me. It was nothing dramatic or startling. I just felt a sense of peace, contentment, fulfillment, and joy.

At the meeting's conclusion, Peyton and Norwood announced that the Full Gospel Business Men's Fellowship International would like to host a dinner for the Prime Minister, cabinet, and other dignitaries of Guyana. The plan was simple enough. If these most prominent individuals in the nation accepted Christ, others, too, would accept. Water runs downhill, and those at the grass-roots level would be persuaded to follow the lead.

"The invitation doesn't have much chance of acceptance," I told Peyton, "but why not write a letter to the Prime Minister?"

"Leaders in Costa Rica, Puerto Rico, Honduras, and elsewhere have accepted a similar invitation," Peyton replied.

The letter was sent November 17, the day before the Jonestown tragedy. Suddenly, to everyone in the world, Guyana, an unknown blob on the map, became identified with Jim Jones and the murder, mass suicide, or massacre which made headlines for weeks.

"Now you don't have a snowman's chances in hell of the Prime Minister accepting," I told Newman Peyton.

Here was a virtually unknown American religious group, wishing to honor our Prime Minister and Guyana after the holocaust brought about by another American, Jim Jones. Peyton was not disturbed. "We will be praying," he said. "With God, all things are possible."

"It would be a miracle," I replied.

And a miracle it was, for Prime Minister Forbes Burnham readily accepted. The Fellowship then airlifted from America its founder-president Demos Shakarian and forty other top business and professional personalities—bankers, engineers, geologists, space scientists, judges, and attorneys—to honor Guyana and its leaders, and to lift up Jesus.

On March 1, 1979, one of the largest banquets in Guyanese history was held at Queen's College, with television coverage for the world. Six men, speaking from their hearts, publicly proclaimed their deep and abiding love for Jesus, and what

He meant to them. The Prime Minister was so impressed with their sincerity and purpose that he met with them again, the following day, at his home.

Evening meetings continued for several days. The Holy Spirit was certainly active in Guyana. Large numbers received Jesus daily. It was, truly, an unforgettable experience, seeing so many proclaim their faith in Jesus. The fact that Demos Shakarian, the movement's founder and a very special person, was present, brought particular meaning to the gatherings.

(Since then, I have met Demos's family: his wife Rose, whose beauty and charm provide the presence of a woman dedicated to the service of Jesus, and his sons Steve and Richard and their families, all devoted to bringing the gospel to all peoples.)

Being with these men showed me that acceptance of Jesus, by the mental processes, by rational thinking, was not enough. Acceptance had to move from head to heart, and I had to give myself entirely for Him, and use whatever talent and ability I had for His glory. For the first time, I realized that the achievements in my life were not mine, but *His* through me. I felt truly grateful for my 232 successful murder defenses, four honors from the Queen, service as Ambassador for two independent territories in England and Europe (unlikely ever to be repeated), and having been saluted by *Guiness Book of Records*.

Clearly, Jesus had given me honors so that He might use me to bring others to an appreciation of what it means to accept Him fully, without reservation or compromise. He was now my personal Saviour.

These honors of the material world were now meaningless to me. What mattered was Jesus, who now was in my heart.

Let me put it in another way. Intellectually, I had always accepted God and Jesus. Spiritually, I was starved. The food that was missing was the Word of God. When Jesus touched my heart, I realized that there had been a void within me, and Jesus now filled that void. To know Him, and to obtain His complete fellowship, I had to go back to the Holy Bible.

Aside from occasional intellectual samplings of it, the Bible had been a comparative stranger to me. It had been a large and beautiful book which remained on the side table of my large desk. Someone had pressed leaves and a flower between certain pages. It remained seldom touched. Today, the Bible is more than a panorama for intellectual exploration, an object of decoration, or a repository for memorabilia. It is for use, for feeding, for seeking, for loving. It is alive, the living Word of God.

Through passage after passage, I seek God's enlightenment, underscoring, with various colors of ink, passages which illuminate my mind, heart, and spirit. Whenever I see the word "Jesus," that name is no longer something apart from *me*. I possess Jesus, and He possesses me, and I write the word "my" before His name. When He died on the cross and was resurrected, He died and was resurrected for everyone who believes in Him and accepts His sacrifice to wash away sins and gain eternal life—and for me, personally.

I pray that, by persistent reading and study of the Bible, I will be enriched with the full purpose and beauty of God's words, so that I might witness more effectively to my personal experiences and life-changes.

I have scrubbed from my life past activities which have lost their savor—owning race horses, daily betting, and club life. During the days, I am in courts. In the evenings, I prepare legal work, after which I read the Bible to fill enormous gaps of ignorance. I have no time for anything else, and I enjoy doing just that.

Noting the difference in my lifestyle, some colleagues were sarcastic at first. "Are you getting a dose of religion?" one of them asked.

"If by religion you mean coming closer to Jesus, then yes," I replied. Actually, the skeptics could only see the surface me. I hope that they will someday know the peace, tranquillity, and calmness which I now enjoy.

Jesus, ever since my decision for Him, directs my life, and I serve however He wishes. If this means continuing in the law, serving as an advocate for Christ, or working in any capacity—ministering to the sick or troubled, or speaking with those who have not accepted Jesus—this, any, or all will I gladly do. My life belongs to Him. With this knowledge, my heart has fulfillment.

What I know is that I must obey the command of Jesus to go and tell, for did He not advise all who accepted Him that they should go to the ends of the earth and teach all creatures (Mark 5:16)?

In my view, little purpose is served in speaking to the converted. Rather, I speak with agnostics or atheists—the unbelievers—remembering, always, Ezekiel 33:8: ". . . O wicked man, thou shalt surely die; if thou dost not speak to warn the wicked of his way, that wicked man shall die in his iniquity, but his blood will I require at thine hand."

No longer will I sit still in my joy, satisfaction, and peace. I must bring these to others, so that they may enjoy a personal relationship with Jesus. It is as if I had discovered something more wonderful than a cure for cancer. I have. Jesus has shown me a cure for death.

What has happened to me since November, 1978? When I spoke in Barbados on the subject "Christ Is the Answer," ninety-two persons publicly received Jesus into their hearts. After the meeting, Newman Peyton observed, "Lionel, you spent some forty years and saved 232 persons from the rope. Yet, in one hour, God used you as the vessel to save ninety-two persons from eternal death."

Since then, I have spoken at conventions of the Full Gospel Business Men's Fellowship International in India, Central America, the Caribbean, New Zealand, London, and many states in the United States—not as a preacher, but as a layman who has made the most important decision that a man could be called upon to make.

Belief without action is dead. Faith without action is dead. No purpose is served by Christians saying, "I believe," if they are not willing to stand up for Jesus and bring others to Him.

Everywhere, I reveal that faith in Christ is not a leap into the dark, but, rather, a leap into the light. I also speak to members of the legal fraternity about the legal basis for the acceptance of the testimony of Jesus in the Bible. I use my legal knowledge to bring into focus the trial of Jesus before the Sanhedrin, Pilate, and Herod, and to show how legal principles were twisted to crucify an innocent person. Yet, it was because of His blood and stripes that our sins are washed away, and we can move from death to life.

In my travels with the Fellowship to New Zealand, Toronto, Canada, Belize, St. Maartens, Barbados, and nine cities in Germany, the most rewarding sight to me was seeing brother lawyers stand up and accept Jesus, confessing with their lips that He is their personal Saviour, and openly accepting Jesus as the Son of God, who rose from the dead. In Guyana alone, twenty-seven lawyers and judges stood up for Jesus at one breakfast meeting. Already, I am receiving letters from those who are experiencing what I have experienced—a complete change of life, a peace and joy which pass all understanding.

Over the past year, I traveled over 130,000 miles. If anyone had told me, two years ago, that I would be doing this, I would have regarded him as mentally deranged.

One of the statements that comes up in my testimony is that, "as a member of the Full Gospel Business Men's Fellowship International, I do not seek to represent any denomination. I accept, as my authority, the Holy Bible. I have accepted Jesus, and getting Jesus from my head to my heart has brought regeneration to my life."

Nicodemus, who was a lawyer, was not satisfied with his learning, scholarship, or religion. He came to Jesus, searching because of a void within him. Conscious of this, Jesus then provided the answer for eternal life: unless a man is born again, he cannot see the Kingdom of God. Everyone who believes in Him will have eternal life.

With Jesus in our hearts, there is peace; with the Holy Spirit abiding in our bodies as His temple. We are given the power to go forth in strength as ambassadors for Jesus.

In the final analysis, this is my position: we are all one heartbeat away from eternity. Young or old, the only two things of which we can be sure are (a) that we will be taxed, and (b) that we will die. We can do little about the former, but we can do something about the latter. We can assure ourselves a place in God's Kingdom.

No one knows how many minutes or seconds he or she has left. I came within three hours of missing Him, when I almost turned down the invitation of the Full Gospel Business Men's Fellowship International.

Perhaps, as I once did, the world regards my victories in the courts as a success; but, to me, the success is in making the decision in which I proclaimed Jesus as my King and Lord of glory. He is the Way, the Truth, and the Life. Only through Him who shed His blood for all can we attain eternal life.

Jesus loves us all, and is knocking at the doorway of our hearts, longing for the opportunity to enter. It is up to each of us.

I made my decision for Jesus.

This is now your moment of decision.

Lionel Luckhoo

(Top above) Lionel, age four and determined.

(Center) "Mummy"—Lionel's mother, Evelyn Luckhoo.

(Right) Lionel the medical student.

the first photograph ever permitted in England of this ceremony, Lionel is knighted by Her Majesty Queen Elizabeth II.

Lionel with his three youngest children: (from left) Marina, Mark, and Sharman.

The Luckhoo family had incredible luck on the turf. Here Sir Lionel leads one of his champions.

Sir Lionel as Lord Mayor of the City of Georgetown.

(Above) "Brothers in law" Lionel, Lloyd, and E.V. The o instance legal memories can recall of three brothers all having taken silk (become Queen's Counsel). With them (second right) is another lawy Prime Minister Forbes Burnham.

(At left) Sir Lionel Luckhoo, KCMG, CBE, SC. Photo taken becoming one of Her Majesty Counsel (Q.C.), 1954.

(Left) Sir Edward Luckhoo, former Chancellor of the Judiciary, now High Commissioner for Guyana in India.

(Below) Gowkarran Persaud, who refused to have any lawyer other than Lionel Luckhoo. Under Lionel's tutoring, he successfully defended himself on a murder charge.

(Above left) Noor Mohamed, defendant in Lionel's thirteenth murder trial and suspected of poisoning his first two wives, seen here with third wife and young daughter. Lionel fought the case to the House of Lords before winning.

(Left) Lionel as Ambassador to France, with President de Gaulle.